I'm not eating any of that foreign muck

(travels with me dad)

First published in 2005

Allen & Unwin
83 Alexander Street
Crows Nest NSW 2065
Australia
Phone: (61 2) 8425 0100
Fax: (61 2) 9906 2218
Email: info@allenandunwin.com
Web: www.allenandunwin.com

National Library of Australia
Cataloguing-in-Publication entry:

Thacker, Brian, 1962- .
I'm not eating any of that foreign muck : travels with me dad.

ISBN 1 74114 531 7.

1. Thacker, Brian - Journeys. I. Title.

920.71

Typeset in Australia by Bookhouse, Sydney
Printed in Australia by McPherson's Printing Group, Victoria

10 9 8 7 6 5 4 3 2 1

Contents

To Harry and Judith

Introduction

My Dad has two fingers missing on his right hand. He nibbled them off one day while he was chewing his nails. Or at least, that's what I believed until I was seven.

When I eventually figured out that nibbling on your fingernails didn't result in the loss of any digits, Dad told me what really happened. Apparently he got his fingers jammed in a machine gun during the Second World War.

The only problem with that tale was that Dad had never fought in any war. But just after the war he was a cook on a submarine in the British Royal Navy. That was how he really came to lose his fingers—cutting up some carrots and missing.

After a few years, in which I only ever sliced up vegetables with the utmost care, I finally found out the truth. Or so I thought.

For about twenty years I was under the impression that Dad lost his fingers in a machine on a motorcycle assembly line at the BSA factory in Birmingham, England. It wasn't until recently that I discovered the real story behind Dad's mysteriously missing digits. Mum and Dad were over for dinner one night and—as I was cutting up some carrots—I said, 'So Dad, how old were you when you lost your fingers at the BSA factory?'

'I didn't lose them at BSA,' he said. 'I lost them in a moulding machine at a plastics factory.'

What I really discovered that evening—or what finally dawned on me after all the false impressions I'd been under—was that I actually didn't know much about my Dad's life at all.

Dad and I talk a lot. It's just that we talk a lot about football and not much about anything else. Most of our conversations are about Manchester United. We can talk for hours about whether Ryan Giggs should play as a midfielder or a striker. I've tried on a number of occasions to get Dad to talk about his life but there have always been more pressing matters to deal with . . . such as whether Manchester United would beat Wolverhampton Wanderers in the Carling Cup.

I did know some things about Dad's life. I knew he was born in Britain in Royal Leamington Spa, Warwickshire, in 1931 and that he was one of eight children including four brothers named Jimmy, Johnny, Freddy and Gerry. Dad's name is Harry. I also knew that Dad had spent time in a children's home when he was young and served in the Royal Navy as a cook. He met Mum at a dance hall in Birmingham and emigrated to Australia with four kids in tow in 1967. I knew that Dad had an irrepressible love of feeble puns, tasteless jokes and tall stories and a penchant for wearing socks with sandals. In fact, when it came to reliable biographical information, I knew more about Ryan Giggs's life than my own father's.

I decided then that as well as wanting to know more about my Dad, I also wanted to really get to *know* my Dad. I decided I would take him on a physical and emotional journey back through his early life. When I explained my idea to him he wasn't exactly wildly enthusiastic: 'I suppose I *could* come . . . but I'm not eating any of that foreign muck!'

I took Dad to the pub for lunch to get an abridged version of his life so I could plan our itinerary and I learnt more in that afternoon than I had in the preceding forty years. I learnt that his Mum died when he was seven and, because his Dad was stationed in India with the army, he was sent to a children's home. I learnt that he joined the navy at fifteen and was stationed in different barracks at far-flung places all over Britain. And, although I had already known he had been stationed in Malta, I didn't know he had also spent long periods in Gibraltar, Sri Lanka and Singapore. The little jaunt back home to Mother England I was planning had suddenly turned into an around-the-world adventure.

At least (and at last) I would find out who my Dad really is, and in the process discover a little bit more about who I am. Our two-month odyssey would take us to his birthplace; the children's home in Warwick; the naval barracks in Wiltshire, Yorkshire, Kent, Suffolk, Gibraltar, Malta, Sri Lanka and Singapore; Mum and Dad's honeymoon hotel in Blackpool; my birthplace in the suburbs of Birmingham; and to the Butlins Holiday Camp in Minehead where we spent our summer holidays when I was a kid. Of course, if we happened to go past Old Trafford along the way, it would be a criminal waste not to pop in . . .

I hoped that in our two months travelling together I'd finally be able to get Dad to open up and tell me who he is and how he got that way—and, more importantly, that we would finally be able to resolve whether Ryan Giggs should play in the middle or up front.

England

1

Glutinous rice cakes with Sayur Lodeh and chilli sauce for breakfast anyone?

The last time my father and I flew in a plane together, I threw up on him. I was five years old and it was my first time on an aeroplane. Our family were emigrating to Australia and the British Eagle International Airways turbo-prop tin can with wings that bounced around and shook us silly took fifty-two hours—via Kuwait, Colombo, Singapore, Darwin and Sydney—to get to Melbourne. Our return trip to London thirty-odd years later (minus the pit stops and vomiting) would take only twenty-two hours. On that flight alone we would spend around twenty hours longer together than on any other occasion I could remember.

There was an air of trepidation and a bewildered 'what-the-hell-are-we-going-to-talk-about-for-two-months?' look on both our faces when Dad and I met up at my house before we headed off to the airport. At least our first conversation was easy. It was about Manchester United. They'd played Millwall in the FA Cup final the night before. Dad had called me that morning and as soon as I picked up the phone I'd blurted out, 'Don't tell me the score. I've taped the game and I'm just about to watch it.'

'All I'll say,' Dad sighed, 'is that I was very disappointed.'

'Oh gee, thanks Dad,' I moaned.

I watched the game and was surprised to see Manchester United take the silverware with an easy three to nil win.

'Why were you disappointed?' I asked Dad when he arrived.

'We should have won six–nil,' he grunted derisively.

Although I'd been back to the Old Dart quite a few times, it almost felt as if I was returning for the first time. The England I was going to now was not only the England of my father's childhood, but of my childhood as well. Mind you, I have very few memories of my early life there. And most of them are in black and white. Quite often what you think are real memories are only your recollections of an old photo, not the time itself. According to our family album, I spent most of my younger years playing with my willy. There is a faded photograph of me standing in our backyard in Spark Hill, Birmingham, clutching my willy so tightly it looks as if I was holding it in place. I do look very happy, though. There are other photos of me—at an amusement park, standing in our drab 1960s lounge room, and in an informal family portrait with my two brothers and sister—and in every shot I'm looking ever so cheerful with my hand firmly in place.

On the plane there wasn't any talk about the trip, our family or my childish insecurities. I did learn something new about myself, however. I learnt where I'd picked up a habit that some people find rather annoying: *both* Dad and I kept ourselves busy flicking through each and every audio station and watching five movies all at once on our personal TV screens.

On the second leg of our Emirates flight out of Singapore we were upgraded to Business Class (I'd emailed the airline and told them I was a travel writer—try it sometime). I'd never been in Business Class before. Neither had Dad, although he said he knew someone who had. For years I'd trudged past the rows of fat men in suits sipping champagne, thinking how smug they looked lounging in their spacious seats with their extra leg-room and complimentary in-flight socks. I had this theory that if I only ever flew Economy then I would stay happy because I wouldn't know what I was missing. It's a bit like my car. For years I had a car without air-conditioning and I was happy to wind down the windows and put up with the occasional scorching from the armrests. Then I got a car with air-conditioning and spoiled myself. There was no way I could go back to steaming underpants again. I was worried the same thing would happen with the Business Class thing.

As I lounged in my leg-friendly seat, sipping champagne and trying my very best not to look smug, the rabble in Economy were probably thinking, 'How can a scruffy-looking bloke like that afford Business Class?' Dad looked like the King of Muster. He ordered a second glass of champagne before we even took off. It may have been three in the morning, but that wasn't going to stop Dad from taking full advantage of our brief sojourn in the high-life in the sky.

There was Lobster Thermidor on the menu. Sadly (and I mean *very* sadly, because I love my lobster) we'd missed it. That had been dinner on the first leg out of Australia.

'What do they have in First Class, then?' Dad asked as he sipped his glass of 'fine' port.

I thought about it as I contemplated ordering another freshly squeezed orange juice.

'They probably have an entire slow-roasted antelope, hand-fed to them by nubile maids.'

Our only foray into the culinary delights of Business Class would be breakfast. Dad screwed up his face in disgust when I pointed out, amongst the toast and cereal, the Nasi Himpit on the breakfast menu. 'It's glutinous rice cakes served with sayur lodeh and chilli sauce,' I explained. Although glutinous rice cakes did seem an odd replacement for Rice Bubbles, it doesn't take much to disgust Dad when it comes to food—I just have to mention the wildly exotic dish of spaghetti and he screws up his face.

•

'I've had a good life, I can't complain,' Dad announced as I drove the hire car out of Heathrow Airport. Although Dad was itching to drive, I wasn't letting him anywhere near the steering wheel. He was too old and too expensive. As soon as you hit seventy, the insurance premium hits the roof. So, it would appear does your tendency to panic.

'Look out for the runway!' Dad bellowed into my ear. Yes, the runway was parallel to the road that we were on, but there was a three-metre-high fence in between.

'Watch out for that car!' Dad shouted, gesticulating wildly a few seconds later. The oncoming car was about half a kilometre away. I was a nervous wreck by the time we hit the first roundabout out of the airport. And, to make me even more apprehensive, Dad was navigating. We didn't have a map, but I had put him in charge of my AA Route Planner (and no, it wasn't full of directions to the nearest alcohol-free establishment). On the Automobile Association website you simply enter your starting point and destination (including exact street addresses) and you are presented with a detailed plan, indicating every road and roundabout with a few pubs thrown in for good measure. For example, 'At roundabout take 3rd exit' would be followed by 'Pass The Slirpin' Sausage (on right)'. You'd really need to visit the other AA if you stopped at every pub marked on the Route Planner!

I thought it would be relatively easy to follow. That was until we got to the second roundabout after the airport and I asked my appointed navigator which exit I needed.

'I can't figure the bloody thing out! It's too complicated,' Dad said.

'Do we need the M4 West or East?' I barked as we passed the first exit.

'It says to go forward. We're already going bloody forward.'

After three laps of the roundabout and me pointing out to Dad that 'Forward (signposted 'West') to join Motorway M4' wasn't really that complicated, as we finally joined the M4 and headed north past the outskirts of London. According to the Route Planner, the journey time to Royal Leamington Spa was one hour and twenty-seven minutes—that's three hours with 'Dodgy Navigator'.

Royal Leamington Spa is not quite a tourist town, but it is in Warwickshire, which is home to two of England's biggest tourist attractions: Shakespeare's birthplace in Stratford-upon-Avon and Warwick Castle. Dad lived a hop, step, and jump from both attractions for fourteen years and hadn't visited either.

I didn't have a map of Royal Leamington Spa because Dad had told me that he knew the town backwards. As we drove around (and around) the town, I got to know it backwards, forwards and sideways.

'I recognise that building,' Dad would say as we passed it for the third time.

As part of our impromptu tour we drove through the centre of town, which was filled with fine, eighteenth-century façades that put a pretty face on such fine British institutions as KFC and Burger King. There was a sale on at the Woodwards department store and a neat queue of oldies in grey coats was waiting patiently to rush in so they could get ten per cent off grey coats. Seeing them, an odd thing struck me. There didn't seem to be anyone in the town under sixty. Indeed, the majority of the shops seemed to cater for a wrinkly population. There was an inordinate abundance of optometrists, funeral parlours, pharmacists and cute little shops that sell cute little porcelain ducks.

After a few more laps of the town we pulled up out the front of Dad's cousin's house. As Dad knocked loudly on the door, a woman popped her head out from next door and said, 'What are you doing, you silly old man?' Dad was banging on the door of the wrong house and the woman was my Aunty Barbara. I hadn't met my Aunty Barbara before. She lives in Canada, but when she found out that her brother was popping over to England she'd decided to pop over too.

Dad's seventy-year-old cousin June lives alone in a large (well, large for England) and extraordinarily neat terrace house.

'Ello me doocks, would you like a cup of tea?' June asked before we even had a chance to put our bags down. June, who was wearing her best frock but had a large apron on over the top of it, ushered us into the lounge room. I stood in the centre of the room too scared to move. Every shelf, table and most of the floor was dotted with porcelain clowns, swans, horses and ducks. Sitting uncomfortably in the middle of a gaggle of porcelain geese was Dad's oldest brother Fred. He'd driven down from Birmingham to greet us and was dressed up in jacket and tie. I'd met my Uncle Fred on a number of occasions and he was always perfectly coiffured and elegantly dapper. I wouldn't be surprised if he donned a three-piece suit just to pop down to the shop for a pint of milk.

Each one of Dad's immediate siblings has a different accent. Fred has a Brummie (as in Birmingham) accent, Barbara has that Canadian twang, Gerry 'Ey-oops' like a Mancunian (from Manchester), Gladys (the only sibling to stay in Leamington) has a Warwickshire accent and Jim sounds like a pirate (he lives in Devon). After thirty-eight years in Australia, Dad still pronounces words like someone from *Coronation Street* but has picked up that uniquely Australian habit of ending each sentence as a question?

'So what's your book going to be about, then?' Barbara asked.

'It's about me travelling with the old fellow here,' I said, pointing across to where Dad was sitting amongst a herd of horses.

'You're not really telling everyone he's your father, are you?'

Barbara (the second youngest of the Thacker clan) was born in 1934—three years after Dad. She went to Canada for a holiday and decided to stay. That was close to forty years ago. Fred was another overstaying sightseer. When he left the army in 1954, he visited Birmingham for a long weekend. 'I stayed for fifty years,' Fred said. 'Now that's a *loooong* weekend.'

Although Dad's family are very distant geographically, they seemed very close and they hugged, joked and teased each other a lot. Dad certainly loved to tease June. When she waltzed into the room balancing a tray crammed with cups of tea and five varieties of gooey pastry, Dad said, 'So they haven't put you in a home yet?' June just smiled, looked at me and said, 'Int' he a cheeky booger, me doock?' In the three days we stayed with June not once did she call me Brian. I was always 'Me doock' and Dad was either 'a cheeky booger', 'a dozy sod' or 'a right pain in the arse'.

I'd just polished off a large piece of cream cake when June announced that our dinner was almost ready. Five minutes later, Dad and I were escorted into the dining room. 'Bloody 'ell!' Dad snorted. 'We're in the special room. This hasn't been used since I was last here five years ago.'

June, Barbara and Fred had already been out for an early dinner, but that didn't stop June from preparing us a mountainous roast dinner. There was roast chicken, roast potatoes, carrots, beans, peas, pumpkin and a slice of Yorkshire pudding as big as Dad's suitcase. I shovelled food into my mouth for fifteen minutes and didn't even put a dent in the pile on my plate.

'I can't finish it, I'm sorry,' I groaned to June, who was hovering over me waiting for me to finish.

'That's okay,' June clucked as she swept the plate away and immediately returned with two towering bowls of homemade apple pie.

I waddled into the lounge and collapsed on the couch just as June sauntered into the room with another tray piled high with Boston buns and cups of tea.

'No thanks, I just couldn't,' I squeaked.

'Would you like some biscuits?' June asked, looking worried because I wasn't trying to eat my body weight in food. 'What about some chocolate? A muffin? bread and butter pudding? A rack of lamb?'

When Dad's oldest sister Gladys arrived we had four out of the remaining six Thacker kids (Iris and John had passed way) together in the one room. When Gladys was having her third child about forty-three years ago she had a stroke and lost the use of her left arm. She was now in a wheelchair. Dad's nickname for her was Rigor mortis, which everyone, including Gladys, thought was hysterical. Gladys got so excited that when she spoke she would forget to breathe and every few minutes Barbara would say, 'Take a breath! Take a breath!' Gladys was full of life and loved nothing more than a good ol' chinwag. In the space of one cup of tea (and a round of scones with jam and clotted cream) I was bombarded with more information about my Dad's family than I had heard in the previous forty years.

To begin with I found out my Grandma's name—Violet. I was quite surprised to hear that she had died from an aneurism. Dad was just as surprised—he thought his Mum had died of a heart attack. The reason why I was so surprised was that my Mum had died from an aneurism when I was nine. So even though Grandma and Mum weren't related, they both died from the same thing at roughly the same age. I'd never really stopped to think that Dad and I shared the experience of losing our mums when we were young. It's just yet another thing that we had never talked about.

I also learnt that my Grandpa Fred was one of fifteen children and his Dad was a chimney sweep. Apparently the house was always full of soot. Grandpa Fred fought at Dunkirk during the Second World War and watched his brother Arthur die on the battlefield and couldn't go over to save him.

One story about Grandpa Fred that did make me laugh happened when he came home from the war. He met a London lass when he was stationed in Devon and married her. They'd been married for a few months when one morning over breakfast he said, 'Darling, could you please pass the sugar and . . . by the way, did I tell you I've got eight kids?'

Meanwhile, back in Warwickshire, Barbara thought her Dad had died in the war. She didn't even know she had a Dad until she was twenty-eight.

I was beginning to OD on tea and the jet lag had really kicked in. My body thought it was four in the morning and my head thought it was next week. Everyone was quickly bouncing off each other now.

'Uncle Albert died of a heart attack . . .'

'No, that was Uncle Cyril and he had gout . . .'

'Oh, that's right, there was a terrible smell in the house and everyone was looking for bad fruit until they found his body slumped behind the radiator . . .'

'Wasn't that John's Dad?'

'No it was Len's and it was after he married Mary Sykes.'

'Oh, yeah, and he wasn't allowed into the house with his shoes on.'

'Yes, and Aunty Mary used to hang out the washing with no clothes on.'

'Her family's all in prison now and she lives in Grotting Poop Road.'

'No, she's in Wallywiggen Way.'

Before my head exploded, I crawled upstairs to bed.

•

My breakfast was the size of a small country. It was fried everything.

'No wonder there's an oil crisis,' quipped Dad.

'Int' he a dozy sod, me doock?' June said as she ladled more grease onto our plates. June was still in her apron. I hadn't seen her out of it yet. When she wasn't cooking, she was cleaning. As soon as we'd finished eating breakfast, June whisked the dishes away from the table and they were washed, dried and put back in the cupboard before we even got out of our chairs (which were immediately stacked on the table when we got up). The floor was swept and mopped by the time we'd collapsed with bloated bellies on the couch.

I asked June to join Dad, Barbara and me for a drive around Leamington, but she said she had lots of cleaning to do. As we left, I heard the vacuum cleaner start up. Barbara told us she hoovers every single day.

I almost hit a lady in an electric scooter as we were driving to the house where Dad was born. That was because Dad would say, 'Turn left here,' and Barbara would scream, 'No, it's right.'

The Thacker family home at 7 Willes Road was a gorgeous three-storey Georgian terrace house. 'We only lived on one floor, though,' Dad said.

'No, we didn't.' Barbara was shaking her head. 'We had the entire house!'

In 1931, the year Dad was born, England was in the middle of the Great Depression. After the Wall Street Crash of 1929, the US economic collapse caused a ripple effect across the globe. By the time Dad popped his tiny head into the world, British industry had virtually come to a standstill. Almost overnight unemployment jumped from one to three million and exports had fallen in value by fifty per cent.

Dad's father was lucky. He was in the army (just like his father and grandfather before him), so the family never had to suffer the full impact of the Depression.

'Did your family have a car?' I asked Dad.

'No, a car cost more than a house!'

I thought Dad was either making stuff up again or he was a tad confused until I checked up on his story later. He was almost right. The average price of a semi-detached house in 1931 was £395. A new standard model Jaguar cost only slightly less at £385. Just to put that in perspective, at today's prices it's the equivalent of spending £170 000 (A$440 000) on your family runabout. At that price you'd want to park it in the lounge room or sleep in it at night.

Dad was child number four. By 1937 there were eight of them: Iris, Gladys, Freddy, Harry, Jimmy, Johnny, Barbara and Gerry. This was a rather impressive rate of production when you consider that Fred Snr was quite often away with the army. By 1938 he was in India as a Sergeant Major in the cavalry. That was the year Grandma Violet died (no one in the family knows which month it was or even where she is buried). Fred stayed in India, so the kids were sold off for medical experiments. Well, not quite, Gladys and Jim were sent to live with their grandma in Leamington but the other six were sent to a children's home in Warwick.

I pictured the children's home as being like something from *Oliver Twist*, with kids in rags surviving on stale bread and watery tasteless soup and sleeping on the hard floor of a windowless room filled with coal dust. So you can imagine my surprise when we turned off a leafy country lane halfway between Leamington and Warwick into a broad sweeping driveway that led through meticulously groomed grounds to a neat row of chocolate-box Georgian buildings. Myton Hamlet was picturesque and romantic and nothing like I'd imagined it. The home is now a hospice for cancer patients and what was once seven separate houses is now all joined together to form one building.

The Thacker boys and girls were split up and put into different houses. Each house had two bedrooms with six beds in each room plus a room for the 'Mother' who, I imagine, spent most of her time chasing a cheeky young Harry Thacker around the grounds.

Less than twelve months after Dad moved into the home, the Second World War started. By the time the war ended and Dad had moved out of the home, he'd been there for seven years. He couldn't remember the actual start of the war, but he did remember spending many nights over the following months sleeping on the floor of a windowless room filled with coal dust. And no, it wasn't part of my *Oliver Twist* fantasy, it was the underground air raid shelter that Dad was quite excited to find when we wandered around to the back of the hospice.

Although Warwick or Leamington weren't bombed during the war, the nearest large city was. On 14 November 1940, the Germans unleashed one of the biggest bombing raids on England when four hundred bombers targetted the sleepy city of Coventry. Within a couple of hours, the entire city was ablaze and over forty-two thousand people were killed. Dad said that it didn't worry them at all, though. Coventry was too far away. Coventry is less than ten miles away from the home?!

According to Dad and Barbara, life in the home was all rather pleasant. Even so, I did screw up my face when Dad told me that for dinner most nights they had steamed pudding—sago pudding, tapioca pudding, rice pudding or semolina pudding. And you didn't want to spill any of that pudding on your clothes—each child had only one set (plus one set of gym clothes that were worn only on Saturdays when the other set of clothes was being washed).

As we were poking around the back of the hospice, looking suspiciously as if we were casing the joint, a fellow came out to see what we were up to. As he kindly took us through the hospice and into the expansive gardens out the back, he explained that adults who had spent time in the home as kids often called in for a look. A group of patients were sitting under the shade of a massive one hundred and twenty-year-old oak tree enjoying the warm spring morning. Barbara said the scene reminded her of the weekly show that the children would put on to entertain wounded soldiers, who'd sit under the very same oak tree.

'Harry would tell jokes,' Barbara said.

'I think he's still telling the same ones today,' I said.

When I suggested to Dad that we walk to his old school in Warwick he snapped, 'I'm not doin' that bloody walk again. It used to take us over an hour.'

'We'd do that walk four times a day,' Barbara added, 'Because we'd also come home for lunch.'

That was over five hours of walking a day. It wasn't always a lovely little stroll through the fields, either. On one occasion, Dad had to dive to the ground as a German fighter plane flew over and let off a burst of machine-gun fire that missed him by only a few feet.

'At least it made the walk home interesting,' Dad observed cheerfully.

St Mary's School looked like something out of Legoland. It was tiny. Next to the school was another building only one step up from Lego size: St Mary's church. Dad told me that every Sunday morning he was supposed to make the long trek to attend mass (if you hadn't already guessed from the prolific breeding, the Thackers were

Catholic). On most Sundays, however, Dad and his posse of cohorts would just amble down to the much closer St Nicholas's, which happened to be a Protestant church.

'We knew all of the Protestant hymns,' Dad said. The vicar couldn't have been very convincing, though. Dad is now a staunch atheist.

'I've got a better story,' I replied proudly. 'When you used to drop us off at St Joey's [after Mum died, Dad felt obliged to go on taking us to church] we would rush inside, steal money from the poor box, buy ice-creams from the shop, then spend the rest of the time playing on the roof of the church.'

Far from being horrified by this revelation that his little darlings had wreaked havoc and committed robbery when he thought we were learning valuable moral lessons, Dad tried to trump me.

'Well,' he guffawed, 'when we did go to St Mary's it was my job to pump the organ. Halfway through a hymn I would stop pumping and hide. All of a sudden the music would slow right down and it would sound like a groaning ghost.'

So much for the Thackers and their immortal souls.

Behind the church was the rectory. 'Go knock on the door,' Dad said.

'What, and run away?' I squeaked.

'No, to see if we can have a look in the school.'

A silver-haired Irish priest opened the door with a cheerful smile. He was quite excited to see a couple of old St Mary's students. Dad, Barbara and the priest then went on (and on) telling stories and comparing lists of the missing and the dead. The Father from Dad's time was long gone, but one of his old teachers was still alive. 'Mrs Broadley is ninety-seven,' the priest said.

'She used to chase me around the class with a cane,' Dad beamed.

Barbara told the Father the organ story and he said to Dad, 'That was you? You're famous!'

The school is now a social centre. The inside was so small there wasn't enough room to swing a cat—or a very naughty ten-year-old Harry Thacker.

We returned to June's to find another roast dinner waiting for us. This time it was pork, and the dining room table was sagging in the middle with the weight of the plates.

'Are you ready for puddin'?' June asked as she took away my half-eaten main course. No, but I was ready to collapse into a blubbering (and blubbery) heap.

When I shuffled downstairs desperately needing a lie-down, the talk was of dead people again.

'Florrie McDonald is gone now. The poor thing had diphtheria . . .'

'That's what Ena Sharples had . . .'

'No, that was Albert Tatlock. Ena was hit by a runaway bus after Betty Alberge ran off with her husband . . .'

After fifteen minutes of this I realised they weren't talking about real people—they were all old characters from the TV series *Coronation Street.*

•

'Whither thou goest I doth not knowest . . . and all that crap,' Dad said when I surprised him with two tickets to see *Romeo and Juliet* at the Royal Shakespeare Theatre in Stratford-upon-Avon. Dad had never been to the Royal Shakespeare Theatre and I had never even seen a Shakespearean play (I left high school at sixteen to go to art school, so I missed the whole Shakespeare kerfuffle). I'm not a huge fan, but I certainly am impressed by his contribution to the English language. Here are just a few of the words Shakespeare invented: barefaced, leapfrog, monumental, castigate, majestic, obscene, frugal, radiance, dwindle, countless, submerged, excellent, gust, hint, hurry, lonely and summit. He also coined such well-known phrases as: in a pickle, vanished into thin air, the milk of human kindness, you've got to be cruel to be kind, soldier on, that will be cold comfort to you and it's all Greek to me (he was referring to his own writing then, I believe).

As we drove through the Tudor heart of Stratford-upon-Avon (for the first of four times) one of the signs I saw directed traffic towards, 'Shakespeares birthplace'. Maybe the local council thinks apostrophes are too modern for Ye Olde Town Centre.

'Shall we have a drink at The Dirty Duck?' I asked Dad. 'It's a noted haunt of thespians.'

'I'm not going to a place that's full of lesbians,' Dad grunted back in Carry On style.

We had a quick pint at The White Swan (which was light on lesbians) then wandered along the banks of the Avon River, past an array of brightly coloured narrowboats, to the Royal Shakespeare Theatre. I rushed upstairs to the toilet before the play started and was quite surprised to see a condom-vending machine for the convenience of patrons overcome by those racy Shakespearean romances. There was even a choice between 'Extra Safe—Be just and fear not' and 'Ribbed—The course of true love never did run smooth'. Actually, I made up the Shakespearean flourishes, but it would have been a fitting touch.

'No wonder Juliet fancied him,' I whispered to Dad as Romeo sprang onto the stage. He was wearing incredibly tight tights and was rather well endowed. For the first half an hour I had to concentrate like mad trying to understand the language. There was a lot of 'whither thou goest I doth not knowest' and all that crap going on. What really surprised me (and most of the people in the theatre) was when an incredibly loud coffee percolator started up right next to me. Except it wasn't a percolator, it was Dad. He was slouched down in his chair and snoring his head off. I was even more shocked than the rest of the audience since Dad had told me that he never snored. With the prospect of spending much of our trip in shared rooms, I'd grilled him before we left about any annoying nocturnal habits I should be prepared for. He neglected to mention that he did expert impersonations of a clapped out jackhammer.

'What's that? What's going on?' Dad said as he awoke with a start. Dad had been asleep for almost an hour and a half when he was woken abruptly by the audience breaking into rapturous applause at the end of the first half (or whatever act we were up to).

We stepped outside where a crowd of well-dressed people, including a couple of dashing chaps wearing cravats, were milling about. 'I don't think I'll go back in,' Dad grumbled. 'It's just a pack of pansies prancing about in tights. I'll go to the pub and you can meet me when it finishes.'

'You missed all the best bits,' I said. 'You missed "O Romeo, Romeo! Wherefore art thou Romeo?" for a start. That's like missing Arnie saying "I'll be back" in *Terminator*.'

'I dozed off when that bloke [Mercutio] kept waffling on and on,' Dad said.

'Oh, he was killed,' I said happily. I had to agree that his waffling had been a bit much so I was quite glad when he died. 'There was a massive fight with swords and knives. The stage was full of people shouting and screaming and there was blood everywhere.'

'No!' Dad was outraged. 'I don't believe you.'

'Look, they've got the entire story in the program . . . he was stabbed to death.' I then went on to read out the abridged version of the story.

'Well, we know how the story ends now. Let's go to the pub for a pint.'

I was keen to stay to the finish. By the second act, I was actually quite enjoying it. When I got used to the whole thee, thou, thouest lark, I started to get right into it. A beer, however, did sound like a smashing idea and I'd already sat through two hours with an hour and a half still to go. And besides, I am my father's son. It may have been brilliant, but it was still just a pack of pansies prancing about in tights.

•

After another artery-clogging repast we finally talked June into coming out with us. Just as soon as she'd swept the floors, vacuumed the house and dusted her entire porcelain menagerie. Our first stop was Dad's former senior school. We could have taken Dad's old short cut, but that would have meant driving through the grounds of Warwick Castle. Instead, we drove down a leafy lane that was flanked by the imposing walls of the Castle on one side and magnificently restored Elizabethan houses on the other. We passed a peacock sitting proudly on a high stone wall and Dad said, 'We used to have lots of fun with the peacocks.' Barbara rolled her eyes as Dad continued, 'On the way to school, we used to jump on their tail feathers and when they flew off we'd end up with a handful of long feathers.'

'What did you do with the feathers?' I asked.

'Oh, nothing. It was just good fun.'

Dad started at St Peter's in 1942. That was the year of the massive thousand-bomber raid on Cologne (which, incidentally, inflicted vast damage on the city for the loss of just forty planes).

'I'll never forget that,' Dad said. 'The planes flew right over our school for hours. The noise was incredible. But there was one good thing . . . we couldn't hear the teacher!'

St Peter's was no longer a school. Unless I was mistaken, it had been turned into a train. The inside of the glassed entrance area looked like a train carriage, with neat rows of train seats on either side of the room. A fellow with mad-scientist hair invited us inside after I told him that Dad had been a student there. The school had closed down in 1962, Peter the mad scientist told us.

Since then it had been a pine furniture warehouse, a carpet shop and a youth centre. Now it housed a company that designed, among other public transport bits and pieces, train seats. What had once been four separate classrooms were now one big airy room filled with IKEA-esque desks and enormous computer screens. As we walked in, I noticed one of the screens had a large picture of a Melbourne tram on it. This tiny design firm in the suburbs of tiny Warwick was designing a tram that would run past my very own front door back home.

Within minutes, Dad had the entire staff gathered around him as he regaled them with tales of his rascally deeds at school.

'We used to tie our coats together and lay them across the road,' Dad said chortling to himself. 'And when the posh kids from Mynton Grammar rode past on their posh bikes we'd pull the line of coats up and knock 'em off . . . My favourite trick, though, was when we used to tie string from the door handle of the principal's house to the handle of the one next door, then we'd knock on both doors and watch them try to get out.'

After fifteen minutes of stories I said, 'Dad, we should let these people get back to work.'

'Yeah okay . . . Anyway, we used to go into the cake shop across the road at the end of the day, ask if they had any cakes left, then say, "Well, you shouldn't have baked so many" and run out.' He was still telling stories (and laughing at his own jokes) as I dragged him out the door.

Although Dad had walked through the grounds of Warwick Castle almost every day for three years, he'd never actually been inside the castle. I asked June if she'd been to the castle and she said, 'Oh yes. I went there a few years ago.' A few years ago, all right—when pushed June finally figured out that she had last visited the castle when she was fifteen. That was fifty-five years ago. I had visited Warwick Castle seventeen years before, so that made me the resident expert.

The castle may be one of the best-preserved mediaeval castles in Europe and impress millions of visitors every year, but June wasn't so easily pleased. According to her, the windows needed a good clean and the bloke dressed in an authentic mediaeval costume at the entrance needed to give his shoes a polish.

William the Conqueror built the original motle-and-bailey wooden Warwick Castle in 1068. Over the years the castle was gradually rebuilt in stone and, by the late fourteenth century, Thomas de Beauchamp had transformed the defences of the castle, adding a huge gatehouse and barbican and two massive towers that still dominate the castle today. Formerly home to some of the most powerful noblemen in the whole country, the castle was taken over in 1978 by a bunch of dummies. Madame Tussaud's Wax Works now owns it and the rooms are filled with a cast of gruesome mediaeval characters.

'Oh, my giddy aunt!' June exclaimed as she tackled the second set of steps down to the first room. 'I'll need some new knees after this.'

'You'll have to go to Africa,' Dad shook his head gravely.

'Why?' June said.

'Because that's where the nee-groes.'

I made a mental note to get Dad a new joke book at the first opportunity.

The Kingmaker Room portrayed Richard 'the Kingmaker' Neville's last battle in 1471, when he ruled the roost as the power behind the English throne. One of the delights in the room was a mediaeval toilet, or gardrobe, complete with authentic stench.

This time Dad, who has a joke for every occasion and is never afraid to use it, came out with: 'When good King Gilbert ruled the land, and gardrobes weren't invented, they pulled up grass to wipe their arse and went home quite contented.'

After shuffling around all the rooms and dummies in the castle, we went for an amble around the grounds (well, with June in tow we rarely got past a shuffle and only once or twice did we actually hit an amble). We pottered past the impressive Rose Garden, dawdled through Pageant Field, which was flanked by two-hundred-year-old Cedars of Lebanon, then tottered down to the river.

A group of ten-year-old schoolboys were feeding a peacock when Dad stepped in front of them.

'Don't do that! Look what it did to me!' Dad bellowed as he held up the famous hand with two fingers missing. As I chalked up yet another tall tale about those once-bloody fingers, the kids all jumped back in fright and quickly checked their hands to see if they had any missing digits.

'We have to walk up to the top of that tower to get out,' Dad told June pointing to Guy's Tower, which is about the height of a five-storey office building. 'It's got five hundreds and six steps,' he added.

'Oh, my giddy aunt!' June stammered.

'Don't worry June, you'll be all right,' he said. 'They'll winch you up on a rope.'

'He's just being a cheeky booger,' I reassured June, who was relieved to discover that there were no steps (or winching for that matter). What worried her most, though, was that she might not get home in time to make us another roast dinner.

Our roast of the day was beef and all the trimmings, followed by trifle, followed by a couple of my arteries seizing up. Too full to move far, I made it only to the couch. June had already cleared up and was settled in for her evening soaps. The opening line in *Coronation Street* was, 'Mah broother's a bender.' His mum (sorry, moom—the show is set in Manchester) responded with, 'It's not mah fault, mah soon's a perv.'

Coronation Street is like *Neighbours* with cold weather and a bad case of depression. Most of the show seemed to take place in a dreary-looking pub full of pasty, miserable-looking people.

'I didn't bring 'im 'oop,' the moom continued. 'I dragged 'im 'oop on a diet of egg 'n' chips.'

Eastenders was next. This was the same except with cockney accents and lots of 'Know wha' a mean?' Amazingly, and a bit frighteningly, *Coronation Street* came on again after *Eastenders*. I couldn't stand watching any more pasty, miserable people sitting in a dreary pub, so I grabbed Dad and wandered up to the pub on the corner where we had a pint sitting with a few pasty, miserable people in a dreary pub.

2

Chicken tikka masala (food that looks like diarrhoea)

Not long after the Second World War ended, Dad left school, moved out of the home and headed north to Manchester to get a job. He was fourteen years old. 'We grew up fast back then,' Dad said. Grew up fast, all right. When I was fourteen, I wasn't even making my own bed. I was immature, lazy, irresponsible and incorrigible (I still am today, but that's not the point). I asked Dad why he chose Manchester and he said, 'Because that was where Manchester United came from.'

Dad had found a room at a boarding house near the city centre and a job stacking wood at Bennett's Timber. He wasn't totally self-sufficient, though. Mrs Weston, who owned the boarding house, served up a hearty home-cooked meal every night.

Another heart-stopping greasy breakfast awaited me on the kitchen table at June's house on our last morning in Leamington. 'I'm really sorry, June,' I whimpered, 'but can I just have some Weetabix?'

As we stepped out of the door to leave, June vacuumed the carpet behind us. Barbara was joining us on our drive to Manchester. Now there were three of us to get totally and utterly confused by the motorway signs.

'Why can't they just bloody say where the hell they're bloody going?' Dad said, shaking his fist at the motorway sign. He was right, though. The large green motorway sign read 'M6 Northeast to A1522 [B1796 ÷ A4676=A119 Southwest to the North]'.

The motorway signs in England tend to direct you to towns that no one visits or no one wants to visit. Our two-hour trip, via Great Snoring and Pratt's Bottom, took us four hours (not really, although they are real towns in Britain). It probably would have taken us two days if it weren't for Barbara. After our third loop of the ring road around Manchester, Barbara cried out from the back seat, 'PLEASE turn . . . ANYWHERE! I beg of you!'

We were staying with Maggie (Gladys's daughter) and Peter (Maggie's husband) in their neat house in a row of neat modern houses in the neat suburb of Reddish. And, gosh, I had thought June's house was neat and tidy. The interior of Maggie and Peter's house looked as if it had been set up for a *Vogue Living* photography shoot. The bathroom was my favourite. It was perfectly, even obsessively, coordinated. The entire room was sparkling white, but everything in it was lavender. And I mean *everything*. The towels, curtains, soaps, candles, toilet cover, toilet brush and toothbrushes were lavender. Even the shampoo, bought solely for its colour not its quality, matched the toilet brush et al.

Fred, who was looking his usual dapper self, had driven up from Birmingham to meet us. His car journey had taken only an hour and a half.

'It's easy,' he said. 'You go straight up the M6 and get off at Junction 27.'

After being welcomed with the usual nice cup of tea and biscuits, we piled back into the car for a tour of Dad's old Manchester haunts.

'Brian's not driving, is he?' Dad asked as we stepped outside.

'I'll drive,' Peter said.

'Good, I've run out of clean underpants.'

It didn't turn out to be much of a tour. Every building that Dad attempted to point out had been torn down or turned into a home for wayward graffiti. When it came to tearing down, they didn't muck about either. The entire neighbourhood surrounding his old boarding house had been demolished and replaced by large blocks of ugly 1960s' council flats. You don't need a war to destroy a city. A handful of dodgy architects will do the trick nicely.

There wasn't much left of any of Dad's old haunts. The once grand Ardwyk Wrestling Hall, Gaumont Long Bar, Ritz Dance Hall and even a few streets had all been bulldozed.

'When you left,' Peter said to Dad, 'They had to tear everything down so they could fumigate the place.'

We arrived back at the house to a party in our honour. There were second cousins, third cousins, fourth cousins twice removed and my fifth cousin's best friend's cat. Gerry, the youngest of the Thacker siblings (born in 1937) rocked up and immediately started trading navy stories with Dad.

Gerry is still in uniform. In fact, it's a bit of a family joke that Gerry hasn't been out of uniform since he joined the navy when he was fifteen. After he left the high seas, he joined the Salford Police. Then he became a warden at Strangeways prison and he is now, at the age of sixty-seven, a security guard at Manchester's largest shopping centre.

Dad spent a great deal of the night teasing the boyfriend of Maggie's daughter Kellie. Ben is a Manchester City supporter.

'City will do all right next season,' Dad said, when he was introduced to Ben (first as a Manchester City supporter and only second as Kellie's boyfriend). 'They've just signed two top Chinese players,' he continued, 'We Wun Wunce and How Long Since.'

The rivalry between Man United and Man City fans is intense to say the least. Mind you, Man City might not have been too successful of late (okay, they're CRAP!), but they have plenty of anti-Man United chants. Some of these delightful little ditties, that almost an entire stadiumful of people would sing, include: 'The shitty Man United went to Rome to see the Pope, and this is what he said ... "Fuck Off! Who the fuck are Man United?"' and 'Ryan Giggs is illegitimate. He ain't got no birth certificate. He's got AIDS and can't get rid of it.'

Manchester United fans simply retaliate with, 'Man City are the shit of Manchester. Man City are the shit of Manchester.'

Peter and Maggie's son Wayde would have belted out a few anti-Man City chants in his time. Not only does he have an entire wardrobe full of Manchester United tops (which are in the same price range as Armani and Versace) he also has a large Manchester United Red Devil tattoo on his arm.

Ben was outnumbered. After taking it in turns to give him grief, it was time for bed. I wasn't looking forward to it—I had to share a double bed with Dad. To be fair, though, it worked out quite well. I could easily give him a good elbow to the ribs whenever he started snoring. So it was just his farting that woke me up.

•

'Oh, that looks lovely,' Dad gushed as Maggie gave him an overflowing plate of grease and lard for breakfast. I tried my best to look excited at yet another opportunity to increase my chances of having a coronary.

On our itinerary for the day was one place that had changed dramatically since Dad lived in Manchester, the docks of the Manchester Ship Canal in Salford Quays. Until recently it was desolate; now it was home to ultra-modern glass apartments and offices and a bunch of large museums that were made, gathering by their appearance, out of Meccano and old tin cans. Even so, for a pile of old baked bean cans, the towering and audacious Lowry did look mighty impressive. The Lowry is principally an art gallery named after L.S. Lowry, who is famous for his bleak paintings of matchstick figures in bleak industrial landscapes (gee, he sounds like the life of the party).

'Do you want to go in for a look?' I asked Dad.

'I'm not going in there,' he grunted. 'It's full of bloody art.'

The Imperial War Museum was different from the Lowry. It was made out of *aluminium* cans. Designed by architect Daniel Libeskind (he's German ironically) and opened in 2002, the structure consisted of three massive silver steel chunks that represent shards of a globe shattered by war (or someone who got really angry with a can opener).

The interior of the museum was a massive open space. The dramatic effect of this enormous area was generated by its curving walls and roof, by the towering, silo-like sub-galleries that broke up the space, and the way in which the exhibits—notably an ex-US Marines Harrier AV8A Jump Jet, like some monstrous winged insect—seemed to peer around the corner at you.

The whole Manchester clan had made the trip out to the museum, but no sooner had we stepped inside than we lost each other. I could have easily spent hours in the place. It didn't glorify war or Britain in any way, nor was it full of badly dressed department store mannequins scrambling under barbed wire accompanied by a tinny soundtrack of guns and screams. The museum adopted a more human approach, examining people's experience of a world destroyed by war, using the mementos and memories of ordinary people. The stories of heroism and of helplessness, with heartbreaking stories of lives and futures ruined, could not fail to move you. One of the most bizarre pieces was an elaborately ornate Gold Mother's Cross, which was awarded to German mums who had more than eight children.

As we wandered around, Dad and Fred were reminiscing about powdered eggs, gas masks and exploding sausages (wartime sausages contained so much water that they tended to explode when fried—hence the nickname 'bangers'). Fred got very excited when he saw a uniform from his regiment (the Royal Engineers) and a rusted Ghurkha kukri (a large, fearsome boomerang-shaped knife).

'I've got two of them at home,' Fred said proudly.

'He uses them to carve up the Sunday roast,' Dad quipped.

Just before we left, the entire clan gathered around a small computer screen while I searched for Great Uncle Arthur (the computer listed all the servicemen and servicewomen killed in the two world wars). It took only a few minutes to find his name and I was amazed to discover that the family was finding out for the first time when he died and where he was buried. Arthur was a gunner with the Royal Artillery and he died in Dunkirk, where he is buried, on 27 May 1940.

As we shuffled out, twenty-two-year-old Kellie said, 'Was there only one from our famlay killed in t' war?'

'Yes,' Fred said.

'Is that all?' She seemed quite disappointed about that.

Dad and I went on alone after the war museum. We were going to a place where the two of us would share together a deeply moving experience. There was a very good chance it would become quite emotional. We were going to the 'Theatre of Dreams'—or Old Trafford, the home ground of Manchester United.

I've only really been a football fan for the past ten years. When we arrived in Australia I was teased about being a Pom so much that I started joining in with the jibes about wogball and was soon running around kicking an Australian Rules footy and shouting, 'Fair dinkum,' 'Beauty', 'Bonza, mate', 'Where's the dunny?' At the age of twenty-four, when I told Dad I was going to live in England for a couple of years, he was amazed.

'I thought you hated England.' I suppose he was right. Up until then I had virtually disowned England. I have a Greek friend who was the same. He hated everything about Greece for years, then almost overnight became proudly Greek again and no longer thought it was silly to dance the Zorba (he may have gone a bit far there).

Although I consider myself Australian, there is still a place in my heart that is English. My football heart, however, has switched codes. I still love my Australian Rules football, but 'The Beautiful Game' is my passion. I support Australia in every sporting pursuit (and Australia has a good go at most of them) except international football, where I'm as one-eyed, fervent, frenzied, impassioned, incensed, bitter, uptight, devoted and impatient as every other England supporter.

This pathological devotion to the English team was on show all around us on our drive out to Old Trafford. The European Football Championships were due to start in ten days and there were England flags (white with the red cross of St George) everywhere. Even the most zealously patriotic Australians don't show this much obsession with their flag. Every third car had a small plastic England flag and pole mounted on the roof and just about every house had a large flag draped out of a window. That's a lot of devotion to a team that hasn't won a major tournament since 1966.

That was also how long it had been since Dad saw his last game at Old Trafford (he saw his first in 1947). After he told me he hadn't seen the Red Devils play in all that time, he went on to recite the whole team from thirty-eight years ago: 'Bobby Charlton, George Best, Nobby Stiles, Dennis Law . . . those were the days.'

They may have been the days, but Manchester United has certainly done all right since then. Our tour of the stadium started in the trophy room and there was no little glass cabinet in the corner. The entire room was lined with floor-to-ceiling glass cabinets jam-packed with trophies.

Our tour leader Julie (Jew-lah) didn't take long to have a dig at Manchester City supporters. As we made our way out towards the pitch she said, 'There are three jails in the stadium. One for males, one for females and one for Manchester City fans.'

I'd been to Old Trafford previously to see a couple of games (as recently as eighteen months earlier I had come up from London with Peter and Wayde on a quick overnight trip to see Man United give some Greek team a shellacking), but the empty stadium with its sixty-seven thousand empty red seats really was a remarkable sight. The three Japanese tourists on the tour evidently thought so, too. They methodically went about photographing every single one of those sixty-seven thousand seats. Julie told us that only three thousand are reserved for away fans.

'During the last FA Cup tie against Manchester City, though,' she continued, 'another six thousand Man City fans were put in the top stand. That brought in piles of complaint letters from Man United fans. They said it was too hard to throw empty bottles *up*.'

In the tiny dressing room everything was bolted down. 'Fans have stolen the clock so many times,' Julie said, 'and the door knobs and even the toilet paper.' I wondered if the thieves kept the toilet roll in a glass cabinet at home.

In the corridor on the way out a local Mancunian who was on the tour said, 'It's cleaner in 'ere than Manchester 'ospital.'

The Manchester United Mega Store is so named because you need mega bucks to buy anything. And you really could buy anything. Besides the usual football paraphernalia, there were Manchester United cameras, chocolate bars, jelly beans, nappies, dinner sets, sheets, underpants, radios, players' footprints cast in bronze and even Manchester United wedding rings (weddings take place on the pitch on most weekends). Although I was tempted by the Red Devil underpants, I didn't feel too guilty about not contributing to the club's estimated annual merchandise sales of around £100 million.

•

'Do you know what England's national dish is?' I asked Dad over a cup of tea back at Maggie and Peter's.

'Roast beef and Yorkshire pudding?'

'No.'

'Fish and chips?'

'No, try chicken tikka masala,' I said.

Dad gave me a you're-pulling-my-leg look followed by a don't-bloody-wind-me-up look.

'It's true,' I said. And it is. In 2003, the Leader of the House of Commons Robin Cook 'officially' proclaimed chicken tikka masala as Britain's new National Dish. Not only that, it is Britain's most popular dish—over 23 million portions are sold in restaurants around the UK every year. It is also the most popular pre-cooked meal sold at Sainsburys supermarkets, and they sell a whopping 1.6 million serves a year (Sainsburys also sell chicken tikka masala pasta sauce, crisps, pizza, sandwiches and chicken tikka masala kievs).

'We have to eat a curry at least once while we're in England,' I said to Dad.

'I'm not eating any bloody food that looks like diarrhoea,' Dad growled.

Dad's 'foreign' culinary repertoire amounts to French toast and the odd slice of Swiss roll. This was essentially my foreign repertoire as well until I moved out of home when I was twenty-one. Not long after I had moved in with college friends, my flatmate's girlfriend presented me with this incredibly weird and alien-looking plate of food. It was pasta . . . but it was green! And flat. It also had a sauce that wasn't bolognaise; it was a cream sauce with the addition of wildly extravagant things like oregano and garlic. After the initial tentative tasting, I was soon devouring this revelation known as fettuccine carbonara—and have since gone on to have an almost obsessive appetite for foreign muck. Up until that point in my life, I was fed on a diet of chops and three veg, roast beef and Yorkshire pudding, fish and chips and sausages and mash. Now and again Mum (let me just interrupt myself to explain that I have two mums: the Mum I have now is actually my stepmother, Judy, who married my Dad over thirty years ago—two years after my original Mum died. It would be much less confusing if I called them Old Mum and New Mum or Real Mum and Step-Mum, but I think you can already sense the problem. I don't want to make either of them sound like less of a Mum—so you'll just have to concentrate and work out which one I mean from the context) would make us something as exotic as spaghetti bolognaise, but Dad would have a separate meal of bangers and mash.

All things considered, I was amazed that Dad now agreed to come out for a curry with Peter and me. Mind you, he only agreed after Barbara nagged him with, 'Brian paid for your airfare, so the least you can do is go out to dinner with him.'

We were heading to the Madras Mecca of Curry in Manchester (if not all of Europe). One single road in the suburb of Rusholme contains over fifty Indian restaurants and is known as Curry Mile. As we cruised down the road I rechristened it Vindaloo Vegas.

There was a neon war going on and each restaurant was trying to outdo the others with dazzling displays of bilious colours and flashing lights.

We already knew where we wanted to go. Ben, who was a regular on Curry Mile, had recommended a restaurant called Shaanesh. Or Shaajan. Or maybe even Shaajart. You see, Peter couldn't quite remember the full name, but he said it should be easy to find as the name started with the letters 'Shaa . . .' There just happened to be an abundance of restaurants that started with 'Shaa . . .' After Peter made a quick call to Ben, we finally stepped inside Shaandar Fine Indian Restaurant (incidentally, there was a good chance it wasn't really Indian, since more than ninety per cent of Indian restaurants in Britain are owned and run by Bangladeshis).

As soon as we sat down, an Indian (or Bangladeshi) waiter approached and said in a thick Mancunian accent, 'Ay-oop, would you lark a beer t'start?'

'Would you like a Kingfisher beer?' I said to Dad. 'It's from India.'

'As long as it's not made with water from the Ganges.'

Dad was looking around the restaurant and at the other diners as if he'd landed on another planet. Even the Indian music playing in the background was too much for Dad.

'You'd think they'd put some bloody decent music on,' he grumbled. As plates of food, including Britain's new national dish plus some rogan josh, rice and naan bread, were being set on the table Dad screwed up his face and said, 'It looks like the dog's eaten something that's upset it.'

There was only a few mouthfuls of food left on Dad's plate as he wiped his mouth clean and announced, 'That was the best Indian meal I've ever had.' It wasn't quite an Indian meal, though. He'd ordered omelette and chips.

Before we headed back to Peter's house I wanted to take Dad to Canal Street. This formerly neglected and seedy part of Manchester had been transformed (it's contagious) into three blocks of trendy canal-side cafés, bars and restaurants. It certainly looked like the place to be as we wandered down the narrow cobblestone street, which was abuzz with revellers drinking and enjoying the warm spring evening. As we picked our way through the crowd I leant over to Dad and said, 'Dad, this is one of the biggest gay villages in Europe.'

Dad's face dropped. He hadn't noticed that the crowd was predominantly men, and that we'd just walked past a large nightclub called 'Queer'. Peter and I dragged a rather dazed-looking Dad into a pub for a beer.

'Bloody hell,' Dad whimpered, 'There's more poofs in here than you can point a stick at.' I'd never seen Dad look so petrified. Halfway through his pint of beer he said, 'I'm dying for a piss, but I'm too scared to go to the toilet.' We did have to drag him out of the pub, though. He was staring, with his tongue out, at two lesbians having a good snog.

As we rushed out of the pub a very camp-sounding fellow shouted out behind us, 'Harry! Harry!' Dad almost wet his pants. The fellow, who was large and black and wearing no shirt, was calling out to one of his friends.

'Bloody hell!' Dad cried, 'Get me out of here.'

As Peter and I jogged after Dad past the entrance to Canal Street, I noticed that the street sign had been tampered with. Someone had blanked out the first letters of each word. For once, I don't think Dad saw the joke.

3

Butt & Oyster's fish and chips

On Dad's first day in the Royal Navy he was asked, 'Can you swim?'

'No,' he said.

'Then learn.' He was then unceremoniously pushed into the deep end of a pool.

In September 1946, at the age of fifteen and a half, Dad started twelve months of basic training (or 'lots of bloody marching' as Dad called it) with the two thousand other boy seamen at *HMS Ganges* Boys Training Establishment (a new intake of two hundred recruits was inducted every five weeks). The original *HMS Ganges* was a square-rigged sailing ship that was presented to the Royal Navy by the East India Company in 1779. After almost one hundred years of active service, the *Ganges* was anchored in Harwich's harbour and became the boy seaman's training ship. In 1905, the boys moved ashore to a land base near the village of Shotley in Suffolk. By the time *Ganges* closed in 1976, over one hundred and fifty thousand boys had been literally thrown into the deep end.

HMS Ganges itself is now a ghost 'town', but some enterprising old Ganges boys had opened up the *HMS Ganges* Museum which, I was disappointed to discover, only opened on the weekends.

I emailed George Athroll, the secretary of the museum, to ask for some info since we would be unable to make it there on a weekend. In response, he kindly offered to open it up just for us. As if in some wartime clandestine operation, I was instructed to pick George up at ten minutes past one at the junction of the A14 and the A137.

'How will I recognise you?' I asked.

'I'll be wearing a long grey trench coat and carrying a violin case,' he whispered.

He didn't really. He actually said, 'I'll be the old fellow standing on the side of the road.' Mind you, he wouldn't have wanted to wear a trench coat. Although it was only May, the weather bureau had predicted a blistering, and very uncharacteristic, top of thirty-one degrees (Celsius). When I'd hired the car I had the option of paying extra for air-conditioning but I said to the desk clerk, 'This is England. We won't need air-conditioning.' Famous last words.

Even with all the windows open we were soon sizzling away in the hot midday sun. As we drove down the A14 towards Ipswich, however, I felt very lucky indeed despite my sizzling rear end. Just outside Cambridge the traffic on the opposite side of the motorway had come to standstill behind a rather messy twelve-car pile-up. We drove for miles and miles past very hot and bothered people sitting in hot and bothered cars. They looked as if they'd been there a while, too. A lot of people had stepped out of their cars, including some girls sunbaking in their underwear and one hefty truck driver who was pissing on the grille of his truck. We later saw on the news that the traffic was held up for six hours.

Poor George certainly looked hot and bothered when we picked him up from the side of the road (we were a bit late because—surprise, surprise—we got lost). Once inside, however, George soon forgot about the lack of air-conditioning when he discovered that both he and Dad had joined the Royal Navy in 1946 and, even more amazingly, had both left in May 1957. They didn't know each other, but that didn't stop them from talking like long-lost friends. I had no idea what they were talking about. It was all navy-speak, like: 'Ahoy there, I was a jack dusty on a frigate that was aloft from the quarter deck and the slops.' 'Really, I was a petty officer on depth charges and bulkheads in the scullery and we'd hang 'em up from the yard arm.'

Our first port of call (so to speak) was the old barracks. Dad was like an excited boy seaman on his first day of leave as we drove up to the once impressive but now derelict gatehouse. Inside the buildings were crumbling, their windows and doorways were bricked up and the old parade ground was neglected and overgrown with weeds. Standing proud, but a bit the worse for wear, in the centre of the parade ground was the *Ganges* mast. This was an actual ship's mast and it was erected to give the boys experience aloft (as they say). It would once have had a massive safety net underneath it and sailors in training clambering all over the 143-foot mast and rigging. On parade days, seventy-seven well-balanced young boys would stand on the beams of the mast. Perched precariously on the very top would be the 'button boy', who would stand on the six-inch wide button with a lightning rod clenched between his knees as the only thing stopping him from performing some impromptu trapeze act.

Dad and George huffed and puffed for a while about how sad it was (the site was soon to become a housing estate) then started comparing tattoos. Dad got his now very faded naval sword and serpent tattoo on his forearm when he was drunk in Malta.

'The tassels are missing from the sword,' Dad said, 'because I sobered up halfway through and ran out.'

'I got this one done in Hong Kong,' George said pointing to a large 'Mum & Dad' tattoo. 'When I showed my girlfriend she said, "Where's mine?" so I had to go get another one.'

The museum was in an oversized, glorified tool shed down by the waterfront. Inside, however, was an outstanding collection of *Ganges* memorabilia. George and Dad sifted through old group photos (Dad was trying to find a picture of himself—although all the kids appeared identical in their Navy uniforms) while I wandered around examining the collection of stiff-looking uniforms and framed photos of little kids playing a game of war—the fresh-faced recruits looked no older than ten.

On one wall was an extensive display of knots. Some of the names looked harder to remember than the elaborate knots themselves: the 'Portuguese Spiral Sinnit Diamond on the Bight Knot' was sitting above the 'Two Hearts Beat as One Knot'. Thinking back, I could recall Dad on camping trips tying the most elaborate twisting double-backed loopity-loop knots on the tent pegs (and I'm pretty sure I had the Two Hearts Beat as One Knot used to tie up my shoelaces when I was a little kid).

I asked George to join us for lunch (I had to drag them both out of the museum) and we were soon basking in the beer garden of the Oyster Reach hotel with pints of bitter in hand. '*Ganges* made me,' George said. It was obvious that George's navy days were very dear to his heart and by the end of his first day he was hooked. In fact, when he came to *Ganges* he couldn't believe how luxurious it was.

'They had electricity *and* a bath. *Plus*, we got three meals a day, *and* we got paid for it!' Dad and George earned twenty-five pence a week as boy seamen (fifteen pence of that was kept by the navy as enforced savings). I sat and listened as the two old navy boys laughed and swapped stories.

'I changed my religion at *Ganges*,' Dad said. 'I told them I was Jewish so I didn't have to work on Saturdays.'

When Dad and George started trading denture stories ('My top plate cost me bloody three hundred pounds!'), I took it as a sign to leave. After we dropped George home in Ipswich, we headed back towards Shotley, where I had booked a night at the Hill House farm B&B. After leaving the motorway at the wrong exit three times, we finally cruised down a quintessential English country lane that was exceedingly fetching in the afternoon sunshine. The hedgerow-lined lane was flanked by fields of red poppies and yellow buttercups while pheasants and grouse fluttered across the road in front of us. The 'farmhouse' was a dazzling white mansion set on top of a hill with views of more green rolling hills and the Orwell River dotted with yachts.

I felt quite chuffed with myself for discovering this gem of a place, and the inside was just as impressive as the outside. We were shown to our commodious bedroom by Hazel, the farmer's wife, who had that 'absolutely soooper, frightfully nice' type of English accent. We also had our very own lounge room and dining room, and a bathroom that was bigger than your average London flat. Hazel told us that they grew sugar beet, potatoes, wheat, barley and had two hundred and seventy pigs.

'So do you slice a few fresh rashers off for breakfast then?' asked my not-so-frightfully-nice father. Can't they keep the riff-raff out of these upmarket establishments?

Hazel's husband Richard suggested a pub in the nearby village of Pill Mill for dinner (he should know the area quite well—the farm has been in his family for eight generations). The Butt & Oyster pub was set right on the waterfront of the Orwell River in what was once a smuggler's haven. Although it was only just down the road from *Ganges*, Dad hadn't been to Pill Mill before (boy seamen could go no more than a mile out of the base and were given a good hiding if they went inside a pub). This neglected little corner of England (as in neglected by hordes of tourists) was genuinely charming and the pub itself was a delightful old seventeenth-century whitewashed building with water lapping around its foundations. Most of the tables outside were full of people with bright red faces enjoying the balmy evening (a mere glimpse of hot sun and the bulk of the populace will try their very best to fry themselves silly). It was after seven but the sun was still blazing down and wasn't due to set till around 9.30.

I love English pub names. I asked the barman how the pub got its unusual moniker. He was an authority on the subject: 'Um . . . something to do with oysters and er . . . butts I think.' In Australia, pubs tend to have the most uninspiring names—often just the name of the town they're in: the Frankston Hotel, the Blacktown Hotel, etc. The English, on the other hand, can get wonderfully silly. My favourites include: The Cat and Custard Pot, The Leg of Mutton and Cauliflower, The Inn Next Door Burnt Down, The Poosy Nancies, The Donkey on Fire and—totally fanciful—The Jolly Taxpayer.

After a delicious meal (I had the baked crab; Dad had the fish and chips) we went for a stroll out into the Orwell River. Well not quite, but the tide had gone out, leaving miles of mud flats, so you could walk right out into the middle of it. When we had arrived at the pub, the wide estuary was filled with boats of all shapes and sizes bobbing gently in the water. Now they looked like a giant's discarded toy boats, lying slumped on the mud. It really was a magical sight as the sun sank over the river, turning the wet sand around us orange.

This was the first occasion on our trip that Dad and I were truly alone and it only really just dawned on me then how special it was spending this time with my father. Although he was possibly the world's worst navigator and a bit grumpy at times, I was really enjoying his company. Even when he let out a loud fart and said, 'Gee, there's a lot of frogs around here.'

As Hazel served us breakfast in our own Grand Dining Room (and I might add it was the best B&B breakfast I've ever eaten, with scrumptious homegrown bacon, eggs, tomatoes, mushrooms and not a drop of grease) she told us that the farm had a bit of a connection with *Ganges*. For many years, the farm would get the slops from the mess (kitchen to us landlubbers) to feed the pigs and they would find *Ganges* stamped cutlery among the mashed potato and gravy. We hadn't noticed, but Hazel had laid out some *Ganges* cutlery especially for Dad.

'We've got a drawer full of them,' she said. Just as Dad took a bite she added, 'We use them mostly for feeding the dogs now.'

4

If it's Tuesday, it must be bangers & mash

'That's the dead centre of Chatham,' Dad announced.

'Where?' I asked, craning my neck to look out on the other side of the car. It was a cemetery.

Every time—and I mean every single time—we passed a cemetery in the car when I was growing up, Dad would crack this tired old joke (along with, 'People are dying to get in there' and, 'You need a skeleton key to get in'). I couldn't believe I'd fallen for it again. But, we were on our way, via the cemetery, to Chatham Dockyard Museum (formerly Chatham Dockyard and Naval Base). When Dad had finished his basic training at *Ganges*, he was shipped to *HMS Pembroke* at Chatham, on the River Medway in Kent, for six months. Like *Ganges*, Chatham is no longer a naval base (it closed in 1984).

Chatham's real claim to fame, however, remains the Royal Dockyards. More than four hundred ships were built on the site from 1613. Over the next two centuries, the Royal Navy achieved and maintained an unrivalled mastery of the seas. Many of the naval battles of the American War of Independence and French Revolutionary wars were fought by ships built at Chatham. The most famous of all was *HMS Victory*, Nelson's flagship at the Battle of

Trafalgar. In the eighteenth century alone, Chatham Dockyard built and launched a staggering one hundred and twenty-five ships. In the years before the Industrial Revolution the dockyard was the largest manufacturing site in the world. Chatham Dockyard is now a navy museum with over eighty acres of storehouses, dry docks, officers' barracks, officers' offices, smithies, roperies, mills, stables and sailmakers and a few old ships thrown in for good measure.

Dad was looking forward to visiting the museum, but I almost left him behind. On purpose. Another hot day was predicted so Dad had gone for the short shorts, long white socks and sandals look.

'I'm not going anywhere with you dressed like that,' I said. 'You look like an old Pommy tourist.'

'That's because I am an old Pommy tourist,' he retorted.

It certainly was shorts' weather. As we pulled into the car park of the museum, the temperature gauge in the car flicked over to thirty-three degrees. Most of the museum was 'open air' and I could almost feel my thongs melting as we walked across the old bitumen parade ground.

'I was in a film with John Mills called *Morning Departure* that was shot here,' Dad said matter-of-factly. I stared at Dad. I couldn't believe he had never told me that he'd been in a film.

'Yeah,' Dad continued, 'there were five thousand of us marching on the parade ground.'

I had thought it would be nice to get out of the hot sun, but the bowels of *HMS Cavalier* were more like the bowels of hell. Dad had been on a similar ship called *HMS Chequers* (well, not that similar—the *Cavalier* was a destroyer and the *Chequers* was a frigate, or a maybe even a friggin' destroyer . . . I get confused).

'It must have been like working in an oven,' I said to Dad (Dad was also a cook by that point).

'The opposite, more like,' he said with a shudder. 'We were in the North Sea during the winter and it would sometimes get down to minus thirty. And what made it even worse was that the food had to be carried from the galley across deck to the mess. Sometimes in a blizzard you'd almost get blown over the side.'

There would have been a lot of scampering across the deck as well—there were around two hundred crew on the ship. Philip Mountbatten (who would later become Prince Philip, Duke of Edinburgh, Earl of Merioneth and Baron Greenwich and the Queen's hubby—among other claims to fame) was on *HMS Chequers* briefly with Dad.

'He got the biggest promotion of all time,' Dad huffed. 'He went from Lieutenant straight to First Lord of the Admiralty.'

'Did you ever speak to him?'

'Nah,' Dad said. 'We all reckoned he was a woopsy, anyway.' I believe the royal consort speaks very well of Dad, too.

The inside of *HM Submarine Ocelot* was even hotter than *HMS Cavalier*. Not only was it hot, it was also akin to crawling around in a large tin can. Dad sailed (or sank?) to Sri Lanka in one of these overgrown sardine cans, *HM Submarine Artemis*. I was amazed (and terrified) by how cramped the whole thing was. The Captain's quarters were the size of a toilet, the toilet was the size of a closet and the closet was the size of a shoe box—I'm not sure where they kept their shoes, though. You couldn't even swing a leg of lamb in the galley. No wonder Dad won't go anywhere near a kitchen now. Cooking in one of these for a few years would scare me off making even toast.

Pinned to the wall of the galley was a week's menu dating back to the 1960s (the *Ocelot* was completed in 1962—the last warship built at Chatham). I stared at it with disbelief. It was basically Dad's meal plan for the past seventy years. There was roast beef and yorkshire pudding, cod and chips, sausages and mash, baked beans on toast, steak and kidney pie, corned beef and, for dessert, bread and butter pudding and trifle. It didn't phase Dad at all that he had based his entire culinary life on a Royal Navy weekly menu plan.

Dad was loving revisiting this claustrophobic part of his life and was soon swinging through the hatches like a boy seaman as he followed our toothless guide Bill, who himself had been at *Ganges* in 1949. 'The new nuclear subs are real posh,' Bill said. 'They even have a gym and a swimming pool.'

'Swimming pool?' I said.

'Oh, aye, a huge one outside.'

After trudging around looking at old sheds and other similarly really important historical buildings, we got back in the car and drove up the road to the University of Greenwich. Dad wanted to fulfil his dream of enrolling in an accountancy course. Okay, that's not true. The university was formerly the barracks of *HMS Pembroke* and once housed five thousand sailors, including one Harold Arthur Thacker.

We drove down the main street inside the university grounds, between rows of red-brick buildings. 'That was Anson . . . and that was Nelson . . .' Dad was reeling off the names of the old barracks, most of them built when *HMS Pembroke* opened in 1903 as the home of the reserve, or stand-by fleet. I asked Dad what he actually did at Chatham, but he wasn't too sure.

'Um . . . guard watch and stuff,' he said.

'What, so everyone was on guard watch?'

'No, we also did cleaning duty and things,' Dad replied.

'I see,' I said. 'So half of you watched over the other half who were cleaning.'

Dad's old guard watch and cleaning headquarters was called St Mary's. I did a quick search on the Internet before I left and discovered that St Mary's barracks was haunted. According to the website, the haunting took the form of 'A Haunting Manifestation—with the sound of someone walking around with a peg-leg late at night'. It was even spookier than that. It wasn't just haunted; it had totally disappeared. There was now a motorway where Dad thought the barracks had been located.

'Are you sure it was here?' I asked Dad.

'Yes, it's disappeared!'

On the way out we passed the old barracks administration building, which was now a student pub called The Drunken Sailor. We were staying at another pub that was once part of the Naval Dockyards, the Ship & Trades pub, which was only four years old but was housed in a large building on the waterfront that in its former life was an engineering shop. Nautical pub names are nothing new to the town of Chatham. While I was researching somewhere to stay I happened upon the following: The Beacon Arms, Jolly Caulkers, Shipwright Arms, The General at Sea, The Ropemakers Arms, The Upper Bell Inn and the Botswain & Call. I assume that last one has something to do with the sea—either that or it's one of those TV detective series.

We checked into our room and wandered downstairs to the bar. I always find that staying in a pub can be a bit dangerous—there's just too much temptation to get rolling drunk. The dinner choices looked as if they'd photocopied the menu from the submarine. Dad was so excited he couldn't decide what to have.

We were quite sensible and didn't get rolling drunk, but the rest of the pub seemed to be. That brought to mind an anomaly in UK law, which still insists that 'It is illegal to be drunk on licensed premises'. From my experience in British pubs, most of the populace break the law on a weekly basis—27 million pints of beer are drunk every single day in Britain. Then again, quite a few other people would be breaking another old statute that says, 'A licence is required to keep a lunatic'.

When the pub closed, and we were lying in bed, we could hear all the drunken lunatics leaving. One fellow was shouting, 'I can't fookin' walk!' which was shortly followed by the same fellow sitting in a car yelling, 'I can't fookin' find reverse!' Another lunatic, whose licensed owner probably should have kept him on a tighter leash, stood right below our window for twenty minutes hollering 'Fookin' bollocks!' over and over.

5

Steak with just a hint of mad cow's disease

There was something real fishy going on in Corsham. While doing research on the net about *HMS Royal Arthur* I kept stumbling across references to a lot of hush-hush cloak-and-dagger stuff going on. An organisation called Truthseekers claims the base takes reports of UFO incursions into British airspace and secretly investigates them. And . . . not only is there the secret UFO project, but also an MI5 (Military Intelligence) facility and Britain's largest underground bunker complex to be used for housing key personnel including the Royal Family in the event of an emergency. Apparently, somewhere in the main part of the underground bunker there is a town—some people say a city—with roads, pubs, shops, recreational areas and special lighting that simulates daylight for those who may have to spend long periods underground.

Another source (I can't tell you his name or I'll have to kill you) reckons it's the UK government's nuclear command centre. Not far down the road from the base is the Corsham Computer Centre, known as CCC, which is in 'fact' the entrance to the underground nuclear command centre. Down below there is a complex rail and conveyor belt system that is used to safely transport sensitive weapons such as, and this is just between you me, nuclear warheads. Apparently, billions of pounds sterling had been spent on the project and the ministry of defence (MoD) constructed it as a 'black project' without the knowledge and approval of parliament.

Also, there is a rumour that Corsham may be the UK's command centre for Operation Abacus, which has something to do with the seven-times table, I believe.

Even the Corsham Tourist Office thought it was a bit suss. The chap behind the counter told us that in 1991 all of the buildings were totally renovated, including the replacement of *every* window, then suddenly two years later the entire base was closed down and no one has been allowed in since. When Dad mentioned that he had been based at *HMS Royal Arthur*, the tourist officer told us that they get a lot of ex-servicemen ringing the tourist office trying to find old flames. 'I've had about five calls asking if I knew an Ethel Smith,' he said.

'I think I went out with her, too,' Dad said with a cheeky grin.

I must say that I liked Corsham very much. I couldn't find it in any guidebook anywhere, but it was a delightful little town full of splendid buildings, mostly built from the local Cotswold stone, which is a fetching beige colour. Although it was ever so charming, the high street wasn't full of Ye Olde Worlde Tea Shoppes or taken over by, thank the lord, McDonald's, KFC or any of those other annoying global invaders. From the high street you could hear the cries of peacocks prowling the nearby formal gardens of Corsham Court, an Elizabethan stately home built on the site of a former Saxon royal manor in 1582. Tucked just behind the high street was a vast chunk of farmland, also part of the ancient estate of Corsham Court, which was home to a large flock of extraordinarily fluffy sheep. When Dad and I went for a stroll along the path that ran through the estate we stopped at a gate with a sign reading: 'If you don't mind could you please shut the gate as our sheep might get out'.

'There's more barbed wire here than at Colditz,' Dad said, and we hadn't even got to the main base yet. A cyclone fence topped with barbed wire surrounded what looked like a paddock next door to the base. Every fifty metres or so along the fence was a small sign proclaiming: 'This is a prohibited place within the meaning of the Official Secrets Act. Unauthorised persons entering the area will be shot—no questions asked'. Or something very similar. On the corner of the road leading into the base was a factory called SP Plastics.

'That's code for nuclear warheads,' I said to Dad, tapping my finger on my nose.

'They make pool linings,' Dad noted.

'Yeah,' I said, 'pool linings *and* nuclear warheads.'

HMS Royal Arthur looked like a place in one of those virus-kills-off-the-entire-world's-population-type movies. The buildings inside simply looked abandoned while the grounds were completely overgrown.

'My whole navy life has gone derelict,' Dad groaned as he stared at the once beautifully manicured lawns and gardens.

'That's not the original gate,' Dad said as we stood next to the bricked-up gatehouse. What had once been essentially a large garden gate was now a heavily fortified metal gate topped with razor wire. In fact, the entire fence around the base was crowned with what looked suspiciously like sparkling new razor wire. I had originally planned to sneak in for a bit of a snoop around but there was no way to gain entry without tearing parts of your body into strips. Besides, I wasn't too keen on getting shot or being fed to aliens or becoming part of some radiation experiment where my testicles got nuked.

Princess Diana was running the B&B where we were staying. Not only was our hostess a dead ringer (so to speak), but her surname was Spencer. The B&B was in a three hundred-year-old house that was a maze of corridors, exposed beams and hidden nooks and crannies. Diana had over-booked, so I was put into her room (but sadly not *with* her—I always had a big crush on the Princess). Di and her (new?) husband were camping down in one of the nooks and crannies somewhere. Naturally, as soon as I got in to the room I started rifling through her drawers but I didn't find any pictures of William and Harry or even an old tiara.

After a quick and decidedly tasty bite at The Flemish Weaver we walked across town to the Corsham British Legions Club. I thought we might visit a legions club at some stage during our trip, so I'd told Dad to bring his membership card along with him. The old fellow behind the bar didn't even bat an eyelid at the fact that Dad's membership card had expired in 1972. Mind you, that was probably because the barman thought it was 1971. Not only was the dimly lit windowless room decorated in that fetching seventies ode-to-brown-and-orange formica, but all ten patrons were dressed in that fetching seventies ode-to-brown-and-orange polyester.

A group of old timers invited us to join them at their table and before I even took my first sip of beer they started reminiscing with Dad about the good ol' days. Rex, who was eighty years old and only had three teeth, had joined the Royal Navy in 1940. He, along with two other mates, came to the Legions Club just about every night. Despite his lack of molars, Rex actually looked quite well for a man who lived on a diet of stout, rum and cigarettes.

'Oh, I used to love our daily rum ration in the navy,' Rex croaked as he sipped his drink.

'We used to get one-eighth of a pint of rum every single day,' Dad told me. In fact, up until 1970, all sailors over twenty years old were given their daily 'tot' as the ration was called, when at six bells (just before midday) the boatswain's whistle signalled for 'Up Spirits'. The British had a centuries-long tradition of serving rum on board Royal Navy ships. One pint of neat rum was first served to English sailors in Jamaica in 1655. In the early 1900s the rum was diluted with water (to produce what was known as 'grog') and was reduced to one-eighth of a pint. Funnily enough, too many people were falling overboard before that. When the daily ration was suspended on 31 July 1970, it became known as Black Tot Day, which was observed with solemnity and sadness as the end of a cherished (and tipsy) era.

When I asked Rex if he knew what was going on down at the old navy base, he looked around nervously and said, 'It's all hush-hush.' I got the same response from a local at the Methuen Arms pub when we stopped for a nightcap on the way home from the Legions Club. He did say, though, that if there was 'an explosion down there' the whole south-east of England would turn into a 'big bleedin' hole'.

For such a small town, Corsham has a very generous selection of homely, snug pubs with inviting names like The Duke Of Cumberland, The Hare & Hounds, The Great Western, The Royal Oak, The Three Brewers, The Pack Horse and The Two Pigs. The Methuen Arms was a wonderful old pub. We ended up staying there for a couple of hours, chatting to the barman and every other patron in the place while we had a few tipsy games of skittles.

'I could almost live in Corsham,' I said to Dad as we waltzed down the handsome high street back to the B&B. 'I could get a job in one of the underground city pubs serving beers to the Royal family when the world ends.'

•

In 1948, at the age of seventeen, Dad decided to become a cook.

'I hated the seaman's uniform,' he said. 'Because I was no good at ironing, I was always getting pulled up for badly pressed pants.' A cook didn't have to press his pants. This meant a transfer to *HMS Ceres* in Wetherby in Yorkshire for nine months of training. Mind you, nine months seemed to me a very long time to learn how to make bangers and mash. Dad was a cook for ten years, but whenever Mum went out and left Dad to make dinner, his culinary expertise would only ever extend to chip butties (chip sandwiches). I never complained—when I was twelve I would have happily eaten chip butties every single night.

On the drive to Wetherby I stopped to make one of the most exorbitant and extravagant purchases of my life. I bought a plastic tub of fruit salad at the motorway services, as the large service station and restaurant complexes are known. We'd stopped for a cup of tea and, feeling a bit peckish and in desperate need of food that didn't include any lard, I spent a week's wages on a small bowl of fresh fruit. It was delicious, but so it should have been when I could have had one of Melbourne's top chefs come to my house and prepare it for about half the price. While I was eating my preposterously pricey fruit I dropped a grape on the ground and Dad said, 'Whoops, there goes two pounds!' According to Dad, fruit salad was one of the harder dishes to prepare when he was a cook in the navy.

'It was a bugger opening all those tin cans,' he moaned.

HMS Ceres was—wait for it—closed. The base closed down in 1958 and it had, according to Dad, been torn down and turned into housing. He was half right. The old Moorlands site had been torn down but the Yorke Road site (Dad's old barracks) was still there. I didn't tell Dad what it had been converted into, though. I wanted to surprise him.

'Is this another UFO base?' Dad asked as we drove towards the old base. 'The whole place is surrounded by razor wire.' Then he saw the sign: Wetherby Young Offenders Institute. His old barracks was now prison cells.

'It's been a prison for over thirty years,' I said as we drove into the car park.

'Can we go in for a look?' Dad asked the prison guard at the main gate.

'You're not allowed in,' the prison guard said with a broad Yorkshire accent. 'Well . . . ah c'n let you in,' he whispered looking around, 'but ah can't guarantee we c'n let you out.' How could the prisoners take prison officers seriously, I thought, when they all sounded like they were part of a Monty Python sketch?

'We're not called t' Yoong Offender's Institute anymore,' the guard said. 'They've changed the name to Wetherby Secure College of Learnin'. We're not allowed to even call 'em prisoners. They're now trainees!'

'Yeah, trainin' to fight'n' smash bloody windows,' another guard chipped in.

'Do you have a lot of trouble here?' I asked.

'Joost t' usual,' he smiled cheerfully, 'smash'n' toilets, smash'n' oop their rooms and smash'n' oop each oother. They're real boogers soom of 'em.'

Real boogers, all right. Although the prison . . . sorry . . . Secure College of Learning was for fifteen- to eighteen-year-olds, the place was full of murderers, rapists and your general common garden variety thugs.

'What happened to my old barracks?' Dad asked pointing beyond the main building.

'Oh, the boogers burnt it down last year.'

•

After checking into a B&B on the high street and then dragging Dad away from the TV—Dad loves his TV—we wandered into town to The Angel Hotel. I'd found out about The Angel and its £5.50 Wednesday steak night on the *knowhere.co.uk* website. This site is quite handy for getting the lowdown on towns because it is an open forum contributed to by locals. The only downside is that most of the contributors are teenagers, so most of the postings are about the best places to ollie on your skateboard, the best parks to get pissed in and the best place to get your battered sausages with curry sauce. One of the hot tips in the entry for Wetherby was: 'The best hanging-out spot is the doorway of the Spar supermarket'. For the ultimate dining experience 'the chinky' (as in the Chinese) comes highly recommended because it 'supplies the best prawn crackers EVER'. For a nightclub, look no further than The Engine Shed Club where 'the over 30s night is good cos all the customers will drink proper beer, not alco pops and won't spew up on you at the end of the night'. The Angel Hotel was noted as a place that was 'a bit more for the oldies'. That was fine by me. At least no one would spew up on me at the end of the night.

The pub itself was actually an 'oldie'. It was once the principal coaching inn on the Great North Road with stables for over one hundred horses out the back. When Dad lived here he used to drop into the pub for a shandy when he was off duty and 'went ashore', even though the base was almost a hundred kilometres away from the sea.

We were there to meet an old friend of mine who I hadn't seen in twenty-nine years. Mark Connolly was my best friend in primary school and he'd emigrated to Australia from Huddersfield in Yorkshire the same year that our family made the big move. His mum got homesick for cold weather and battered sausages, so they moved back to England in 1975. I hadn't heard from him for over twenty-five years until he got in touch with me twelve months earlier through one of those school reunion websites. I recognised him as soon as he walked into the pub. He still had that cheeky thirteen-year-old boy's grin that I remembered. Mark brought out some old school photos in which we looked like brothers, mainly because both our parents favoured the old bowl-on-the-head haircut. There was a lot of chat about what happened to whom, although Mark remembered more than I did. We had a 'crack'n' night and the £5.50 steak was, in Mark's words, 'loofleh'. Dad told Mark that was because mad cow disease gives the meat a lovely sweet flavour.

6

Death by chocolate

In 1957, after twelve years in the Royal Navy, including stints in Gibraltar, Malta, Sri Lanka and Singapore—all of which Dad and I still had to visit (or revisit in Dad's case)—Dad took extended leave and got himself another job. He had planned to go 'back on board' when he finished his leave but he lost his fingers and was no longer considered fit to serve—he couldn't salute properly for a start. Since there was no work in his beloved Manchester, Dad dossed at his brother Fred's mother-in-law's house in Birmingham while he looked for work there.

His first job while on leave (pre squashed fingers days) was at the BSA motorcycle factory. Incidentally—for all you motorbike heads out there—BSA stands for Birmingham Small Arms. The company was originally set up to supply guns and ammunition to the British government during the Crimean War. In 1903, they began manufacturing motorcycles and, by the 1950s, after purchasing Triumph, BSA became the largest producer of motorcycles in the world. By 1965, however, competition from Japan and Germany was eroding their market share and by 1972 the motorcycle business was so hard-hit that all the factories were shut down. Dad probably played a small part in the downfall of the company.

Not long after beginning work at the factory, Dad started sending motorcycle bits to his father in Devon. He began with small things like a throttle and a suspension coil. Then, as he became more confident he sent a fuel tank and wheels. When the engine was delivered, Dad had managed to send an entire bike in the post. Not long after the last piece was sent and, after a short time tinkering in his garage, Grandpa Fred wheeled out a brand new BSA motorcycle. After all, Fred was a motorbike mechanic after the war and he worked right up until he died at eighty. Before Dad was tempted to send motorbikes to everyone he knew, he left and took a job at a plastics moulding factory. It was there, after only a few weeks, that he lost his fingers. Well, when I say 'lost' they were really, as Dad explained it, 'squashed like a banana'.

While Dad was at BSA he started dating a girl named Doreen Hill, who he'd met at the Harp Irish Ballroom. After a few weeks of courting—going to Laura Dickson's Dance Hall and kissing in the lane next to Doreen's parent's place—Dad leant over to her one night at the movies and whispered, 'We should get married.'

Doreen (my Mum) was born in Birmingham on 1 January 1925—she was six years older than Dad for those who are not good at maths. I found all this out for the first time as we sat with Mum's sister Ann in her house in Solihull, Birmingham, flicking through old photo albums. I knew very little about my Dad's life, but I knew virtually nothing about my Mum's. I stayed with Aunty Ann and Uncle Colin on my first Big Trip OS. When I told Ann that I was staying with a friend in Blackrock, Dublin, she said, 'That's where your grandparents are from.' I didn't even know they were Irish.

'Are they still alive?' I had asked rather sheepishly. They weren't, but I really didn't know until then. I had felt so embarrassed with my lack of knowledge about my family history that I didn't ask about my Mum's life at all.

Among all Ann's photos was a pile of photo albums full of pictures of our early life in Australia. Mum, I discovered, was terribly homesick and would write long letters to Ann every single week. Every few months she would also send another of these lovingly compiled, voluminous photo albums. It was really nice looking at photos of my Mum. I have only ever had one photo of her, with Dad on their honeymoon in Blackpool. Ann gave me a photo of Mum as a beaming twenty-four-year-old bridesmaid at Ann and Colin's wedding, standing in front of the very same church where she ended up marrying Dad.

After leaving photos scattered all over Aunty Ann's lounge room floor, Dad and I jumped in the car and drove to that church—he hadn't been there since he got married there in September 1957. The English Martyrs Church was in the middle of what Dad dubbed Little Islamabad.

'The whole place is full of Pakis!' Dad said.

'Dad, you really can't say that any more,' I said wincing. At the beginning of the trip, whenever Dad mentioned 'Pakis' to other people I would squirm. I soon discovered that a lot of the white English people called them that or even a lot worse, including the Catholic priest at the English Martyrs Church. The Father was outside tending the garden when we arrived. I told him that we were from Australia and the first thing he said to us was, 'So, have you seen a white face yet?'

'It's amazing, isn't it?' Dad responded.

'Don't get me started,' the Father said, glancing around. 'I'll get in trouble.'

The Father, who was Irish so a foreigner himself, went on to tell us that he had only about fifty parishioners left and they were all over sixty.

'They're the ones who didn't get out in time,' he grumbled. 'When they all die off there'll be no one left.'

'Have you tried converting them?' Dad said motioning to a couple of Muslim men dressed in robes walking on the opposite side of the road.

'Oh no, you wouldn't have a chance in hell.' If most of the population think like this, I wonder who's eating all that chicken tikka masala?

We had a quick look inside the church—it was nice and looked like . . . a church—then we drove around the corner to Shaftmoor Lane to check out a very large and very grey factory. This was the former home of Lucas, which made alternators and other similar car bits that are a complete mystery to me. Mum was working on the assembly line at Lucas when, not long after they married, Dad got a job there as a production controller. The factory, which looked incredibly run-down, is now the home of a multi-national called Denso, which makes alternators and other similar car bits that are a complete mystery to me.

We couldn't go inside the Denso factory, so I'd organised for us to visit another one—I wanted to see and feel what life was like toiling away in noisy and often dreary and dank surroundings. It's quite extraordinary how many world-renowned brands originated in the 'city of a thousand trades', including Typhoo Tea, Brylcreem, Bakelite, HP Sauce, Norton, Ariel, BSA motorbikes, MG, Rover, Dunlop tyres and Morris, Mini and Austin cars. The only factory we could visit was way out in the suburbs. That it just happened to be the Cadbury chocolate factory had nothing to do with my sudden fascination with production lines.

Cadbury is one of Birmingham's oldest companies, expanding from humble beginnings when John Cadbury opened a shop selling drinking chocolate—the original 'chocolate bar'—in 1824. Back then, drinking chocolate was a luxury and only affordable for the wealthy. It wasn't until the early 1850s, when the government reduced the high import taxes on cocoa, that Cadbury set up a factory to manufacture drinking chocolate and cocoa. Not long after, the Swiss added condensed milk to produce chocolate bars (bless their little Heidi socks). Cadbury got in on the act in 1903 when they started rolling out what is probably the world's best known chocolate bar: Dairy Milk. Today, Cadbury products are available in nearly one hundred and sixty countries and the company, including their merger-partner Schweppes, employs forty thousand people around the world. The brand is so synonymous with chocolate that in India cocoa trees are called Cadbury trees.

It's nice to know that I'm personally responsible for the wages of at least a dozen Cadbury employees. Okay, it's time to confess: 'My name is Brian Thacker and I am a chocoholic.' Rarely a day goes by when I don't eat chocolate, so for a chocoholic like me a visit to the Cadbury factory is akin to one of the Muslim employees doing the hajj to Mecca. Now, repeat after me: 'All chocoholics who are physically and financially able are obliged to make the pilgrimage to the Cadbury factory at least once during their lifetime, pay homage to the Beloved Chocolate, abandon this illusory world and be welcomed into the House of Cadbury'. Over five hundred thousand people a year make the pilgrimage to the Cadbury chocolate factory—or Cadbury World, as it's better known.

I was looking forward to abandoning the illusory world, but I was a little worried that I might do an Augustus Gloop—the fat kid in *Willy Wonka & the Chocolate Factory* who ate so much he fell into a river of chocolate and was sucked up a pipe. I had it in my mind, or I was hoping at least, that Cadbury World would be like Willy Wonka's factory. Well, it wasn't too far off. There were no Oompa Loompas, but there was a train ride through an enchanted forest with chocolate waterfalls and cocoa beans with arms and legs doing things like fishing and ice-skating. And, as in Willy Wonka's factory, there didn't seem to be a way out.

As soon as we walked into the factory we were given a bag with a solitary Dairy Milk chocolate bar in it.

'*One* chocolate bar! Is that it?' I squealed. I was expecting at least . . . well, ten—the factory does produce one million bars of Dairy Milk a day. I was only devastated for a minute, though—I discovered that at just about every turn after that a chocolate bar of some sort was thrown into my bag.

We shuffled down endless bright purple corridors full of screaming kids with chocolate smeared all over their faces. Some of the children were on leashes like pet dogs and when we sat down in a theatre to watch a film on how to make chocolate, one parent said to her little leashed Oompa Loompa, 'Sit down! Sit!' followed by, 'Good boy, good boy!' One Augustus Gloopesque boy escaped from his mother's grasp and ran under a fence into a room full of large vats of hot gooey chocolate. I was almost tempted to join him.

Almost two hours later we found the exit. But first we had to pass through the world's biggest chocolate shop. Actually, it was more like a supermarket. People were wheeling around shopping trolleys piled high with massive bags of chocolate off-cuts and broken bits. There were 'I'm a chocoholic' t-shirts for sale, but compared with all the other shoppers I didn't feel worthy enough to buy one. I hadn't bought one of the chocolate bars that was as big as a small car and, more importantly, my arse was nowhere near large enough.

There was an ambulance with its lights flashing parked out the front of the factory.

'That fat kid probably fell into a vat of chocolate,' Dad said. Lucky sod, I thought.

•

After yet another roast dinner at Ann and Colin's—I barely touched it as my stomach was still churning hot gooey chocolate—Dad and I went for an amble around the corner to visit Cheryl, Ann's daughter. The suburb of Solihull doesn't fit my image of Birmingham at all. There are no soot-washed, sandwiched houses in drab narrow streets, but instead lots of wide clean streets lined with majestic ancient trees and large front yards with flawlessly green lawns. Admittedly, Solihull is quite a posh suburb but I expected to see at least one discarded HP sauce bottle or just a little bit of soot here and there.

'Do you know what?' I said to Dad as we strolled down the street. 'I don't even know what date Mum died.' I knew it was November 1971 but I didn't know the day.

'It was November 30th,' Dad said, 'the day before Mick's twelfth birthday.' (Mick is my older brother.)

This was the first time in my life that I remember us talking about Mum's death. So I told Dad that I'd somehow blocked Mum's death from my mind and couldn't remember anything about it besides asking Dad where Mum was and being told that she had gone shopping. In fact, and a psychoanalyst would no doubt have a field day here, I seemed to have blocked out most of my memories of Mum. Back in Australia there never seemed a 'right' time to talk about Mum, but not only were we walking the streets of Mum's birthplace, I was feeling that already on our trip we had developed a much closer bond. Dad told me how he had had to 'just move on' and pretend everything was okay for us kids. The hardest thing, he said, and one of the most gut-wrenching things he's ever had to do, was calling all the relatives in England to tell them the sad news.

Cheryl was seventeen when Mum had died but was thirteen when we left England. By the sound of it, she was almost glad we left. 'Please Mum, not the *Thackers*!' she would scream when we came around to visit.

'We'd hide all our toys,' she told us over a glass of wine that night, 'because you Thackers would wreck 'em all. One time,' Cheryl continued, 'you'd all left and we were amazed that there was nothing wrecked. Then we went upstairs. Mick had covered the walls of Mum's bedroom, plus the bed and the mirror, with hand cream and lipstick.'

I found out that Mick was quite a cheeky monkey. I also learnt that he got up early one morning, when Dad was in the middle of painting our house in Spark Hill, and decided to paint the furniture with my brother Colin and me as his apprentices. And the carpets and the curtains. Another time, he pulled down all of Dad's freshly laid wallpaper. My favourite tale of naughtiness, however, was the time he snuck behind a large display of cans at Ann and Colin's supermarket and had a rather large crap that wasn't discovered till two days later. We Thackers were—and still are—all class.

As we left Cheryl's house she was crying and laughing (Dad's jokes tend to do that to you). She was actually sad to see us go this time. Dad is her only uncle and this was probably the last time she'd ever see him. Well, that's what he told her. After he'd milked the tears for a while and we had finally waved goodbye, Dad smiled cheekily and said, 'See you in three days.' We were coming back to Birmingham after a quick visit to Blackpool and the Yorkshire Dales.

7

Death by fried lard

In my faded black-and-white photo of Mum and Dad on their honeymoon in the seaside resort of Blackpool, they are walking arm-in-arm down the Promenade dressed in their Sunday best. Mum is wearing a skirt, jacket and gloves. Dad looks like a dashing young Dean Martin with jet black hair and blazer and tie. He told me he even wore his jacket and tie to sit on the beach.

It couldn't have been more different as we drove down the wide promenade—known as the Golden Mile—which was packed with folk parading up and down gorging themselves on hot dogs, hamburgers and ice-creams as big as my head. The gentlemen's attire of choice was shiny tracksuit pants and the latest (and largest!) England football tops—tattoos and mullets optional. The ladies favoured tight jeans with stomachs just bursting to get out—tattoos and screaming kids optional. Most of the snotty nosed kids were wearing full football kits—shirts, shorts, socks and even 'mock' football boots—predominantly Liverpool, which was only half-an-hour's drive south of Blackpool.

'Those football kits cost heaps,' Dad said, although most of the folk don't look terribly well-heeled.

'They can afford it,' I said, 'with the money they save by not going to the dentist.' Missing molars also seemed to be very much the fashion in Blackpool.

The Golden Mile was made up of tacky amusement arcades, bingo parlours, pubs, greasy food shops and McDonald's, which is much the same thing, really. My first glimpse of the sea was of grey, muddy water and grey, muddy sand that wouldn't even pass as a nice sewage outlet in Australia. It wasn't all horrid, though. Handsome tram cars of all shapes and sizes were gliding along the seafront and rising majestically at the end of the Promenade was Blackpool Tower—a sort of squat and portly Eiffel Tower.

I pulled up on the busy Promenade in front of the tourist office and Dad rushed inside to get a map. I hadn't booked anywhere to stay, as the whole of Blackpool is virtually one big B&B. In fact, with one hundred and twenty thousand holiday beds, Blackpool has more tourist beds than the whole of Portugal. What is even more amazing (and frightening) is that Blackpool attracts eleven million visitors annually, which is more than twice the number of people who visit Australia every year.

The map of Blackpool was utterly useless—you needed a magnifying glass to read the street names. But if you wanted to actually read the street names, all you had to do was send a postal cheque for £1.30 to the Blackpool Borough and they'd send you a larger map. The only problem is that you'd get it a week after you returned home.

I couldn't find (or read the name of) the street that Dad and Mum stayed in, so I turned down the first street off the Promenade. Not surprisingly, it was wall-to-wall B&Bs. The first one we tried had a vacancy sign, but the proprietor told us that they only welcomed 'couples and families'. I understand they do this to deter rowdy revellers, but I'm pretty sure Dad and I don't look like the sort who would tear up the sheets for a toga party and piss in the sink.

A sign out the front of Douglas House B&B promised 'impressive bathrooms'. The bathroom certainly was impressive. It was very impressive that they had managed to squeeze a toilet, a sink and a shower into a bedroom closet.

'You can tell who this hotel's biggest clientele is,' Dad said standing in the closet—I mean bathroom. 'They've got a denture's mug.'

'The bed's a bit lumpy,' I said as I bounced up and down on it.

'This is a good bed,' Dad observed cheerfully. 'On our honeymoon the mattress was filled with straw.'

The only real downside to our clean and compact room was the amplified voice coming in from next door saying, 'Two black ducks, twenty-two . . . legs eleven . . . lucky for some, thirteen . . . two fat ladies, eighty-eight . . .' The B&B was next door to Pat's 10p Bingo Hall.

I was so hungry I could have eaten two fat ladies. It had taken us ages to get to Blackpool and miraculously it wasn't because we took a wrong turn for a change! Rather, we were stuck on the M6 motorway on a Bank Holiday Monday. It was incredible. In the space of one hour we moved half a mile. To be honest I got a little upset.

'What the *fuck* is going on!' I screamed out the window on a number of occasions to all the other motorists. There was no accident or lanes closed, it was just the sheer volume of traffic. Then again, the M6 has nothing on the M25, the ring road around London. Traffic on it moves so slowly it causes around five hundred thousand motorists to waste the equivalent of twenty-nine years of their lives. True! No wonder the M25 was voted the worst place to visit in Britain—the Millennium Dome was second and good ol' Blackpool was third. So now I was really hungry.

Food is not Blackpool's strongest point. Food comes largely in one variety—deep fried. We opted for deep-fried fish and chips in a restaurant on the Promenade. At least we knew where the food came from—Birds Eye and McCain.

Mum and Dad spent most days on their honeymoon strolling up and down the Promenade, browsing in shops, flitting small change away in the amusement arcades, hiring deck chairs on the beach (even though it was warm, they never went for a swim) and 'taking in' Pleasure Beach, Blackpool's colossal amusement park. As a drawcard for tourists, nothing comes close to Blackpool's Pleasure Beach. It is the most popular attraction in the UK with 7 million visitors annually, outdoing the British Museum by almost two million. Why bother with ancient treasures when you can shove ping-pong balls down a clown's throat?

'Has the Promenade changed much?' I asked Dad as we slogged our way down towards Pleasure Beach.

'No . . . and I think it's still the same rubbish on the ground.'

The Pleasure Beach stats are mind-boggling. There are 145 rides including 13 roller coasters, 54 restaurants that sell one million ice-cream cones, 550 000 burgers, 500 000 candy flosses and 47.5 miles of hot dog sausages every year, and more people wearing football shirts than at a World Cup Final. The park is free to enter, but you do have to pay to go on rides. I only wanted to go on one. The Big One—Europe's fastest and tallest roller coaster. It travels at over a hundred kilometres per hour around steep bends and over dips and causes near decapitation. It is so high, it needs to have aircraft beacons on the top to warn aeroplanes of its presence. Dad passed up my offer to buy him a ticket.

'The Big Dipper was scary enough for us,' Dad said. The Big Dipper was built in 1921. Dwarfed by the Big One, it now looks like a toddler's ride.

The climb to the top took forever. I was just starting to enjoy the view . . . then came the drop. For the first few seconds I thought I was going to drop something in my pants. It was terrifying. No, it was fun. No it wasn't. Yes it was. My favourite bit, however, was when the loudmouth sitting behind me lost his sunglasses when they went flying off his face towards the sea. As we got off the ride, I heard him yell to his mate, 'Those fockin' sunglasses cost me four 'undred fockin' quid!'.

We caught a rattling topless tram to our B&B rather than face the long walk back, and for a brief respite from all the football shirts. I made us a nice cup of tea (well, with powdered milk, it wasn't actually that *nice*) but the kettle hadn't even boiled before Dad was fast asleep. I kept forgetting that Dad was seventy-two—not to mention that we'd been frantically on the go since the trip began. I still had to throw a book at him, though—he was sounding like a runaway train again.

•

I couldn't face any more fried food for dinner and I don't think my travel insurance covered death by lard. There wasn't much alternative on the Promenade, though. Besides the six McDonald's (yes, that's *six* McDonald's in just over a mile), the main option was dodgy looking burgers topped with cheese, sausages cut in half and a generous dollop of grease.

'That one there,' Dad said, pointing to a particularly scary looking burger, 'was there in 1957.' We had to eat something, so we had a double hot dog each for 50p. Surprisingly, it was quite nice and, best of all, neither of us had a coronary.

In the middle of all the unashamed tackiness that is Blackpool stands the Blackpool Tower Ballroom. After working our way up through the tower's layer after layer of noisy entertainment—Tower Circus, Jungle Jim's Zap Zone, Charlie Cairoli Fun House, Dawn of Time Ride, Aquarium, and the Traditional Fayre Carvery Restaurant—we stepped back into 1957. The magnificent rococo ballroom with its extraordinary sculpted and gilded plasterwork, murals and chandeliers was alive with folk of Dad's vintage gliding around the dance floor to the sound of a gloriously grandiose Wurlitzer. This was where Mum and Dad came every single night of their honeymoon and they had danced to the very same Wurlitzer, and the very same tunes. Reg Dixon was the organist back in 1957 and he went on to play at the Blackpool Tower Ballroom for fifty years. He would have played 'Oh I do like to be beside the seaside'—and I'm not exaggerating here—around thirty thousand times!

We sat down and had a beer and watched the dancing couples perform the most elaborate and complicated steps. This was the original *Saturday Night Fever*. A lady of the blue-rinse variety waltzed up to Dad and asked him for a dance. Her name was Mary and she'd been coming to Blackpool at the same time every year for over forty years. Her husband had died three years before, so she now came alone.

Dad made an excuse about his rubber-soled shoes before I urged him on: 'Go on Dad, it would be impolite if you didn't.' Mary was an accomplished dancer with a grace that belied her years, but I have to say I was also quite impressed with the old fellow's twinkle-toes as they strutted around the dance floor to 'Darktown Strutter's Ball'. Dad may have been a bit rusty but he had the moves and he only stood on her toes twice. And totally bowled her over once. When they finished Dad whispered to me, 'That'll fix her. She won't want another dance now.'

It was dark when we stepped back onto the esplanade, where feckless youths were parading up and down the street smoking and drinking cans of lager. The dazzling lights of the amusement arcades were enticing people in with the promise of, as Slots of Fun amusement arcade put it, 'So much fun you can taste it!' Stalls lined the Promenade selling 99p 'Tassels for a Titter' nipple adornments, plastic bosoms and the ever-popular 'Wicked Willie' caps. We were too early for the Illuminations—from late August, the entire Promenade is lit up with thousands of electric and neon lights. In 1957, when Mum and Dad were in Blackpool, the Illuminations were lit by Jayne Mansfield. Since then, the celebrity light-switcher-onners have included Dr Who in 1975, Kermit the Frog in 1979 and Status Quo in 1993.

As we walked past the tiny booth of International Palmist & Clairvoyant Leah Petulengro (as seen on TV), I noticed a series of photos of her standing with The Beatles, Tom Jones and even Prince Andrew—she told Andrew, back in 1999, that he would remarry Fergie. She had been reading palms on the Promenade for over thirty years. If Tom and John had got their palms read by Leah, then so would I, even if I did think the whole thing was a load of bollocks.

After paying my ten quid Leah sat me down and, after a cursory glance at my palm, announced that I would lead a happy and prosperous life. Gee, that's a new one. I bet she didn't use that line very often. In my ten-minute 'reading' I also discovered that I was going to be rich, live to a ripe old age, have something special happen to me on 8 December (8 December has since passed and nothing that special happened—oh, except the mixed softball team I play in won). Leah also told me that my daughter Jasmine will be in the limelight and possibly even a star. 'I think she'll be in . . . music,' she added—she had probably read my last book in which Jasmine, as an eleven-month old, performed at the Tamworth Country Music Festival. She also told me that Dad had a dodgy hip. At the end of our reading she asked me if I had any questions. I sat in silence for a minute. What do you say . . . can you give me the lottery numbers? Then I asked, 'How will England go in Euro 2004?'

'Um . . . well . . . they will perform admirably,' she said musingly.

' . . . and then get knocked out in the semis, right?'

'Um . . . I'm not sure.' Leah made subtle motions that the session was over (she stood up, opened the curtain and turned off the light—I bet she didn't do that to Tom) and I joined Dad in the street where he was chatting to Leah's husband (he ran the mobile phone accessories store next door).

'England won't make it past the semis in Euro 2004,' I said to Dad as we traipsed off down the Promenade. 'Oh, and you've got a dodgy hip.'

I rarely pass up a chance for a bit of karaoke, but I did hesitate at the door of Jim's Karaoke (twelfth season), which was next door to Pat's 10p Bingo Hall. The place was packed with pissed folk of that speaking-incoherently-dribbling-flashing-your-bare-bottom type, and there was some poor bloke up on the stage who, judging by his gut-wrenching wailing, was obviously being tortured. I dragged Dad in, but we didn't get very far. Our feet had stuck to the carpet. A large sign next to the stage read, 'Anyone swearing, swinging mikes or chanting football chants will be cut off'. Most of the crowd was made up of blithering drunkards from separate buck's and hen's nights. Blackpool is now the buck's and hen's party capital of the UK, whereas in Dad's time it was the honeymoon capital—Ann and Colin, Fred and Dianne, Gerry and Brenda and June and John all had their honeymoons in Blackpool.

A succession of people wailed into the mike, before one guy, wearing an Osama Bin Laden mask, which had better looking teeth than he did, got up to sing 'I will always love you'. After I sang a song, for which I got rapturous applause because I didn't fall off the stage, I went upstairs to the loo and walked past one of the hens giving one of the bucks a head job in front of the ladies' toilets.

It was on that note that I decided to call it a night, although I had to stop Dad from going up for a look.

•

Because I've actually paid for the breakfast part of B&B, I always feel I should eat it but in order to lessen the impact on my blocked arteries, I said to Jane, 'I'll have no fried bread . . . and no fried sausages and also . . . hold the fried lard, too please.' There wasn't much left to have. After breakfast, Jane and her husband Tony joined us for a cup of tea and a 'quick' two-hour chat. Most of that time was spent talking about junction numbers on the motorways.

'So is it junction 21C off the M6 or junction 17A-minor off the M5 to get to the B61/62?' I asked Tony. In the end he felt so sorry for us and our dismal navigational skills that he gave us his brand new Collins UK Road Atlas. To be honest, I don't know how we'd got this far without one. I'd had just about enough of the AA Route Planner. Dad was right when he said, 'I can't figure the bloody thing out!' The drive to Blackpool included this helpful directional advice: 'Straight ahead on the M6 to the M6 junction which joins the M6.' But it may not have been all the Planner's fault. As we got into the car, Dad said, 'This Road Atlas is not much use.'

'Why's that?' I asked. It looked pretty good to me.

'Because I can't read maps.'

'Didn't you learn how to navigate in the navy?' I asked.

'If I'd been a navigator in the navy,' he huffed, 'we'd still be at sea now.'

8

Animal-all-sorts pie

'These people are all bloody mad!' Dad snorted. The surrounding fields were full of hikers in anoraks traipsing through the drizzling rain. Actually, they're not called hikers in England. They are called 'ramblers' and they go 'rambling'. Whatever you call them, that lot *were* all absolutely bonkers. Personally, I love a good ramble, but I find it remarkable that people want to tramp around getting sopping wet, sloshing through mud and sheep shit while unable to see twenty feet in front of them. Dad thought anyone who walked anywhere at all was odd.

'Why the hell would you bloody walk,' Dad said, 'when you can drive?'

Dad and Mum had driven through the Yorkshire Dales on their way back home from their honeymoon but had only stopped for lunch. I thought it would be really nice for me and Dad to go for a stroll together in the countryside. Well, that was until I discovered that he absolutely abhorred walking.

'If I'd wanted to walk,' Dad grumbled, 'I would have joined the army.'

A ramble was obviously not on, especially in that weather. Mind you, we couldn't really complain too much about the rain. We'd been in England for two weeks and we hadn't seen a single drop up until then. But how could we feel we'd been in England unless we'd had a good drenching or two?

Somehow we managed to find our way through the Great Wall of Drizzle onto the Yorkshire Dales—after taking junction 17A-minor off the M5 and onto the B61/62—and we then wound our way down narrow country lanes between meadows of wild flowers, woodlands, waterfalls, bruise-hued moors and past ancient abbeys and snug stone villages.

The village of Malham, where we were staying, looked almost too twee to be true. I could go on about babbling brooks and dells and stuff, but I'll let the writer of a tourist brochure I found describe it:

> This is indeed the stuff that picture postcard villages are made of. Malham is a charming and delightfully quaint little village with pretty stone cottages clustered harmoniously around the picturesque and spacious village green.

In the same short piece of copy the writer also managed to use the words pleasant, lovely, spectacular, peaceful, attractive, glorious and—let's not forget—scenic. What really surprised me, however, was that not once did he or she use the word 'idyllic'. Maybe it was raining at the time.

It was actually quite difficult choosing which village in the Yorkshire Dales to stay in. There are just so many 'delightfully quaint little villages' with even more delightfully quaint little names like Giggleswick, Hubberholme, Horton in Ribblesdale, Starbottom, Appletreewick, Buttertubs, Blubberhouses and the hillside hamlet of Booze, which, by the way, is the only village on that list that doesn't have a pub!

It wasn't just the superlative-riddled brochure that attracted me to Malham, though. There was also the Malham Youth Hostel, which had the unbeatable charm of being a third of the price of all the other B&Bs in the dales. Dad, however, was a bit worried that he'd be refused entry because he wasn't quite youthful enough. He had nothing to worry about. The place was full of grey-haired ramblers. It's funny, but hostels in England are quite often full of wrinklies, while most of the youth hostels I've stayed in around the world are full of your run-of-the-mill tight-arse twenty-four-year-old backpackers.

'Where's the bloody bathroom?' Dad asked, searching the room frantically for a cunningly concealed extra door.

'It's down the hall,' I said, then quickly waved my arm around the room and added, 'But we do have *two* sets of bunk beds each.'

The absent bathroom was bad enough, but Dad was also having trouble getting over having to make his own bed. Ten minutes after I'd finished making mine, Dad was still trying to figure out the 'sleeping sheet'.

I left Dad huffing and cursing over the sheet (he had it inside out and upside down, but he wouldn't let me help him) and went for an exploratory amble around town. I soon discovered Dad was right about the ramblers being absolutely bonkers. Three of them were sitting in the rain on a park bench in the middle of the village green eating, what must have been, very soggy sandwiches. I checked out the three pubs to ascertain which one looked good for dinner then scuttled back to the hostel. When I got back to our room Dad was still trying to figure out the sleeping sheet.

'They've got a plague of ants here,' Dad said not long after we sat down at our table in the Lister Arms pub. He then started scraping the poppy seeds off his bread roll. I ordered game pie and when it was served I asked the waiter what sort of game it was.

'Oh, the works,' he chirped, 'There's pigeon, rabbit, venison and duck.' Dad ordered bangers and mash and looked around to see what other people were enjoying.

'How's your animal-all-sorts pie?' Dad asked the couple sitting behind us. One of the great things about travelling with Dad was that we were never short of company. He'd speak to anyone and within minutes would have them in stitches with the same old jokes I'd heard for forty years. The couple were ramblers who'd spent the day rambling in the rain. Dad told them they needed to get their heads read.

•

I got up early and peered out the window at a brilliantly blue sky. With the other hostel guests being English, ramblers and old people, there was no need to queue for the shower—in fact, no one had been in it at all. Then I trundled down to breakfast. Everyone was at breakfast at eight o'clock on the dot.

'Glorious morning!' I said to an anorak-wearing lady sitting opposite me. She grunted back at me then stared out the window—the hardcore rambler must prefer a good drizzle. I had porridge and fruit while Dad had yet another fry-up. I told Dad that I would have a lot of trouble trying to explain to Mum how he died from an overdose of grease.

I was absolutely staggered when Dad said that he'd come on a hike with me.

'No way am I going for a hike,' he had said the night before at dinner. 'Not with my dodgy hip and all!' Dad wasn't quite dressed for rambling, though. He was wearing a collared shirt, drip-dry slacks and dress shoes. He lasted about a hundred metres, then the track out of town started to incline slightly. 'Sod that,' he puffed, 'I'm going for a cup of tea.'

The track that ran through town was part of the Pennine Way, which runs for 268 miles (429 kilometres) from Edale in Derbyshire to Kirk Yetholm in Scotland. A fit (and, in my opinion, decidedly bonkers) rambler can ramble the entire route in sixteen days. I wasn't quite in the same league. I was doing the rambler's equivalent of walking to your letterbox—the three-hour Malham loop.

Beyond the village, the path twisted up through rolling countryside to the magnificent natural (and magnificently sheer) amphitheatre of Malham Cove. As I clambered up the steep limestone steps I was thinking that maybe Leah the Clairvoyant was almost right—if Dad had come with me he would have ended up with a dodgy hip after this climb. The view from the top was, as the Malham brochure writer would have put it, 'delightfully picturesque and spectacularly peaceful'. The high, open moors were dotted with flocks of shaggy Swaledale sheep and criss-crossed by five hundred-year-old drystone walls that snaked wildly over the slopes. I continued clambering over the walls and through open fields scattered with boulders, following the AA Route Planner-type instructions I'd printed out from some rambler's website. The instructions started out simple enough:

> Follow Pennine Way signpost which leads you right up to the top of the Cove. Admire excellent views. Cross the Limestone Pavement, go over the stile and straight on. Go left onto road, then left again through gate.

It was around this juncture that I figured out I was hopelessly lost. The instructions didn't help, either. There was a touch of déjà vu as they read:

> Go straight ahead on the Pennine Way to the Pennine Junction which joins the Pennine Way.

I spotted a couple of ramblers heading my way, so I scampered over to ask for directions. These were serious ramblers with massive backpacks and, luckily for me, a proper ordnance survey map. When they pulled the map out, I noticed that they had marked every single inch of their rather impressive ramble so far.

'Right,' he said, 'you simply need to go straight ahead on the Pennine Way to the Pennine Junction which joins the Pennine Way.'

'Thanks,' I said and turned around and went back the way I came.

For a change of scenery I thought I'd be clever and take a slightly different route back to Malham. As I approached Malham, and after I'd scaled a dozen farmers' fences and stood knee-deep in sheep shit, I realised I could never be a true rambler. I don't like rain, I can't read maps, my knees look too knobbly in hiker's shorts and, most importantly of all, I don't have a hand-knitted woollen hat.

9

Cockles, whelks, mussels and jellied eels

Dad was too sacred to get out of the car.

'They're not going to bite you,' I said.

'No, I'll stay here. I'm not getting out,' Dad said with a shudder.

We weren't in a wildlife park or even in some dangerous high-crime area. We were in a quiet suburban street in Sparkhill, Birmingham. The street was Ivor Road and it was where I was born and lived for the first five years of my life. The neat line of 1930s terrace houses didn't look even the tiniest bit scary. Dad didn't want to leave the car because he felt uncomfortable being in an area that was full of 'Pakis', who, I had on good authority, don't bite people that often.

It certainly was a different Sparkhill from the one we lived in back in the early sixties. It was now, as Dad dubbed it, 'Downtown Karachi'. To be perfectly frank, I was quite taken aback at how close it really was to being Downtown Karachi. As we drove down the busy high street, we didn't see one single white face—indeed, one-third of Birmingham's population of three million is now non-white—and all the shops had names like Ahmed Real Estate, Azed Supermarket, Al-Faisal Chiropractors, Mushtaq's World of

Beautiful Fabrics and, my favourite, Hussein Brothers Chartered Accountants.

When I told Dad that I was going to knock on the door of our old house he said, 'Don't you bloody dare.' He was probably worried that it might now be occupied by a large, disreputable migrant family headed by a man who'd left his native country to find a better life with sons given to theft and senseless vandalism. In short, a family just like the Thackers . . .

I didn't knock on the door, but I was curious to see what it looked like inside. My rather hazy memories are of a large house with an even larger backyard. It looked positively tiny. I took a few photos while Dad sat nervously in the car. I tried to imagine what it would have been like living there. I remember Dad telling me that in my first-ever winter it snowed so much he had to climb out of the window to shovel snow away from the door. Only the lounge and the main bedroom had fireplaces, so at night we four kids were just buried under massive piles of blankets to keep us warm.

I've always wondered what I would have been like if we had stayed in England. I know for a fact that we would have moved out of Sparkhill, unless Dad had scored a job at Mushtaq's World of Beautiful Fabrics, of course. But where would we have moved to? Would we have moved near Ann and Colin in Solihull? Would I have stayed in Birmingham after I finished school? Would I have still been 'arty' and gone to art college? Would I have travelled so much? Would I still be losing all my hair? It undoubtedly would have been a very different life from the one that I lead in Australia now. There is one thing I can be very thankful for, though. If I had stayed in Birmingham I would have sounded like Ozzy Osbourne. The Birmingham accent is consistently rated England's most unattractive and makes the whole population sound, well, to put it bluntly, thick. Oh, besides my lovely Aunty Ann and Uncle Colin and all my other relatives in Birmingham, of course—they all sound like rocket scientists!

We dropped the car back at Ann and Colin's and hopped on a bus to the city centre. 'I don't like sitting on top,' Dad said as I grabbed the front pew on the top level of the red Midland double-decker bus, 'there's no driver up here.' But I loved being on top with that frisson of exhilaration (now, now) that comes with smashing through overhanging branches and careering around corners on the brink of disaster.

On my last trip to Birmingham I visited the city and was quite astonished when I suddenly stepped off the bus and back in time. The drab office buildings, the drab shops, the drab clothes—and most of the food—were straight from the fifties. The only really 'modern' thing was the Bull Ring, a massive shopping mall that was an architectural tribute to a concrete high-rise carpark. That could help explain why Birmingham's best-known landmark is a tangled mess of motorway known as Spaghetti Junction.

Well, boy, had it changed. The Bull Ring now looks like a four-storey high loaf of bread encased in bubble wrap. I liked it, though. Imaginative, yet sympathetic, modern buildings had also replaced a lot of the old grey monolithic buildings and the once neglected heritage buildings had been given a good ol' scrub. On top of this, everyone around us looked decidedly healthy and prosperous with an I'm-just-so-happy-to-be-living-in-Birmingham look on their faces. Dad pointed out that the reason everyone was so happy was because this was one of the five warm and sunny days that Birmingham gets each year.

With all these wholesale changes, Dad didn't recognise the place. He even had to ask a bobby for directions. The bobby, of West Indian extraction, chatted excitedly to us for ten minutes.

'Australian cops have guns,' Dad told him—British police don't.

'Really!' he squeaked, 'You wouldn't want to give soom of our luds goons. They'd go troppo!'

Dad remembered the Brindley Place canals where 'dead dogs and the odd human part would float by and the entire area smelt of piss'. Brindley Place, and the adjoining canals—there are more kilometres of canals in Birmingham than Venice, by the way—were now home to hip bars, restaurants and boutiques.

The largest bar on the canal was the Down Under Bar. This dinky-di Aussie bar had fifteen different Australian beers to choose from and kangaroo burgers with Kakadu plum chilli sauce and crocodile fillets on the menu.

Although the Skippy burger sounded inviting, we bussed back to Solihull where Aunty Ann's roast beef and Yorkshire pudding was waiting for us. As I filled my face with Roast Dinner No. 16, Dad told me that when we lived in Sparkhill we would sometimes have a surprise dinner—the surprise being that no one, including mum who was cooking it, knew what it was. Ann and Colin, who owned and ran a small supermarket, would often get cans of food without labels. Being unable to sell them, they would give them to Mum and Dad. Once a can was opened it had to be used, so we would have something like baked beans mixed with baby carrots and topped with pears for dinner. Apparently we used to pass up the dog food, though.

It was a struggle bringing up four kids on Dad's wages, so he had two other jobs. On the weekend he would hang wallpaper and a few nights a week he would go from pub to pub selling bags of cockles, whelks, mussels and jellied eels. Dad hadn't stepped into any of those pubs for almost fifty years, so I decided to take him on a bit of a pub crawl. I recruited Uncle Fred as driver and guide and dragged Dave (Cheryl's son) and Steve (June's son) along for the ride.

Steve, who is in his thirties, lives in Birmingham, but couldn't wait to get the hell out of 'this bleedin' shithole' as he affectionately called England. He'd been trying to emigrate to Australia for six years. Although he'd been rejected twice already, he'd finally found a way to get in. All he had to do was to get himself a job in one of the fields cited on Australia's 'most wanted occupations' list. The list included hairdressers, pharmacists, boat builders, piano tuners, dressmakers, chefs—that's just what we need: more bangers and mash—air-conditioning mechanics, welders, mental health nurses, occupational therapists, physiotherapists, medical diagnostic radiographers and sonographers—no one knows what these are, but we need plenty of them anyway. Steve had taken a job in Birmingham as a stainless steel welder as he didn't fancy cutting hair or tuning pianos. All he had to do was work in that job for five years and he was in. He'd been doing it for four years when we were there and he hated it. In fact, as soon as he gets his visa to go to Australia he reckoned he'd 'never look at a bleedin' sheet of steel again'.

Steve wasn't the only one wanting to leave the country, either. On the front page of the *Daily Express* newspaper just the day before we met up was a big, bold headline that announced: 'THIRD OF BRITONS WANT TO EMIGRATE'. The story began:

> A third of Britons are thinking of leaving the country in despair at the state of the nation, citing soaring crime, escalating house prices, petrol prices and long working hours as the main reasons . . .

According to the article, Australia was the favoured destination and the majority of the people leaving (almost two hundred thousand people left the UK for good in 2003) were in managerial and professional occupations, sparking concern that Britain was suffering a 'brain drain' of talent. Mind you, I wouldn't quite class losing Ozzy Osbourne, Alf Garnett, 'Aussie' Joe Bugner and David Beckham as a 'brain drain'.

Some brains had been almost totally drained in the suburb of Sparkbrook. In the dark and dingy car park of The Malborough pub, some morons had smashed the headlights of one car, taken the wheels off another and, in a show of pure genius, thrown a shopping trolley on top of a third.

'This area's a bit dodgy,' I said, glancing around nervously in case there were still some flying supermarket trolleys about. Fred, meanwhile, was rummaging through the boot of his car and dragged out two large and menacing knives. Dad and I were both wondering how dodgy the area was if the pub was BYO knife.

'Look at these,' Fred beamed. Thankfully, we weren't going to slash our way into the pub—Fred was just showing me his Gurkha kukris, which were identical to the one that was on display in the Imperial War Museum, but in much better condition.

'Oh, hello, Fred,' a red-nosed old patron said as we stepped into the pub. Other patrons followed suit: 'Evening, Mr Thacker', 'How are ya, Fred?', 'Look, if it isn't Fred Thacker!' Half the patrons in the main bar, well all the ones with the reddest noses, knew him. That was because Fred had a connection with this pub—he was a barman for fifty-two years and spent ten of them at The Malborough. Yet, here's the remarkable thing: Fred had last worked at (and visited) the pub in 1978. The same barflies who'd been there twenty-five years ago were still propping up the bar.

'The place hasn't changed,' Fred said. 'There's still the same cigarette burns on the cushioned seats.'

'Try lifting one of the stools,' Dad said. I did, and they were incredibly heavy.

'That's so people can't throw them around,' Fred chortled.

Dave loved the pub. 'I'm bringin' me mates 'ere,' he said as we played a game of pool in the empty (and dusty) poolroom. 'There are no pubs like this any more. They've all been fixed up.' I have to say, I liked it too. It was like being in a time warp. Nothing seemed to have really changed, including the décor as well as the patrons, since at least the early sixties. I even noticed that there were authentic 1960s poo stains in one of the toilet bowls.

The next pub we visited *had* been fixed up—there were no poo stains in the toilet, for a start. In fact, it was all a bit 'lah-de-dah'. The car park of the Shaftmoor was filled with Mercs, Beamers and other cars with no supermarket trolleys on their roofs. The carpet looked brand-new and the chairs weren't too heavy to throw around if you got the urge. The bar was packed with people and there wasn't a single red nose in sight.

I was only halfway through my half-pint of lager when Fred said, 'Shall we go?' Everyone else had finished their drinks. Dave, the twenty-one-year-old uni student, had drunk two pints of beer in the time that I'd taken four mouthfuls. Fred, who was driving and therefore drinking lemon squash, was champing at the bit to get going so we could finish the pub crawl and he could start seriously downing pints.

'I have twelve pints of beer on a Fridee night normally,' Fred said.

'I wouldn't be able to stand up or even talk if I drank that much!' I groaned.

To tell you the truth, I was amazed that Fred looked so fit and healthy. Not only does he down a few gallons of beer every week, he used to smoke—literally—like a chimney. In between working in bars he also drove a truck up to Edinburgh a couple of times a week and he would smoke, wait for it, one hundred cigarettes a night! He would leave at midnight and over the thirteen-hour round-trip would smoke an entire carton—one cigarette after the other.

'I don't smoke any more,' he said, 'it's bad for you. The kids keep me fit,' he added. Fred has seven children, thirty-three grandchildren (he had his mobile phone with him because number thirty-four was due to pop out any second) and seven great-grandchildren.

'We didn't have television, you see,' he said with a wink.

The College Arms was full of blithering drunk Irish road workers with bright crimson faces who were constantly hugging each other and speaking in Finnish (well, that's what it sounded like). While we were sitting down, a fellow walked in wearing what looked like a lab coat and bellowed something out.

'He's selling cockles and jellied eels,' Dad said excitedly.

I followed him, along with about half the pub, outside. A crowd had gathered around the boot of his car while Mr Lab coat looked around apprehensively. Ah, so these were highly prized black-market jellied eels. I squeezed in for a look, only to find myself looking at a boot full of bags of sausages. Mr Lab coat was doing a roaring trade, although I imagine that many of the drunken patrons would take their bags of sausages inside, put them under their chairs and promptly forget about them.

Dad told me that he used to do quite well out of selling his seafood, especially since he used a little extra ingenuity. Dad would get bags of seafood from his supplier then empty them all out and put them back into smaller bags. He'd end up with almost double the amount of bags and he'd still sell them at the original price. He used to bring home any spares he had at the end of the night. One of my clearest childhood memories is of eating whelks—a sea snail that looks like, well, a snail. I remember using a pin to pull the little critters out. I think my brother Mick used to make me eat real snails out of the garden, too.

Our pub crawl ended up at the Moseley All Services Club. Dad never sold seafood there—it just happened to be conveniently situated across the road from Fred's flat. As soon as I walked into the brightly lit bar—it was like a 7–Eleven with beer taps—a fellow said to me: 'Hello Brian, you're a funny booger you are!' I had no idea who he was. Another fellow said, 'Gee, you've got a great life there, Brian.' In fact, everyone in the club (well, all eighteen of them) was giving me a wave and a smile. It all seemed very odd.

'Everyone in here has read your books,' Fred beamed. My very proud Uncle Fred had made every single member of the club read all of my books.

After a couple of pints, Fred's ex-wife Dianne turned up to say hello to Dad. Dianne is quite large and she was wearing an even larger red coat.

'Don't stand by the bus stop,' Dad warned her when she walked in, 'or sixteen people will jump on you . . . They'll think you're a red Midlands bus.'

'You've been a foockin' idiot your whole life,' Fred said—while trying not to laugh. 'Why don't you have a day off?'

•

All my relatives in Great Torrington in Devon sounded like pirates. Although I couldn't spot any concealed tattoos, talking parrots or treasure chests about their persons, Aunt Rosie and our other relatives all had such rich West Country burrs I wouldn't have been surprised if they'd burst into a chorus of 'Yo, ho, ho, and a bottle of rum'.

Aunt Rosie was Dad's half-sister. This was where it all started getting a tad confusing. Great Torrington was also the home of Dad's brother Jimmy, his step-sister Maureen and his half-brother's twice-removed identical twin step-daughter. Okay, I made the last one up, but I did learn as we were driving to Devon that Dad also had a half-brother called Derek living in Barnstaple. Gee, ol' Grandfather Fred certainly was a busy little bee.

After dropping our bags off at Rosie's, we popped across the road to visit my great-aunt Violet. She was Grandfather Fred's sister and the sole survivor of the fifteen siblings.

'She must be about 120 by now,' Dad whispered as we stepped through the open front door. Violet was dressed in camouflage—she was sitting in a huge floral lounge chair that matched her dress, the carpet, the curtains and even her slippers. The rest of the lounge room looked like a floral-themed photo frame shop—every available space on ledges, shelves and tabletops was crammed full of framed family photos.

'Which one are you?' Violet croaked, squinting at Dad.

'I'm Gerry,' Dad said with a cheeky grin.

'Ee zart booger Harry,' Rosie said rolling her eyes.

'You're one of Fred's,' Violet said, ' . . . and aren't you dead?'

All things considered, Violet was doing very well to remember that Dad was one of Fred's—she has over seventy nieces and nephews.

Violet hadn't even known that she had a brother called Fred until he came home on leave, walked into the house and said, 'Hello, sis.' Their mum 'just hadn't got around to telling her'. With fifteen kids in tow, she'd probably just lost count.

We sat back with sweet milky cups of tea in hand while Violet regaled us with stories.

'During the war,' she said brightly, 'an American soldier asked me for a walk, so we walked to a field and sat on the grass . . . then the dirty booger took his pants off!' Violet giggled like a little girl for five minutes. Although I wasn't that keen to hear about Violet's hanky panky in the hay, I did finally get one story straight. Dad had told me that his cousin Albert had been mugged and stabbed to death in Singapore, while Fred told me that he was killed in a fist fight in Hong Kong. Not only did they both have the wrong cause of death; they had the wrong continent. Albert was in Cape Town,

South Africa, having an argument with a shopkeeper over change when the shopkeeper pulled out a gun and shot him dead. So much for the legendary Thacker charm.

Violet was still telling stories and giggling as we walked out the door. The minute we stepped into Rosie's house we were ushered into the dining room for a roast dinner. 'I'll only give you a little one,' she said, 'we're having a barbecue at seven o'clock.' Little one? There was enough food on my plate to feed the population of a small country. Beside the fact that there was a mountain of food, it was 4.30 and the barbecue was less than three hours away. I spent most of my time trying to pile what food I couldn't eat onto one side of the plate so it looked as if I'd eaten most of it.

After our lunch (or early dinner), we waddled around the corner to visit Uncle Jimmy. Two years younger than Dad, Jimmy had moved to Torrington to live with his father Fred in 1946 at the age of thirteen. Jimmy was the only male sibling who hadn't joined the armed forces, and that was only because, having asthma, he was refused entry.

I had stayed with Jimmy and his wife Mary sixteen years previously and I mostly remembered arranging our days around the Australian soap *Neighbours*. Mary would watch the early evening screening and then the repeat of the same show at midday the following day. Not much had changed. While Jimmy was telling us more stories about how cheeky my brother Mick was—like when he pushed Jimmy's daughter Michelle down a flight of stairs . . . head first—the phone rang. It was Mary's friend calling to remind her that the evening episode of *Neighbours* wasn't going to be on because of the opening game of Euro 2004.

Although the roast dinner was still gurgling away in my tummy, we had to get back for the barbecue. The whole gang was waiting for us in Rosie's backyard, including Dad's step-sister Maureen, Rosie's ex-husband Dave, a whole bunch of cousins and—I think I've got this right—my half step-uncle twice removed (and once by force).

As soon as I sat down I was given a plate with the equivalent of half a barbecued animal on it. Rosie's two daughters Lisa and Lindsay (my half-cousins?) were very excited to see me. Lindsay kept hugging me half to death, but that was probably because she was already seriously drunk. I really don't know what our life would have been like if we'd stayed in England, but I do know that we would have been surrounded by the loveliest relatives. Every cousin, aunt and half-step third nephew we'd stayed with or met was not only hospitable beyond words—and they all made a mean roast dinner—but were also simply just good fun to be with. Then again, if some of my relatives had their way, they'd be in Australia with us. Lisa and her husband Andrew were desperate to emigrate to Australia.

'We don't have enough points,' Lisa said, 'and neither of our jobs are on *The List*.' Andrew was a roofer and Lisa was a dental nurse. 'There is a slight chance we can get in if we live in Adelaide.'

'They *pay* people just to live in Adelaide!' Dad said.

'What about Tasmania?' Lisa asked. 'Is that nice?'

'It's okay . . . but they've all got two heads,' Dad said gravely—and in true (mainland) Australian tradition.

'There should be plenty of work for you, then,' I said to Lisa. 'Everyone has two sets of teeth to work on.'

When Lisa told me that she'd married her second cousin (Andrew), I said, 'You'd fit in perfectly in Tasmania then.'

'That's nothing,' Lisa said, 'there was a girl at my school whose father was also her grandfather.'

I'll let you figure that one out.

10

Mushy pea fritters and a nuclear accident

On my fifth birthday, a beaming Des O'Connor presented me with a birthday cake and crooned 'Happy Birthday'. Yes, the Des O'Connor who went on to release thirty-four albums with sales of over fifteen million, and who has hosted a television series in the UK every year since 1963. Back then, he was a Redcoat at the Butlins Holiday camp in Minehead, Somerset. Redcoats were the über-jolly uniformed camp (often in more ways than one) entertainment officers and Butlins Minehead was where Mum and Dad took us on our annual summer holiday until we left England. Overseas holidays were virtually unheard of when we first went to Butlins in 1963. In fact, up until Billy Butlin opened the first Butlins Holiday Camp at Skegness in 1936, most Brits never went away on holidays at all. Butlins changed that with its shrill, plastic, thigh-slapping technicolour antidote to the grim reality of factory life.

All the Butlins camps provided countless activities for the kids and plenty of places to drink for the adults. Back in the sixties, Mum and Dad and the rest of the parents would go out partying every night and leave the kids alone in the chalets. Childcare consisted of parents leaving a hankie on the doorknob to advertise the fact that a child was asleep inside and to alert the Child Patroller (CP), who would walk past the chalets a couple of times every evening. If the CP needed to raise the alarm, a bell would ring in all the drinking spots and everyone would go perfectly silent. An announcement would come over the loudspeaker saying, 'Baby crying in Chalet 22', then suddenly a couple would scuttle off out the door. Actually, it was probably only the 'little woman' who left . . .

An evening's entertainment for the adults at Butlins consisted of a stout or two for the men and a Babycham for the ladies at the Pig & Whistle pub, followed perhaps by a romantic dance to the dulcet tones of The Vibratones in the Beachcomber Ballroom. The décor of Beachcomber could only be described as Early Sub-tropical Rainforest. It came complete with a lagoon, artificial tropical storms every twenty minutes, and a papier-mâché volcano that would spectacularly erupt at regular intervals.

Mum and Dad would start their evening at the Pig & Whistle then head over to the Old Time Ballroom where, according to a brochure from 1964, you could do 'modern dancing or "Old Time" dancing or maybe even the latest Butlins vogue—Square Dancing'. Dad said, 'Oh no, we only ever did the old time dancing.'

As there were no televisions in the chalets, they would sometimes go to Prince's Lounge to catch the latest instalment of *Coronation Street*—that show has been running since 1960! Dad has a couple of old postcards from our trips to Butlins and one of them is of the Prince's Lounge. It looks like the departure lounge at Bucharest airport, but not as exciting. Another postcard shows a whole bunch of people doing exercises outside a line of what look like prison camp huts. It looks more like Stalag Butlitz than a holiday camp.

There are now only three Butlins left—at its peak in the sixties there were around a hundred registered holiday camps in the UK, including ten Butlins. The three remaining Butlins camps are

Minehead, Bognor Regis and Skegness. The first sounds like the name of a heavy metal band, while the other two sound like terrible medical ailments that involve boils and flaking skin.

I'd booked a four-day Long Weekend package at Minehead, but to be honest I was expecting more of a ghost town than a party town. I just couldn't imagine (or fathom) why people would go there any more. Given the glut of cheap overseas holidays to tempt holidaymakers, and the fact that it was early June, nowhere near England's two weeks of summer in August, I thought that we would just about have the place to ourselves. Boy was I in for a surprise. As we stood in the queue in the jam-packed reception area, a lady in front of us asked if she could change rooms and the ever-smiling counter girl said, 'I'm sorry, we are totally booked out. There isn't a spare bed anywhere.' No spare beds? That meant that all six thousand five hundred beds were taken. Later I discovered that the three remaining camps still play host to a staggering one million happy campers every year.

I know that Butlins has done its best to shake off its Hi-De-Hi image, with its knobbly knee competitions, glamorous granny competitions, cringe-worthy cabaret, cramped chalets and square dancing in the Bucharest airport departure lounge, but I never expected the camp—sorry they're called resorts nowadays—to be full to bursting. Mind you, the brochure makes Butlins look like paradise. It's full of photos of perfectly slim and gorgeous people frolicking joyously in the warm sun. Every single shot is of a cloudless day—and this *is* England we're talking about. Even the photo of the hip young couple picking up some frozen peas from the resort supermarket made it look as if they were having the best time of their entire lives.

We had been allocated a chalet—sorry, they're called units nowadays—in the two-storey blocks of Plantation Quay (the other exotically named blocks included Lagoon Bay, Pacific Wharf, Oyster Bay, Coral Beach and Sunset Wharf—which may have been just a tad misleading). Although the outside of our 'Gold Class' apartment looked like a cross between a housing commission flat and the set of Play School, the inside was modern, bright and clean with two bedrooms, a lounge with wide-screen TV and DVD player and a kitchen. I loved the place as soon as we stepped through the door—on the kitchen table was a complimentary bottle of wine and a gigantic box of chocolates—stuff the tiny chocky on the pillow when you can have an entire box!

There are four levels of accommodation at Butlins: Standard, Superior, Silver and Gold. When we stayed at Butlins almost forty years ago, our entire family of six stayed (and slept) in one tiny room. It was brand spanking new, though—Butlins Minehead opened in 1962, the year before we first went there. There was no ensuite then, however, just a shower block at the end of the line of chalets—another convenient excuse for Poms like us not to wash very often.

As we were 'half-board', we were having an intimate dinner with a few thousand other Butlinites in the Ocean Drive Dining Room. Before dinner Dad and I set out to explore the camp. The centrepiece of Butlins is the Skyline Pavilion, a vast covered area, which, in Dad's memorable phrase, 'looks like a circus tent with tits'. The massive indoor loitering centre housed pubs, amusement arcades, bingo halls, a sports bar, a bowling alley, shops, boutiques and restaurants—not that I'd call Pizza Hut and Burger King restaurants. It was all like a clean, neat and organised Blackpool. They even had the same dress code—football tops, loud shorts, tatts, beer bellies and missing teeth (and that was just the women). The place was full of families, all in matching football gear. Dad said that back in the old days there was a married section and a singles section. 'The singles section was just one big brothel,' said Dad with a longing gleam in his eye. You can take a bloke out of the Navy, but . . .

There were arcade games everywhere—out the front of the restaurants, in pubs and even in the toilets.

'What's this?' Dad chirped standing in front of some noisy pokie-type machine with epileptic-fit-inducing flashing lights. He put in a pound, pressed a few random buttons for about nine seconds, lost his money and said, 'I don't get it.' He did exactly the same thing at the very next machine, except this time he lasted all of eleven seconds. I had to stop him on the fourth machine—one of those crane things that gives you half a micro-second to catch a stuffed Spiderman toy—just what Dad needs—before he squandered my entire inheritance.

On the way to the Ocean Drive Dining Room for dinner we stopped in at the Butlins souvenir shop, which sold Butlins hats, Butlins glass ashtrays, Butlins pint glasses, Butlins ceramic ashtrays, Butlins shirts and Butlins marble ashtrays. This seemed to be a favourite haunt of the Butlins wrinklie population. 'These are probably the same people who came here in 1965,' I said.

'That couple over there,' Dad said, pointing to a couple of very wrinkly wrinklies, 'look like they never left.'

To get to the Ocean Drive Dining Room we had to walk past rows and rows of identical units. These were the original chalets from the sixties, but they had been totally renovated and upgraded and were now the 'Superior' Units. It still looked like a prison camp. The difference was that it now looked like an *upmarket* Stalag 13.

The Dining Room was also in the original building and I wasn't really that surprised to see that they had stuck to the menu from 1963: roast chicken with potatoes, peas and carrots; steak 'n' kidney pie or fish and chips. There's that submarine cuisine again!

'We had waitresses in the old days,' Dad huffed as we stood in the self-serve queue. My cousin Maggie from Manchester worked as a waitress at Butlins in 1972 and got together with one of the serving staff—her husband Peter. If he was anything like the serving staff I could see scampering around, he would have been very skinny and very spotty. We both went for the roast, because we just didn't feel we'd eaten enough of them while we'd been in England.

After dinner we dropped into the Sun and Moon pretend-a-pub for half a lager. The mock traditional English pub was adorned with red and white flags and balloons for England's first Euro 2004 game against France in two nights' time. The crowd was mostly men with large beer guts hanging out of their England football tops (it was nice to see they had dressed up for the evening, though: they'd replaced their shorts with tight jeans). Most of these men kept glancing over at a table full of single women. To be honest, I was just as intrigued. There were six girls and they all had breasts of gargantuan proportions.

'You wouldn't want one of them on your nose for a wart,' Dad whispered as we walked out.

There was a plethora of entertainment options for the night, but we headed straight to The Swinging Shillelagh Irish pub in the Skyline Pavilion where there just happened to be a karaoke night on. Okay, I'm Brian Thacker and I'm a karaoke addict—I couldn't possibly pass it up. When we walked in, an old fellow was up on stage belting out a heavy metal song, although it sounded more as if it was him who was getting a belting. Standing next to him up on the stage were two Redcoats, kitted out in their smart, two-piece red suits, smiling, swaying and clapping their hands as if they were on some sort of happy drug. Their permanent set smiles looked so plastered-on that I wondered if they needed pliers to reset their mouths to normal at the end of the night.

Being able to maintain a permanent smile isn't the only difficult skill one needs to master to become a Redcoat. Like contestants in one of those Pop Idol shows, wannabe Redcoats are assessed on their singing and dancing skills by a panel of six judges, and there are over four thousand applications every year for around fifty vacancies. Most of the Redcoats view the role as a stepping-stone to a career in TV or music, or on stage or as the manager of a McDonald's. Actually, some have done all right. As well as Des O'Connor, other one-time Hi-Di-Hiers who have emerged from Butlins to become celebrities include Cliff Richard, Michael Barrymore, Jimmy Tarbuck, H from the group Steps and the comedian Dave Allen.

I think I would have made a good Redcoat. Then again, if the reaction to my singing at the karaoke bar was anything to go by, the audition judges would have been swinging punches at each other. While I was up on stage singing Frankie's 'My Way'—one of my favourite karaoke standards—a fight broke out at the bar. Two guys tried to beat the hell out of each other while I casually crooned 'I find it allll sooo amusing'.

Dad doesn't mind a bit of karaoke either, but he wasn't happy with the song selection. There were no Dean Martin or Perry Como (or even Des O'Connor) songs on the list.

'There's no Danny Boy,' Dad grunted in frustration, 'and it's a bloody *Irish* pub!'

Most of the patrons who got up to sing looked (and sounded like) patients on day-release from the Somerset Meadows Loony Bin. We had a few beers with Mark from Birmingham, who had a purple face (and no, I didn't ask).

'I live in Wales now,' he said, 'I moved there to get away from the Pakis.' This was the seventh year he'd brought the family to Butlins for a holiday.

'It works out well,' he said. 'I go to karaoke while the missus takes the kids to puppet shows.'

We left just before midnight. When I told Dad that I was going on to Jumpin Jaks nightclub, I was very surprised when he said he'd come too. I never thought I'd see my father in a nightclub with all that 'bloody thump-thump modern music'. Dad stayed for half an hour, but that was only because he was in a state of shock and couldn't move. The look on his face was priceless. He was standing near the dance floor with beer in hand looking as if he'd just stepped into the middle of a voodoo sacrifice ceremony.

'What a load of *bloody* noise,' Dad shouted in my ear before he left. The 'load of bloody noise' Dad was referring to wasn't some thump-thump techno track; it was the sweet-sounding sixties hit 'Buttercup'.

•

Back in the early days of Butlins, sleeping in simply wasn't allowed. A blast of 'Good morning, campers' would be followed by the 'Wakey-wakey' breakfast song, which was piped directly into the chalets. The words to this delightfully annoying little ditty went:

Roll out of bed in the morning
With a great big smile and a good, good morning
Wake up with a grin
There's a new day a-tumbling in
Wake with the sun and the rooster
Cock-a-doodle-do like the rooster used-ta
You'll find it worthwhile
If you roll out of bed with a smile.

I think I would have killed someone—and got away with justifiable homicide—if they still played that. Then again, I did have to put up with the early morning trumpet show out of Dad's bottom every morning.

The sun was out—the forecast was for a blistering twenty-two degrees, so while Dad went back to the unit after breakfast for a nap (the disco dancing had worn him out) I went to find a deck chair to do some intensive sitting in the sun. I asked a passing Redcoat where I might find one and she told me they didn't have any.

'So this is a *summer* beach resort,' I spluttered, 'and you don't have anywhere to sit in the sun?'

'That's right,' she said, flashing me a smile before skipping off to be sweet and nice somewhere else. I decided instead to go for an aimless wander around the camp. As I strolled past the entrance to 'Crazy Golf' I overheard a lady saying to her aged mother, 'Look, you can't do everything today or you'll have nothing to do for the rest of the week.'

There certainly was plenty to do. Just a quick glance at the Butlins weekly entertainment guide revealed a smorgasbord of timetabled events. At 10.00 a.m. you could join Noddy for Storytime, followed at 11.00 by Trampoline Comedy with Jeff Jay, and then move onto the five to twelve year olds' Petanque Championships. Petanque wasn't the only sport on offer, there were sports of all sorts. I walked past the multi-sports area where games of five-a-side football, basketball, volleyball, netball and tennis were in full swing. There were activities for the entire family, too. Signs out the front of the Megazone Laser game complex read, 'It's fun to shoot your kids' and, 'Have fun. Blow up a loved one.'

Besides the sports, however, there didn't seem to be that much adult entertainment until the evening. Back in the sixties there were plenty of events to keep the adults busy. For a start you could begin your day with Holy Communion in the Camp Chapel (7.30 and

8.30 sessions). I found that party-till-you-drop funfest in a 1963 program, and the rest of the highlights for the day included:

9.00 to 10.00 - Fun and Games on the Playing Field
10.00 to 12.00 - Philishave Shaving Competition in the Pool Sun Lounge
10.00 to 10.30 - Light Hearted Exercise on the Green to Music
10.30 to 11.00 - Car Owners Meeting in the Viennese Bar
12.15 to 1.15 - Twenty Questions in the Quiet Lounge
1.30 to 2.30 - Kiddies Holiday Lovelies & Bonnie Babies in the Ballroom
2.30 to 3.30 - Professional Wrestling in the Marquee
3.30 to 6.30 - Rizla Cigarette Rolling Competition in the Marquee
4.00 to 5.00 - Know your Highway Code Competition in the Sun Lounge
5.00 to 5.30 - Glamorous Grandmother Competition in the Montgomery Ballroom
7.30 to 8.30 - Miss Venus & Tarzan Competition in the Marquee
7.30 to 10.15 - Sing Song in the Bars
8.00 to 9.45 - Holiday Princess & Miss She Competition
8.15 to 11.15 - Old Time Dancing in the Old Time Ballroom
11.15 - Goodnight Campers

The Rizla Cigarette Rolling Competition (all three hours of it) would have been my favourite.

I wandered deeper into the resort, past row after row of units with large English flags adorning just about every window. After about twenty minutes, I came across the Standard Units. It looked as if the residents couldn't be bothered walking all the way to Skyline, so they'd camped out on the neat lawn areas between the chalets. Some had brought out their chairs from inside the chalets while others played football or laid on the grass in the sun. Call me unkind, but it looked like a refugee camp full of board-shorted beached whales. Mind you, at £28 for a three-night stay, you could hardly bitch about being a refugee. I discovered later that one former Butlins camp has actually become a refugee camp. I wonder if the Albanian refugees still have 'Storytime with Noddy'.

I met Dad in the Skyline Pavilion at Harry Ramsden's Fish & chip restaurant for lunch. Harry Ramsden's is Britain's biggest chippie chain, with a hundred and seventy outlets serving ten million customers a year. The original Harry Ramsden's in Yorkshire is the world's largest chippie, with a hundred and forty staff serving over five hundred tonnes of fish and chips every year. They may be famous for their fish and chips, but that's not why I wanted to eat there. A whopping poster in the front window was advertising 'Mushy Pea Fritters (2 for £1.49)' and the larger-than-life photo of one of them broken in half looked like a hamburger after a nuclear accident. The outside of the fritter was a lovely golden-brown colour, while the inside was fluorescent green. It looked so horribly unappetising I just had to try one.

The place was packed with porcine Poms. In the six adult years that I spent in the UK, I don't remember having seen so many obese people. Was it because I lived in London and most people there can't afford to eat so much, or was it a condition of the working class or people from 'oop north'? Whatever it was, these people could certainly knock back a plate of chips. If I tell you that the average ten-year-old British kid eats his or her own weight in chips every year, bear in mind that that's the average across the whole population. It's the Butlins kids who account for most of the chips—and more than their fair share of the weight.

The poster for the mushy pea fritters added: 'Can you resist them?' After eating just one, I can safely say yes—it also *tasted* like food that had been in a nuclear accident.

After successfully clogging up our arteries with chips, we threw ourselves into a series of activities for the afternoon. We started with a spot of bowling. Dad, with his missing fingers, had trouble holding the ball and twice threw it into the next lane. Then, when we finished, he walked out with his bowling shoes still on. Crazy Golf was next, followed by table tennis—Dad finally won that one—then snooker. Halfway through our very slow game of snooker I said to Dad, 'Hurry up and take your shot, we've got archery booked in at four, then fencing, some trampolining and a session of aqua-aerobics.'

By the time we'd stopped for a quick ale on the way back to our apartment, had a shower, and I'd dragged Dad away from the TV, it was seven o'clock and time for dinner.

'Gee, everyone must eat early,' I said as I peeked through the window at what looked like an empty dining room. It was empty all right. There wasn't a single diner in sight.

'Dinner is between four-thirty and six-thirty,' the spotty server told us. After I'd kicked up a stink about the incomprehensibly ridiculous and archaic dining hours, we were given a couple of restaurant vouchers—for Pizza Hut.

Just across the way from Pizza Hut and next door to the souvenir shop was the entrance to 'Centre Stage'. This was, according to my Butlins Weekly Entertainment Guide, the major entertainment venue. It promised such exhilarating showstoppers as, 'Dance with Billy Bear' and, the 'Chip Shop Boys (the Pet Shop Boys covers band)'. Mind you, if you didn't want to see a talentless covers band, you could always see a talentless original band. Have you ever wondered what happened to Limahl, the singer with the extraordinary two-tone mullet who fronted Kajagoogoo? Old pop stars no longer burn out and fade away . . . they play at Butlins. Also appearing at Butlins during the summer were Bananarama, Suzi Quatro, Boney M, Doctor & the Medics, Alvin Stardust, Katrina and the Waves, Slade, Brotherhood of Man and T-Rex—they must do that one with Marc Bolan a la *Weekend at Bernie's*.

My disappointment at missing Brotherhood of Man was soon forgotten when we stepped into the Centre Stage ballroom. I stood there with my jaw agape at the size of the room. It was immense—a cavernous space in which a couple of thousand people were sitting at tables. At either end was a bar about fifty metres long, while up the front was a gigantic stage where The Big Beat Boogie Band were bashing out 'Shake your Booty'. The problem was that there weren't many booties doing much shaking on the dance floor. Most of the crowd were parents who sat drinking and looking vaguely bored while their kids slept in buggies or played listlessly with colouring books.

We stayed for a few beers and watched with amusement as a gaggle of Redcoats danced by the side of the stage in an attempt to draw people up onto the dance floor. They all had that rather forced look-how-much-fun-we're-having expression on their faces while they did the twist with ten-year-old girls and overweight grandmas. It all seemed like a hell of a lot of hard work on the off chance that you might become the next Cliff Richard.

•

After another breakfast spent queueing patiently for toast, I left Dad to his own devices while I hit 'Splash Waterworld'. This was the vast, covered water fun park with rides and slides and other assorted gimmicks. I wanted to get in early before all the fat hairy blokes with tatts turned up and put me off my lunch. If there had been a lot of fat hairy blokes with tatts in the sixties, it would have been a frightening sight indeed. The swimming pool back then had vast viewing windows that allowed you to see under the water from a walkway at the side of the pool. There was even a snack bar where holidaymakers could drink tea and eat shrimp-paste sandwiches while watching—through vignettes of plastic coral and fish—swimmers disporting themselves. There was more kitsch above the water: the pool was famous for its plastic decorations and the entire ceiling was festooned with fake birds, leafy plastic vines and tropical flowers.

On the way back to the apartment I dropped into the resort newsagency to pick up a paper. The young fellow behind the counter was French. His name was Jacques and he was on a three-month exchange program from his university in Lyon.

'If I was you,' I said, 'I'd hide under my bed tonight.' England were playing France in their opening game of Euro 2004 and the poor bugger would get eaten alive.

I have to confess, I was getting very excited (and increasingly nervous—the England team does that to you) about the match. There was a real buzz about the place and most of the male population in the camp were already wetting their whistles and singing England chants. And there was still more than six hours till kick-off.

According to a story in the *Daily Mail* newspaper; 'A fifth of the British male population are planning to get up early on the morning of the match to get in their wives' good books. An estimated £25 million will be spent by husbands and boyfriends during the tournament buying their partners new clothes or a restaurant meal as payment for watching the tournament.' More than twenty million people in England alone were expected to watch the game on TV.

After an afternoon of watching highlight packages and preview shows on the telly, Dad and I headed to the dining room at 4.30 for an early dinner—or is that afternoon tea?—so we could grab a good spot in the pub for the 6.45 kick-off. Just about every single person in the camp had the same idea and we struggled to even find a seat. As we left the dining room, Dad said, 'When we last came here in 1966, England had won the World Cup the previous week.'

'That could be a good sign,' I said hopefully.

There were plenty of venues showing the match, but we opted for Jumpin Jaks Nightclub because it was, as the sign out the front said, 'Adults only. No screaming kids allowed'. It was just full of screaming drunken adults instead. The room was filling up fast but we scored a prime viewing position within stumbling distance of the bar. The music stopped briefly while the DJ announced, 'David, your son is at the door.' I could see a little boy waiting patiently at the door, but David wasn't moving anywhere. He didn't want to lose his spot.

Every single person was decked out in red and white—hats, shirts, pants, capes and painted faces. All of a sudden the crowd parted and in stepped a fellow wearing a France shirt and the tricolour painted on his face. It was Jacques. Then the chant began. To the tune of 'Here we go', the entire pub was pointing at him and singing, 'On your own, on your own, on your own . . .' It was all in good humour but I wouldn't have wanted to be in Jacques' espadrilles if France gave England a hiding.

Dad befriended a couple of lads (as he does) and we were soon in a shout with Bob from Bristol and Pete from Leeds. The only problem was that they drank like fish. By the time the match started, Dad and I had three full pints of beer sitting in front of us.

England scored the first goal and the room erupted with a deafening roar. Bob celebrated by buying us another two pints of lager each. With only two minutes to go, and the Barmy Army singing winning chants, France scored two goals. When the whistle blew there was dead silence. I couldn't see Jacques. He was probably being flushed down the toilet.

It was amazing. If England had won, the nightclub would have turned into an instant party. Within five minutes of the match finishing, it was virtually empty.

Dad, who was quite merry at this point, said, 'Bloody England, I'm going to bed.' I stayed with Bob, who was having a whole heap of trouble standing up, and Pete and tried to drink my way through my now rather impressive collection of full pints. After a couple of hours or so—I was in that beer-induced time warp—an old fellow dressed in an England top and wrapped in streamers waltzed in with two tall blonde girls wearing incredibly short skirts draped around him. It was Dad. He'd attempted to go back to our unit, but couldn't get anywhere near it because an all-in brawl was taking place right outside the door. (By the way, what is it about the English that when they lose a game of football they have to beat the hell out of each other?) While he was waiting for the fight to finish he met two young couples from Manchester and they invited him back to their apartment for a few drinks. One of the girl's boyfriends had swapped shirts with Dad, so he was now wearing Dad's fetching stripey number from Target.

Dad was grinning like the Cheshire cat and it wasn't just because he had two leggy girls all over him. He was drunk. I'd never in my life seen my father drunk. In fact, I can't even remember seeing him drink at all when I was a kid. He has a beer or two now, but never gets beyond that slightly silly stage. It's also hard to tell how the grog's affecting him because he's slightly silly most of the time anyway.

'We came here in nineteen-forty-shix,' Dad told the girls as we staggered out of the nightclub. Dad was like a little kid. And I mean really like a little kid. He squeezed into a Postman Pat kiddie ride and put some money in. The rest of us jumped on the roof of Pat's van and we all sang along: 'Postman Pat, Postman Pat, Postman Pat and his black and white cat!' When Dad jumped on the life-sized horsie ride and started belting out the theme from *Rawhide*, I suggested it might be time for bed.

•

Our last morning in England was the first time that I *needed* a greasy fry-up for breakfast. This was also probably Dad's last day ever in

England. It almost felt like the end of our trip, but we had Gibraltar, Spain, Malta, Sri Lanka and Singapore still to go.

We dropped into the newsagency to pick up the paper on the way back to our room and I was relieved to see that Jacques was still alive. 'What happened to you after the match?' I asked.

'I run 'ome very queeckly,' he said, 'becoz ze English are very fierce.'

Gibraltar

11

Judias en salsa de tomate (baked beans on toast)

It was nice to see that the English holidaymakers on the Malaga-bound train were all showing their full support for the English football team and donning red and white. What was really impressive, though, was that they didn't have any football shirts on. The arms and faces of the sickly white English tourists were all bright red from sunburn. We were supposed to be going from Malaga airport to the centre of town (to get the bus to Gibraltar), but we decided to take the scenic route. Okay, I tell a lie, we went the wrong way. And it wasn't that scenic.

The train we were on skirted the coast along the Costa del Concrete past the architectural abominations of Torremolinos, Fuengirola and Marbella. With its Casa del Council Flat holiday apartments and narrow, packed beaches, the unashamedly commercial Costa del Sol looked just as terrible as I have always imagined it would be—amazingly, the number of British people taking holidays in Spain each year far exceeds the population of Greater London and more go to the Costa del Sol than to Italy! After travelling to the end of the line and back, we finally got off at the right stop and jumped on the bus heading three hours south to

Gibraltar, or Gib (pronounced Jib) as Dad and his navy mates used to call it.

It was in late 1948, at the age of seventeen, that Dad was commissioned to Gibraltar as a cook on *HMS Swiftshore*. For three months Dad slept and cooked bangers and mash aboard the ship that was parked—although that may not be the official term—in the main harbour.

'It wasn't like going abroad, though,' Dad said, 'it was just like England . . . except it was sunny.'

As we lurched around a sweeping bend, the Rock of Gibraltar loomed ahead through the heat haze like a shimmering ghostly fortress. Gibraltar is tiny, just six square kilometres, and is mostly uninhabitable because of the Rock. That, however, didn't stop every upstart nation fighting over it like cats and dogs for centuries until Gibraltar became part of the British Empire under the treaty of Utrecht in 1713. Spain has never recognised the legitimacy of the treaty, though, and this has been a source of discord between Britain and Spain ever since. At present, passions in this childish brawl are running high. Although the thirty thousand residents have been promised a referendum on their future (in the last referendum in 1977, only forty-four Gibraltarians voted against staying with Britain—and apparently those forty-four were asked in no uncertain terms to leave not long afterwards—they are worried that Gibraltar will eventually be handed back to Spain). Britain pays their bills, you see. The Spanish aren't likely to step in when a final notice gas bill is slipped under the door of an elderly expat with Union Jack boxer shorts.

The border between Spain and Gibraltar was across the road from the bus stop. After the Spanish guard grunted at our passports, we strolled into Gibraltar and hopped aboard a red double-decker bus heading down Winston Churchill Avenue. Suddenly, the Costa del Sol had become the Costa del Cream Tea.

The bus driver was Moroccan. His wife, who was standing directly behind him, was giving him an absolute earful. In keeping with international female tradition, she was probably telling him how to drive. That would have been okay, but he kept turning around and shouting right back at her. While all this was going on, she was feeding him nuts as if he was one of Gibraltar's famous Barbary apes.

We had to stop at traffic lights for a few minutes while a plane landed. Gibraltar's runway crosses the main road into town. We didn't fly into Gibraltar because the flight to Malaga was only £39—compared to £159 to fly into Gibraltar.

After checking into the Cannon Hotel I was keen to get out and see the town, but Dad had a bit of handyman work to do first. He couldn't help himself. First he fixed the bedhead that had come away from the wall, then he rewired the light switch. Before he moved on to the leaking tap, I dragged him out of the room.

At first glance, Gibraltar looked unmistakably and quintessentially British. Walking thirty paces down Gibraltar's pedestrianised Main Street took you back to the Britain of bobbies on the beat and red telephone boxes. Many of the restaurant and pub menus were straight out of the seventies, too, with prawn cocktails, steak and kidney puddings and peppered steaks featuring prominently. Every other shop had windows filled with alcohol, cigarettes and perfume. Since Gibraltar is free of VAT (value added tax—like the GST), even the prices took you back in time.

'When I was here,' Dad reminisced, 'the streets were teeming with loud sailors.' The streets were now full of day-trippers from the Costa del Sol in loud clothes. We strolled past Marks & Spencers, a Boots chemist and pubs with very English names like the Duck & Firkin,

Pig & Whistle, Three Owls and Hackney Carriage. At the end of Main Street was the open expanse of Grand Casemates Square.

'This was all the old army barracks and the square was the parade ground,' Dad said. It was now full of swanky fish and chip restaurants. We grabbed a table at The Rock fish and chip shop, which was adorned with British flags and framed photos of old Blighty. We ordered cod, chips and mushy peas from the owner and head chip fryer. He was Moroccan.

On the way back to our hotel we dropped into Ye Olde Rock British pub to catch a bit of Euro 2004. The barman was English but after living in Gibraltar for ten years now considered himself Gibraltarian—although he didn't live in Gibraltar, he lived across the border in the Spanish town of La Linea because he couldn't afford to live in Gibraltar. The Euro 2004 match on the big TV screen was between those two European football superpowers: Latvia and the Czech Republic. We were happy just to sit quietly over a beer and watch them slog it out. After about twenty minutes of silence Dad turned to me and said, 'Did you hear about the Latvian and Czech poofters who were living together?'

'No,' I replied.

'The Latvian went to bed and had a dream he'd won the Lotto. When he woke up in the morning he found a Czech up his arse.'

Naval humour, eh? You can't beat it . . .

•

After greasy fry-up No. 27 for breakfast, we went for a wander through empty streets down to the harbour. As we stood on the water's edge looking over the bobbing yachts, Dad said, 'This was full of navy ships. There would be at least ten ships in the harbour at one time, including a couple of aircraft carriers that would hold three thousand sailors each.' There were no British navy ships at all now, just a rather diminutive and very unimposing Gibraltarian patrol boat. The only British vessels in the harbour were the five unseaworthy Safeway trolleys lying in the water.

Dad had never been to the top of the Rock.

'There were no bars up there,' he pointed out. I quite fancied walking up but because of Dad's walking phobia—which I discovered is called, and I kid you not, ambulophobia—we took the cable car. Actually, it was more like an old metal shipping crate suspended from a cable. It creaked and groaned its way up to the 426-metre summit of the Jurassic (as in 150 million years old) limestone monolith. When we stepped out onto the lookout platform at the top, I said to Dad: 'I can't believe you never came up here.' I couldn't believe it because the view was—and I know this is an overused cliché, but it really was—breathtaking. Sitting directly below us like a scale model was the harbour and town; to the west was the Spanish town of Algeciras on a dazzling sweep of bay; to the north, the low brown hills of Andalucía; and, across the strait to the south lay Morocco, with the haze of the Atlas mountains in the far distance.

I talked Dad into walking down to St Michael's cave with me. I may have fibbed a little bit when I told him that it was the best cave in Europe to convince him! On the short, but steep incline to the cave we passed an old blocked-up concrete doorway. This would have been one of the entrances to the complex network of tunnels that lies beneath the Rock. Most of the tunnels, which extend for about thirty-four miles (fifty-five kilometres), were dug in the Second World War and were used as the base from which General Eisenhower commanded the North African landings. The largest of these tunnels was the Great North Road, a thunking great tunnel running a mile and a half through the rocky promontory and wide enough for a four-tonne vehicle to pass through, with off-road parking to boot. Legend has it that the tunnel system stretches to

Morocco and that this is how the Barbary apes came to Gibraltar in the first place.

I met my first Barbary ape on the road in front of the doorway. He smiled at me then scratched his balls. He didn't give a baboon's arse that I was there and totally ignored me when I virtually stepped over him to get past. The rest of the troop was hanging about the entrance like teenagers loitering outside a 7–Eleven store. They were all looking bored and restless. The apes are effectively British citizens on the dole. The municipality's government allocates money to feed and administer them, plus they get free medical treatment! The dole-bludging apes also play a part in the controversy over sovereignty—it is said that if they ever leave Gibraltar, so will the British.

Dad and I were laughing as an ape swiped out at a fat tourist, who tried to get in too close for a photo, when a sprightly young simian suddenly jumped onto Dad's head. It then started swinging, rather impressively I have to say, from Dad's hair. I tried to take a photo, but I was laughing too much. When the cheeky monkey had scampered off, I noticed that Dad was leaning on a sign which read, 'On this site HM Queen Elizabeth II and the Duke of Edinburgh, together with their Royal Highnesses Prince Charles and Prince Anne, made friends with the apes on 10 May, 1954.' I wonder if one of the apes swung from the Queen's hair or Prince Charles' ear. Now that would have been really funny.

Dad got a bit scared in St Michael's cave . . . because we didn't pay to get in. I coerced him into sneaking in with me on the tail-end of a large tour group and he was worried that we'd be caught and dragged off to the police. The interior of the cave, which was a massive limestone grotto, looked as if it had been designed by the Spanish architect Antoni Gaudi. The walls and cathedral-like stalagmites had that melted look of Gaudi's famous Church of the Sagrada Familia in Barcelona. The cave also doubled as a concert hall and Suzanne Vega had played there only the night before. The tickets seemed very expensive, though, considering you'd be getting freezing water from the stalactites dripping on you all night. Then again, I reckon that would be a lot more enjoyable than listening to Suzanne Vega.

'You're trying to kill me, aren't you?' Dad said when I suggested we walk all the way down to the bottom.

'It's not very far,' I said reassuringly.

It *was* very far as it turned out and it took us almost three hours to walk down the steep road. To make matters worse, the runty stunted trees that clung to the rock gave us no shade and therefore no relief from the hot sun. Dad whinged and moaned a bit on the way down but secretly I think he enjoyed it and was quite chuffed with himself for making it down with relative ease. Neither of us was keen to tramp all the way back across town to the hotel, though, so we stopped at a bus stop at the bottom of the Rock. We waited for forty-five minutes, then three buses turned up at once.

'This really is like England,' I said as we hopped aboard.

After a well-deserved long, hot shower, we headed down to the marina for dinner. The first in a long line of waterfront restaurants looked nice enough, so I stopped to peruse the menu.

'How do you like the sound of *bacalao grande con patatas y pure de guisantes*?' I asked Dad.

'Sounds bloody terrible,' Dad said through a grimace.

'How about *judias en salsa de tomate* or *pastel de carne y pure de patatas con salsa*?'

'You know I won't eat any of that muck,' Dad snorted.

'The menu is in English as well,' I observed drily, 'and the ghastly foreign muck I've just described in Spanish translates as fish and chips with mushy peas, baked beans on toast and meat pie with mash and gravy.'

'Oh, that's all right then,' Dad said. 'Just make sure you order it in English.'

As we were escorted to our seats I noticed a poster on the wall for a 'Tercentenary Musical Nights Concert—Celebrating the 300th anniversary of British Gibraltar'. What a spot of luck—we just happened to be in Gibraltar for the 300th anniversary of British rule. The concert was due to start in two hours' time. I later read that the Rock was captured by joint Dutch/Anglo forces in 1704 *before* it was ceded to Britain in 1713.

The tercentenary celebratory concert line-up included regimental bands and pipers, historical re-enactments, songs from West End musicals and a James Bond stunt scene. According to the waiter, there were still tickets available.

After scoffing down our dinner, we headed to the town's main car park and former parade ground, which was the venue for the historic 'Showcase of Gibraltar's British culture'. In our mad dash to get tickets, I didn't notice until we stepped inside the grounds that I stood out like a mangy gorilla at a gathering of the civil-servant Barbary apes. The crowd, which was made up almost entirely of local people, was all dressed up. The men were wearing suits and there I was in a t-shirt, shorts and thongs. At least I fitted in at the bar; they were selling cans of Fosters.

We found a seat in the temporary grandstand just as the setting sun turned the Rock above us into the colour of molten gold. After the regimental band and pipers belted out 'God Save the Queen', we were subjected to a bunch of kids from the local high school singing songs from the musical *Oliver*.

'It sounds more like songs from *Cats*,' I said to Dad as one of the little cherubs wailed her way through 'Where is Love?' Dad absolutely loved it. After *Oliver*, there were songs from *Annie*, *Fiddler on the Roof* and a couple of opera arias. At one point I moved a seat over and pretended I didn't know him—he was singing along so loudly to 'If I were a Rich Man' that he almost drowned out the choir.

During the interval we had a chat with one of the local bobbies.

'So, do you live in Malta?' Dad asked.

'No,' the bobby said looking quite puzzled. 'I live here in Gibraltar.'

'Humour him,' I whispered to the bobby. 'He thinks he's in Malta.' Dad clearly had a bad case of, 'If this is Tuesday, I don't even know what country I'm in'.

The second half was what I dubbed the 'gay set'. First there was a marching band of pretty boys in navy uniforms, which was followed by a sprinkle of Judy Garland and a dash of Barry Mannilow and then a delightful little selection from *Me and My Girl*. The audience jumped to their feet when the thirty-piece orchestra and thirty-voice choir broke into Gibraltar's national anthem, which sounded like another show tune from *Me and My Girl*: 'Mighty pillar, rock of splendour, guardian of the sea, port of hope in times of need, rich in history'. The crowd stayed on its feet for England's unofficial national anthem, 'Land of Hope and Glory'. This time I sang along: 'Land of Hope and Glory, daa da da daa daaaa, da daa daa da daaa da . . .' Amazingly, the Australian national anthem has the same lyrics: '. . . for we are young and free, daa da daa daa daa da da daa, our home is girt by sea'. The finale was a spectacular pyrotechnics display to that old firework accompaniment favourite, the *1812 Overture*.

As we were leaving, the bobby we'd spoken to at the interval said to Dad, 'Enjoy your stay in Malta.'

•

'I thought the war had started again last night,' George said to Dad and me over breakfast. 'I went to reach for my rifle when those damn fireworks went off.' George was eighty-five years old and he'd booked himself into the hotel for the entire summer. This was his first time back in Gibraltar since 1939. He'd joined the Royal Navy in 1933 and was stationed in Gibraltar from 1937 until the Second World War started.

'He's certainly trumped me,' Dad said.

'This will be your last English breakfast for a while,' I said to Dad as he polished off his bacon and eggs.

'What will we have for breakfast in Spain?' Dad asked uneasily.

'We'll be eating *tortillas con patas*.' Dad stared at me with dismay.

'Well, I'll bloody starve then.'

I didn't bother telling him that *tortillas con patas* is nothing more than an omelette.

Spain

12

Deep-fried tripe in hot paprika sauce

'G'day,' Dad said to the waiter who waltzed past us as we sat down in the café next to the La Linea bus station.

'Dad, he has no idea what you're saying.'

'They should all speak bloody English,' Dad grunted.

'We're in their country. They don't *have* to speak English. You should at least try to speak a few words of Spanish, even if it's just hello and thank you.' After Dad moaned a few more times, I taught him how to say hello *(hola)*.

'Thank you is a little more difficult,' I said. 'In most of Spain they say *gracias*, but here in Andalucía they have a totally different way of saying it. You know how in Barcelona they speak Catalonian instead of Castillian? Well, the Andalucíans also have their own dialect.' It took Dad a few attempts to say 'thank you' in Andalucían so by the time the waiter was on his way over with our drinks he was ready to try it out. Just before the waiter reached us, however, I blurted out, 'Don't say it!'

'Why not?' Dad asked.

'You might give the waiter a bit of a shock,' I whispered. 'I've just taught you how to say "suck my balls" in Spanish.'

I know a few words of Spanish—including the phrase I taught Dad which doesn't come up that often in polite conversation—but I didn't know quite enough to pre-book our accommodation. As usual, the Internet came in very handy. I simply went to *babelfish.altavista.com* and translated, 'Can I get a twin room for two nights, please?' into Spanish. Out of interest, and after I'd already sent a fax to two different hotels, I went back to the website to translate my request back into English just to see if it made sense. It made sense, alright. It was just that what I'd actually asked was: 'Can I have a pair of binoculars for two nights, please?'

Mind you, it would make travelling quite interesting if you used *babelfish* all the time. 'Do you have a room with a view?' translates back into, 'Do you have a quarter with a vision?' I tried a few phrases and some actually worked, but my favourite wacky re-translation was of, 'What's a nice girl like you doing in a place like this?' Filtered through Spanish it re-emerged as 'What's a pleasant girl taste of in a place like this?' I would have sounded like quite a philosopher if I'd used *babelfish* to find out if we were on the right bus for Cádiz. I would have said, 'The bus is this, that is Cádiz leading'.

Our journey on the bus that was this took us along a spectacular and craggy coastline dotted with snug fishing villages. Then suddenly we would make a detour inland for ten minutes and we'd be right in the heartland of Australia with its parched brown hills covered in eucalyptus trees and grazing sheep. That's exactly what it looked like.

'So, Dad . . . this is Spain,' I said as we gazed out the window. I decided to take Dad to Spain because he'd told me before we left that when he was in Gibraltar he would peer across at Spain every day and wonder what it was like. He had a passport, which in fact was just his Royal Navy paybook, but the border between Gibraltar and Spain was closed back then. I had originally thought we might go east from Gibraltar to the Costa del Sol, but that's not technically Spain—it's more like a sunny Blackpool. I'd opted instead to go along the west coast to the grand coastal city of Cádiz then up through Serranía de Ronda to a hilltop pueblos blanco (white town), make a quick stop in Andalucía's capital Seville and finish our Spanish journey in Madrid.

Once we'd past through the tedious modern suburbs of Cádiz, and crossed the narrow strip of land that connects the mainland to the small island of Old Cádiz, the bus dropped us off outside the crumbling eighteenth-century walls that surround the old town. We caught a cab through impossibly cramped alleyways to Quo Qádiz Youth Hostel, where we hoped to find a room waiting for us rather than a pair of binoculars.

I must have got the translation wrong again because it seems I'd booked the gay quarters instead. We were given a room with a double bed and I'm sure the lady behind the counter whispered, 'This is the old poof and his toyboy' to the manager. The only other beds available were up on the 'roof'. The look on Dad's face was priceless when we went up for an inspection. Spread out on the concrete roof in the open air was a whole bunch of old mattresses with sleeping bags placed on them.

'This is only one step up from being homeless,' Dad squawked.

•

The incredibly narrow streets of Old Cádiz were deserted.

'The city has been evacuated,' Dad said. 'You'd think someone would have told us.' The city did look abandoned, but that was because everyone was at home snuggled up in bed having their siesta. We went for an aimless amble down perfectly quiet and shaded lanes and through grand but empty open squares. The silence was broken when a car drove past us and did a three-point turn just to get around a corner.

'Imagine you driving in here,' Dad chuckled. 'The car would be covered in dents.'

'Imagine you navigating in here,' I said. 'It would take us a week to get out.'

We stopped at a bakery, which was one of the few shops open, and bought a ham and cheese roll each. Dad looked like a cow chewing its cud as he tried to get his false teeth around the chewy bread.

'A starving crocodile couldn't chew through this,' Dad mumbled through a mouthful of bread.

After lunch, we climbed to the top of Torre Tavira, an eighteenth-century mansion with the tallest tower in the old town, for incredible views of people's underwear flapping on rooftop washing lines. Each house seemed to be standing on tiptoes in order to look over its neighbour's shoulder and raise itself above the thick girdle of ramparts for a view of the sea. It was blindingly bright because every house was whitewashed and the long stripes of vermilion that mark the borders between the houses increased the brilliance of the façades even more. The high, turreted houses may have been faded and literally crumbling from the sea air but the old town was magically preserved. Nearly all the buildings now standing date only from the eighteenth century, but Cádiz lays claim to being the oldest city in Europe—it was founded by the Phoenicians in 1100 BC.

By the time we came down from our tower the streets were filling with people who had awoken from their midday slumber. The town's main beach, Playa de la Caleta, was already packed with locals baking themselves in the hot afternoon sun. We went for a stroll along the water's edge and—I couldn't believe I was doing this with my seventy-two-year-old father—ogled women's bottoms. Surprisingly, there were very few pale tourist imitations rubbing cheeks (so to speak) with the olive-skinned local bottoms. It seemed odd that this charming old town with its fine beaches and countless seafood restaurants was largely ignored by the tourist hordes. Maybe it was because there weren't any smutty t-shirt shops or Red Lion pubs serving bangers and mash.

Dad and I soon discovered that finding a pub in Cádiz wasn't that easy. England was playing Switzerland in their second game of Euro 2004 and we trawled the streets looking for a bar with a TV so we could watch it. I tried asking people in the street but no one seemed to speak any English. Thank goodness for charades. No sooner had I done a great impression of Beckham taking a shot at goal followed by a less easily interpreted mime of me watching TV, than we were directed to a tiny bar not far from our hostel.

We didn't have much trouble finding a seat. There was only one other patron—an old fellow who looked as if he'd been there for a few days. The barman seemed a little disappointed that we'd interrupted his quiet afternoon, but he got quite excited when he discovered that he had two large-as-life England supporters in his bar. Usually, the locals probably locked up their daughters and hid the grog. The bar was certainly a far cry from Butlins and we tried to keep our chanting down to a minimum.

The commentary was in Spanish and the fellow spoke so incredibly fast that by ten minutes into the match he was already forty minutes into the commentary. England won easily (3–0) but after their last-minute capitulation against France we tried not to get too excited until the final whistle. When the game finished it was after 8.00 and way past Dad's dinnertime (he usually has his dinner at 5.30 at home). He didn't believe me when I told him that most restaurants in Spain don't even open till 8.30.

'I tell a lie,' I said to Dad as we stood in front of the closed La Faro tapas restaurant in the old fishing district of La Viña, 'it's not 8.30 when it opens . . . it's nine o'clock.' As an old English couple dressed up in their Sunday best waddled over to check out the menu, Dad broke the bad news: 'It doesn't open till 9.'

'We're usually in bed by then,' said the lady with a sigh.

There were other restaurants open, but I'd set my sights on going to La Faro after reading about its delectable seafood tapas. While we waited for it to open, we sauntered back down to the beach and, although it was after eight o'clock, it was even busier than it had been in the afternoon. It was just as hot, too.

We got back to the restaurant just as the impeccably dressed and bow-tied waiter was opening the doors. The tapas bar was one long room decked out entirely in polished marble.

'Where are the chairs?' Dad asked, looking around for somewhere to sit.

'You stand to eat in a tapas bar,' I said.

'It wouldn't cost much to put a few stools in,' Dad huffed.

A large sunken marble bench top behind the bar was brimming with a mouth-watering array of tapas.

'You order,' Dad said, 'but no funny stuff.' To be honest, I was really quite impressed that Dad had agreed to come to a tapas bar at all. It was only because I told him—quite sincerely—that the prospect of enjoying authentic Spanish tapas was one of the main reasons I had looked forward to visiting Spain.

Tapas is small portions of food that were traditionally served free with a drink. The name *tapa* (literally 'lid') derives from the barman's generous custom of placing a slice of ham or cheese over the top of a glass before serving it to a customer. Andalucía is the home of tapas and there are more tapas bars in Andalucía than in the rest of Spain.

I tried to order things that Dad might eat, although I did enjoy winding him up by telling him that I'd ordered snails in curry sauce and deep-fried tripe in hot paprika sauce. We had cheese balls, potato salad, *pincho moruno* (mini meat kebabs), seafood salad (Dad didn't like the prawns because, 'I only eat them deep fried'), *puntillitas fritas* (fried squid) and the house speciality, which was absolutely exquisite, *tortillitas de camarones* (fried dough made with wheat flour, egg, onion and little prawns).

'Did you like it?' I asked Dad as I polished off the last of the fried squid, which Dad wouldn't even try.

'Yeah, not bad,' Dad shrugged his shoulders. That meant it was good. I actually thought it was the best tapas I'd ever eaten.

It was after ten when we emerged from the tapas bar, but it was only just beginning to fill up. The narrow lanes and open plazas were abuzz with well-dressed locals out for their evening *paseo* (stroll), or dining alfresco in large groups. There wasn't a free table in any restaurant. Businesses were still open, too, and people were trying on clothes in tiny boutiques—in fact, all the shops in the old city were tiny—picking up a loaf of bread or buying a TV. One shop had only two TVs—if they had a rush and sold both the shop would have been empty.

It was a perfect summery evening, so Dad and I joined the locals on their *paseo* around town.

'If this was Australia,' Dad said, 'everyone would be inside watching TV.'

'That's why I just love this place,' I said with a sigh.

After stopping for a quick cleansing ale in a delightfully cosy bar we ended up at Plaza de Mina which, although it was 11.30, was still full of people eating dinner—old couples holding hands, large families with young children happily playing or racing around the table and teenagers lounging around trying to look cool. Everyone seemed so deliriously happy.

'I could easily live here,' I said to Dad.

'You need to be an insomniac to live here,' he replied musingly.

We took the long route back to the hostel (we were trying to postpone getting back to our room and our undersized double bed) past mostly gorgeous twenty-somethings who'd taken over the plaza shuffle.

'I couldn't live here,' Dad said, 'not with all this walking they do.' As we clambered up the four flights of steps to our room Dad said (in between puffs), 'Do you know what? I've walked more in the last few weeks than since we moved to Australia thirty-five years ago.'

13

Goat's balls and real lettuce

As our bus pulled out of Cádiz bus station into busy traffic, the driver stuck his head under his seat. Just as he was about to bowl over a Renault he looked up, swerved sharply, then scratched his head. Ten seconds later he stuck his head under the seat again. He'd lost something pretty important because he even stood up, *while he was still driving*, and rifled through the overhead locker. After searching every nook and cranny within reach he called someone on his mobile phone—by his timid responses I guessed he was talking to his wife—then he spent the rest of the trip scratching his head and muttering to himself.

At our first stop, just outside of Cádiz, a nun hopped aboard, sat next to Dad and immediately began trying to convert him. Well, I'm not sure if that's exactly what she was doing, but she waffled to him in Spanish for about twenty minutes while Dad just smiled and nodded his head.

As soon as we left the suburbs of Cádiz, we entered the classic rural landscape of Andalucía, where green hills under rocky crags are dotted with pueblos blancos like snow-white cloths that have floated down to snag on hilltops and settle in crevices. Arcos de la

Frontera, which is only an hour north of Cádiz, is just one of the many pueblos blancos that dot the region. Serenely beautiful today, the pueblos blancos have a turbulent history. The name 'de la Frontera' tagged onto many a village name reflects the mediaeval boundary between Moorish and Christian kingdoms, which for centuries had been at each other's throats.

The village of Arcos de la Frontera looked out over surrounding fields from the edge of a sheer cliff like a precariously perched white castle. When our bus reached the base of the steep ascent up to the village we transferred to a mini-bus. I couldn't figure out why the side of the mini-bus was covered in scratches until we drove into the village. The bus could barely squeeze through the narrow sun-baked streets of whitewashed houses. It got so impossibly narrow that at one point the bus couldn't go any further without tearing the side mirrors off. The driver solved that problem very easily—he simply pressed a button on the dashboard and the electronic side mirrors swung in. Everyone then breathed in and we squeezed through with only millimetres to spare.

We were dropped off in Plaza del Cabildo (the village square) and walked the last fifty metres, much to Dad's chagrin, up steep, white-trimmed steps to Hostal San Marcos. After checking in and going through our usual routine—I rifle through all the drawers and Dad turns on the telly—we headed back down to the plaza and the windswept lookout. Gazing down from the top of the precipitous wall of rock was like being in an aeroplane—the vast cork forest we'd driven through on the way up had Matchbox cars driving through the middle of it and the forest itself looked like a backyard vegie patch.

'I think we'll go the "Lucky Dip" for lunch,' I said to Dad as we sat down in a tiny courtyard restaurant. Dad gave me a what-the hell-are-you-going-to-feed-me-now? look. The lucky dip is actually *plato combinados*, which is usually two 'surprise' courses and a glass of house plonk for under ten Euros. 'It's probably goat's balls,' Dad grunted. He almost whooped with delight when the first course, a garden salad, came out.

'It's got *real* lettuce,' Dad beamed. 'Real lettuce' according to Dad is iceberg lettuce and he constantly, and I mean *constantly*, goes on about the 'garden weeds and grass clippings' that are served in restaurants in Australia. Dad clapped his hands with glee when the main course was presented to us. It was roast chicken and chips without a single goat's ball in sight. Dad celebrated by making himself chip butties.

We went to another lookout after lunch, which involved trudging down a lane that was so steep one misstep would have sent you tumbling all the way back to Cádiz. The final leg to the look-out was a hard slog up wide steps with Dad puffing and panting behind me.

'If I lived here, I'd be dead in a week,' Dad gasped while catching his breath at the top. 'Either that or I'd never leave the house.'

I was keen to continue our exploratory hike but Dad was worried that 'the undertakers won't be able to get to me when I keel over.' I could hear him huffing and mumbling 'bloody hell!' as he lumbered back up the hill. I went for a hike up and down staircases and winding alleys that at points were so narrow that I just about had to turn sideways to pass through them. It was siesta time and the village was suddenly and magically empty. I couldn't see any locals but I could smell and hear them. The streets were redolent with the delicious aromas of roasting *chorizo*, olive oil and garlic, and I could hear the sound of Spanish TV soaps drifting out from just about every house. With the tortuous, narrow and steep lanes lined with blue-shuttered, whitewashed houses decorated with colourful flower pots, I could easily have been on a Greek island—except there were no postcard shops or mangy cats.

After an hour of aimless wandering I headed back and found Dad sitting outside a café halfway up the hill sipping a beer.

'I'll need another beer stop before I make it back,' Dad said. It was at the second beer stop that I saw a poster for a flamenco show, Ill Concurso Flamenco. Not only was it happening on our one and only night in Arcos, it was around the corner from our hostel at the Teatro Olivares Veas.

'You can't get more authentically Spanish than that,' I said reading the poster. 'A flamenco show featuring Alberto Sánchez Sánchez and José García.' Flamenco is actually not indigenous to Spain, but to just one part of it—the province of Andalucía. I'd been to sanitised and touristy kitsch flamenco shows in Barcelona with the whole dancing girls and castanets thing, but this was *peña flamenca* or pure flamenco with just guitar and vocal. This truly would be authentically traditional (although the addition of stunning Spanish girls wiggling their bottoms isn't such a bad thing) and indeed a privilege, since I later read that it's increasingly rare to see just a singer and a guitarist perform together. Best of all, the show even had authentically traditional prices: it was free.

The show didn't start till 10.00, so after having a nap, which neither of us meant to have—the Euro match between Denmark and Bulgaria we were watching on the TV in our room was so damn boring—we trundled downstairs to the hostel restaurant for dinner.

'Try this Dad, I think you'll really like it,' I said. Dad eyed me suspiciously. 'It's tomato soup.' Dad took a spoonful and immediately screwed up his face.

'It's bloody cold!' he yelped.

'It's supposed to be, it's called gazpacho.'

'Haven't they got a microwave?' Dad huffed.

By the time we finished dinner it was after 9.30, so we rushed to the theatre to secure good seats. When we got there, the show was scheduled to start in fifteen minutes but there were only three old couples dressed entirely in black and staring forlornly at the empty stage. It looked as if a funeral was about to start. Dad and I looked at each other, then said in unison, 'Let's go get a beer.' When we came back at ten, the crowd had ballooned with the addition of another couple. We shuffled in and plopped ourselves down in the middle. By 10.30 there were thirty-eight people in the audience. I was getting so bored waiting that I counted the audience, as well as seats—there were one hundred and fourteen of them, by the way.

Just after 11.00, the guitarist, who was dressed like Don Johnson of *Miami Vice* fame with a lilac suit and open shirt, wandered out on to the stage accompanied by his middle-aged accountant. His accountant, who was wearing nice slacks and a business shirt, sat on a tall stool next to him on the stage. I know that flamenco over the years has fused with blues, jazz and even punk, but I'd never heard of it being fused with tax double-entry bookkeeping.

'Don' José García stretched his long fingers across the fretboard into a chord that even an octopus would have trouble attempting and started playing. His fingers danced around at a mesmerising pace, producing a sound so amazing he could have been playing three guitars at once. Meanwhile, his accountant looked as if he was suffering from a terrible case of constipation. He was rocking and shifting uncomfortably in his seat with a fierce and determined look on his face. It wasn't José's accountant after all, but the singer Alberto Sánchez Sánchez—his parents must have had a stutter. Alberto then started howling in extreme pain. Each note was of such violent emotional intensity that poor Alberto looked as if he was about to croak it any second—or rush to the toilet. I'd read that flamenco songs often express pain, but this was more like inflicting pain. Halfway through the first song, which was called I believe, 'AHHHHHEEEEEEEEEHHHHHHH!', Alberto was sweating like mad.

'If that was a cat,' Dad said in my ear, 'I'd have it put down.' Suddenly, Alberto plunged his hand into his pocket and started groping around while his groaning hit a crescendo. After a minute of jiggling about, he finally pulled out an immense handkerchief and began mopping his brow.

It was at this point that I started giggling like a schoolboy. This is really where a father should tell his adult son to be quiet and grow up, but no, he was too busy giggling himself.

After the second song, which was called 'UGGGGHHHOOOOO-GGGGGHHH!', Dad said, 'I'm just going to the loo. I'll be back in a sec.'

Dad hadn't returned by the time the third song, a moving love ballad entitled 'YAHAAAAAAAAAAAHHH!', had finished. I had a sneaking suspicion he wasn't coming back at all. The next song was a vocal solo. Alberto stood up for this one to get the full groaning effect. It certainly was intense, and he began sobbing and gesticulating wildly as the crowd started to cheer him on—I later read that a flamenco singer tries to achieve *duende*, which is total emotional communication with the audience. Whenever Alberto let out a particularly poignant moan, the crowd responded with an 'Olé!' The longer the moan the bigger the 'Olé!' At one point, Alberto's face was so red I thought his head was going to explode.

I was feeling left out so I tried to get into it by yelling out 'Olé!' as well. I screamed it out with gusto, however, it just happened to be in the wrong spot and I was the only one who 'Olé'd'. The whole theatre, including Alberto, watched me as I slunk out the door.

I found Dad sitting outside a café downing a beer.

'That was bloody terrible,' Dad said.

'The singer had a lot of passion, though,' I said.

'Yeah, but he didn't have much com-passion.'

•

There was no mini-bus service on Sundays, so we had to walk down the steep hill to the bus station. Dad must have muttered 'bloody hell' twenty times before we got even halfway down. Dad's face was almost as red as Alberto's, so—before he collapsed—we stopped at a busy café for breakfast.

When I was organising this trip I had tried my darnedest to make it as easy as possible for Dad so there wouldn't be too much lugging of luggage or long waits at bus stations. Normally when I travel I do such inefficient things as wait five hours for a bus or walk around for two hours trying to find the best cheapest dive in town. I'd planned and organised almost our entire trip so I didn't have to put up with him walking around muttering 'bloody hell' for hours. I had known even before I left Australia that there was no minibus on a Sunday and that if we missed the 9.30 bus to Seville there wouldn't be another one till 4.30. I found all this out courtesy of the Internet. To find out the bus times I simply went to the local Cádiz 'Comes' bus service website and printed out their timetable.

It is absolutely phenomenal what you can find on the net to help you plan and organise a trip. Besides the obvious things like booking cheap flights, hotels and car hire you can check everything from detailed weather reports for every two-horse town in the world, including live weather-cams, to photos of meals in a restaurant thirteen thousand kilometres away. I love the fact that you can peruse restaurant menus, look at the photos of meals, then book a table from the other side of the world. This can also save some embarrassment. The last time I visited Paris I was contemplating taking my wife to Tour D'Argent, arguably the world's most celebrated restaurant, until I went to their website and discovered that the 'cheapest' meal was a AU$240-a-head set menu—and that's without wine or even after-dinner mints. I told my wife that I'd take her there once we'd won the Lotto. And if I win the Lotto twice we might even go to the Seiyo Ginza Hotel in Tokyo, which in 2004 served 'the world's most expensive meal'—this little refuelling exercise cost US$13 000 but it did include the last existing bottle of 1870 Chateau Lafite Rothschild. Oh, and after-dinner mints.

I hadn't looked up any restaurants in Arcos, but the Arcos de la Frontera wheelchair hire website would have come in handy as Dad wasn't keen to walk another step further.

'I'm knackered,' he sighed as he slumped into a seat outside the café. The patrons inside looked as if Central Casting had sent them along for a stereotypical Mediterranean café scene: men with big bushy moustaches wearing cloth caps, grey cotton waistcoats and baggy canvas trousers were talking animatedly as they sipped coffee and downed glasses of sherry—this was their morning heart-starter, they had their real breakfast in mid-morning. Incidentally, sherry originally comes from the town of Jerez which was only twenty-five kilometres from Arcos de la Frontera.

When I asked Dad what he wanted, he looked at me wearily and bleated weakly, 'Just try and get me something that resembles food.' When I returned ten minutes later carrying a tray laden with food and drink, Dad's face lit up with joy and he suddenly didn't look tired any more. I had found him some plain white-bread toast with butter and strawberry jam and a large mug of milky English Breakfast tea.

14

Fish, chips and stewed bull's penis

'Is this Valencia?' Dad stammered as he shook me out of my deep slumber.

'*Valencia*?' I sat bolt upright. How the hell did we end up in Valencia? I was sure we were on the bus to Seville. I had dozed off to sleep about an hour after we left Arcos de la Frontera and I had no idea which direction we had taken. Valencia was on the other side of the country. As we passed through the nondescript suburbs of a large city, I shuffled sheepishly up to the front of the bus.

'Sevilla?' I asked the bus driver as I pointed out the window. He looked at me as if I was an escaped lunatic and said, 'Err . . . no.'

I panicked for a second before I realised that maybe my accent was so bad I'd asked if the city was an electrical appliance. I tried again and he said, 'Si, Sevilla'—pronouncing it Sebeeya. In the end there was no need for my mild panic; Dad had just got a little confused about which city we were actually headed for.

Mind you, it didn't take me long to get confused as we tried to find our hotel. After leaving the busy traffic intersection of Puerta de Jerez, we entered the calmer confines of Barrio Santa Cruz and wended our way through the maze of more improbably narrow, cobbled alleys in search of the elusive Hostal Arias. Barrio Santa Cruz is the city's oldest (it was the mediaeval Jewish district) and most picturesque (read touristy) neighbourhood.

After finally stumbling across our hotel and checking in, we hit the streets to join all the other crazy tourists out and about in the full heat of the of the midday sun. At least it was cool in the twisted lanes of Barrio Santa Cruz, where ancient pastel-coloured houses leant so far towards each other that they almost seemed to touch. Further shade came from the orange trees that were blooming in tiny plazas, the typical *sevillano* patios overgrown with flowers, and creepers thrown over whitewashed walls like coloured lace shawls.

We stopped for a spot of lunch at Bodega Santa Cruz, where locals spilled out into the street, consuming plates and plates of tapas. It was a frenetic spit-and-sawdust kind of place, ideal for taking the pulse and getting the feel of the city. Dad found a seat while I went to the bar to order. The bar was beneath a ceiling adorned with generous cuts of cheese and *jamón* (cured ham), hanging temptingly from wooden beams, as if vying for attention with the dusty bottles of wine stored on high shelves. When I ordered my selection of tapas—I was excited to see that the menu was in Spanish only—the barman scribbled down the prices with a piece of chalk onto the bar. When we had another beer he simply added it on to our list and we paid the total at the end.

I came back with three plates of tapas: delicious fried *boquerones* (bite-sized portions of grilled fish), *patatas bravas* (fried potatoes soaked in aioli) and a serve of *rabo de toro*.

'We've got fish, chips and chops,' I said to Dad as I plonked the plates in front of him.

After we'd polished it all off, I said, 'So Dad, did you like the chops?'

'It was nice,' said Dad with an air of surprise.

'It was stewed bull's penis.' I went and got my shell-shocked father a beer before I told him that it was really only stewed bull's *tail*.

'Let's go find this AFC,' Dad said. I'd stupidly taught Dad this acronym which, when I was a tour leader in Europe, was our affectionate name for a church. It stood for 'another fucking church'.

Seville's most famous church wasn't just another fucking church, though. The dauntingly gargantuan Gothic cathedral is, according to the *Guinness Book of World Records*, the world's largest cathedral. saints Peter and Paul (in Rome and London, respectively) occupy more real estate, but Seville Cathedral's surface area—11 520 square metres to be exact—is said to be a bit larger than either of theirs according to the official Guiness tape measure.

The Moorish tower of Giralda, which is attached to the Cathedral, loomed above us as we turned the corner and saw the Cathedral's spires, towers and delicate network of high buttresses against the turquoise sky. The cathedral's fifteenth-century architects declared, 'Let us create such a building that future generations will take us for lunatics'. I couldn't actually tell if lunatics had designed it because it was so dark inside that I could barely make out Dad standing next to me, let alone the many cavernous chapels. I also walked straight into the enormous monument and tomb of Christopher Columbus, who remains a hero in Spain, even though he was actually Italian. Then I crashed into the knee of one of the four huge figures that held aloft the mariner's massive coffin—he must have been quite a strapping lad.

Not only is Seville Cathedral the world's largest cathedral, it also has the world's largest altar and the world's largest collection of tight-arses—entry to the cathedral and adjoining Giralda tower is free on Sundays, so the chapel was chock-full of tourists.

'There's not a chance in hell you're getting me up there,' Dad grunted when I asked if he wanted to climb to the top of the

Giralda. Sort of Ali Baba meets Big Ben, the one hundred-metre brick tower is Seville's iconic building—and unquestionably its most beautiful. It is also one of the most important examples of Islamic architecture in the world and was originally the minaret of a mosque built by the Moors in the twelfth century. When Seville came under new management, the Giralda was saved from being torn down only because it was converted to Christianity as the bell tower for the new cathedral.

Dad perched in one of the pews while I made the ascent to the bell chamber on a spiralling ramp that was built so ghost guards could ride ghost horses up to the belfry. After my tortuous climb—the outstanding view of the sprawling city from the top was worth it, though—and twenty minutes spent trying to find Dad in the gloom, we retired to our hotel room for a siesta. We had both now adopted and embraced this wonderful Spanish tradition.

•

It was late afternoon by the time we woke up and, after Dad had done a bit more maintenance to our room, we ventured out into the streets again. We headed first to another landmark of Seville, the Plaza de Toros de la Maestranza. This is the country's most famous bullring—it was the setting for the opera *Carmen*—and, for the afficionados, the most beautiful in the world. I was keen to do the guided tour of the stadium, even though I do find the whole bullfighting thing abhorrent. I'll happily eat as many sirloin steaks as you can throw at me, knowing the animals are basically murdered, but I'm pretty sure it's not by poncy men in tights torturing them slowly to death with a letter-opener.

On our walk to the bullring I noticed something rather odd. There wasn't a single person wearing a Spain football top or a Spanish flag in sight. I'd been looking forward to our first night in Seville because Spain were playing the host nation Portugal—the local derby of Euro 2004. I was expecting a hot-blooded Spanish football fiesta but there wasn't a single drunken chant going on anywhere. When we did finally stumble across a crowd, it was for the wrong sport. A bullfight was taking place at Plaza de Toros de la Maestranza, which meant there would be no tour.

As soon as we were within cape-throwing distance of the stadium, a ticket tout accosted us.

'You wonn teek-et? Thirty Euro for you,' he whispered.

'Is this the Spain–Portugal match?' I asked, pretending I didn't know it was a bullfight.

'Si . . . yes,' he nodded. 'Okay for you, twenty-five Euro.' By the time we'd walked around half the stadium, our tout had dropped his price to ten Euros.

'Is Raul playing?' I asked.

'Si, of course. Okay last price seven Euros.' It was only two Euros more than doing the tour, so I took two tickets.

'We'll stay ten minutes then we'll leave,' I said to Dad. Dad was even more reluctant than me to see men in tights torturing cattle.

The inside of the bullring *was* incredibly beautiful, with its brilliant white and ochre paintwork and golden arches (how apt!). The stadium was only half full and most of the spectators seemed to be tourists. The only locals were old men wearing cloth caps and clutching all-day suckers, which is what Dad dubbed the foot-long cigars they were smoking.

A bullfight (or *corrida*) was in progress as we sat down in the uncomfortable concrete bleachers. A large and menacing bull was being tormented by four wusses in tights waving hot-pink capes, as they ducked in and out of the shelters whenever the bull came anywhere near them at all. The brightly coloured capes, by the way, provide more of a spectacle for man than bulls, who are colour-blind and couldn't care less whether you wave a red flag or a yellow beach towel at them.

The *picador* appeared next on his padded horse, which has had its vocal cords severed so its terrified cries don't alarm the crowd, and immediately began jabbing his *pic* into the hump of shoulder muscles, slowly draining the bull of much of its strength. A second *picador* was stationed on the opposite side of the ring in case the bull turned nasty. The third wave of toro-tormenters were the *banderilleros*, who ran at the weakened bull and planted their staves around the wounds administered by the *picador*. The bull was now staggering like a punch-drunk fighter while the *banderilleros* ran around it like bullying schoolkids.

'I can't watch any more,' Dad shuddered. He looked around in disgust at the crowd, then stormed out. As Dad walked out of the arena, the biggest girl's blouse of them all came in. The *matador*. The bull was so weak now that I could have brought it down with a rolled-up newspaper. I glanced around at the crowd trying to comprehend how they could find this entertaining. Amazingly, bullfighting is as popular as ever in Spain. I felt a tad guilty as I watched the bull stumbling about in obvious agony because I had become one of the tourists who keep this horrific 'sport' going. The bull is a cash cow for the Spanish economy—an estimated thirty million spectators a year witness nearly twenty-five thousand bulls being slaughtered.

The *matador* toyed with the dying bull for ten minutes. The crowd was silent as the *matador* raised his weapon of death and sighted along the blade of his sword. For minutes he just stood there. I couldn't take it any more. I stood up and bellowed out, 'PUT IT OUT OF ITS MISERY . . . YOU . . .' The crowd was staring at me.

'YOU . . . PLONKER!' That was the best I could come up with in my sudden outburst. I glanced away as the *matador* plunged the sword into the bull's shoulder. I should have left with Dad. I turned back just as all five hundred kilograms of bull thudded onto the sand. The poor bugger didn't die immediately, though. I could see his head move, nostrils flared and eyes bulging.

A pair of horses dragged the bull from the Plaza de Toros as a brass band struck up some cheerful music. I stayed for the start of the next *corrida,* as I wanted to see how it started. In the end, I was glad I stayed. A protester jumped the fence and ran at the *matador* who, when he turned around, was given a good spiking by the bull. I left as the *matador* was being carried out on a stretcher. I refrained from screaming out, 'Good work, bull!'

I found my rather shaken father standing out the front of the stadium.

'I almost got bowled over by the dead bull,' Dad whimpered. When Dad had rushed off down the corridor, the dead bleeding bull was dragged right into his path.

'The score's one-all,' I said with a triumphant grin. 'The bull got the *matador* a beauty.' The low sun was an appropriate blood red as we walked away from the stadium.

•

The streets were now full of families in their Sevillana Sunday best as they emerged to take their nightly paseo through the streets. I expected to see at least some kids in Spain football shirts, but I couldn't even spot a scarf. If this was England, the locals would be decked out entirely in England colours and starting a fight.

We headed back to Bodega Santa Cruz for some more tapas—the stewed bull's tail didn't quite have the same appeal this time, though—thinking that it might be great to watch the match in a local haunt. The game had already started by the time we got there but only about a dozen people were watching it on the small television set. The rest of the crowd were too busy chatting and looking cool. When Portugal scored the first goal, one drunken Spanish fellow actually seemed quite happy. We had a few too many drinks with a couple of London lads who were off to the England–Croatia game the next day. They could only get a flight to Seville, so they were left with a four-hour bus journey to the stadium in Portugal.

Mark was a journalist for the *Daily Mirror* and he told us that the Spanish don't care too much for their national team and are more interested in their local club teams, as in Real Madrid, etc. At the end of the match a rather inebriated Spanish fellow leant over and waffled something to me in slurred Spanish.

'No comprendo,' I said.

'Spain is . . . shit!' he grunted.

•

'I don't want tost-hardos [tostados],' Dad sighed when he bit into his toast and jam at breakfast. 'I want tost-softos.' Dad was developing quite an obsession about the state of Spanish bread. 'You could put wheels on this and use it as a skateboard,' he added.

The morning was already suffocatingly hot by the time we finished breakfast and it wasn't even the true hot season—it hovers around forty degrees for most of the summer. The interior of the Alcázar, however, was decidedly cool. The Alcázar Palace has to be Seville's greatest attraction. From the outside it looked like your stock standard high-walled fortress, but stepping inside was like entering Aladdin's palace. Well, I was close . . . in the eleventh century the Alcázar housed the great court of the Abbadid dynasty, including al-Mu'tadid the Cruel who had a harem of eight hundred women and a garden full of flowers planted in the skulls of his decapitated enemies. Most of Seville's charm comes from its Moorish influences—Seville was conquered by the Moors in 712, before the

Christians reconquered it in 1248. The Alcázar is the jewel in the city's Moorish crown.

It all sounded spectacular but initially I wasn't sure if we'd even get in. Not only did they have a complicated 'flow-control' system to alleviate the pressure of visitors, they also had pretty strict door bitches. Dad was asked quite rudely for ID when we reached the entrance. It was free entry for over sixty-fives and when Dad presented his licence to provide age proof, the guard looked him over unconvinced. He stared at his face for a while before letting him in.

'He was counting your wrinkles,' I said as we shuffled past.

It didn't take us long to get lost as we wandered through a series of exquisitely patterned, arcaded courtyards and salons, each one leading to another through a succession of horseshoe-shaped arches. Ornamentation was everywhere, but what dazzled the most were the delicate lattices in the plasterwork that looked as if someone had crocheted the walls.

I never like to hire guides when I visit historic sites. As well as being a self-confessed tight-arse, I like discovering places myself, with the help of a guidebook, of course. The only problem was that the maze of corridors and courtyards was so extensive, I had no idea where we were.

'What's this room?' Dad asked as we stood in the middle of a large white room. I studied my guidebook for a minute, then looked up and said: 'This is an old room that's made of bricks.'

After plodding around in the oppressive heat for most of the morning we opted for a sedate afternoon and immersed ourselves in the soothing cloak of exotic greenery at Parque de Maria Luisa. The afternoon was stifling hot so we lazed on a shaded park bench by a large pond for quite a spell. Except for a few families of ducks, we just about had the park to ourselves.

'Even the ducks are having a siesta,' Dad said. It felt like we were the only people awake in the entire city.

When we eventually headed back to our room for our afternoon kip, I found it hard get to sleep anyway. Dad started watching TV again and when I said earlier that Dad watches anything, I mean anything. He was watching *The Flintstones* dubbed into Spanish ('Yabbos-dabbos-doo-os!').

After I managed a bit of Spanish shut-eye we ducked back into the maze of Barrio Santa Cruz and happily got ourselves lost as guitar music leaked out of crooked houses and the intoxicating aroma of tapas wafted out of numerous bodegas. Seville has four thousand bodegas and tabernas that specialise in tapas. We stopped at Bar Enrique Becerra for our now customary nightly tapas. As usual, arriving at opening time meant we were the only people there. As with La Faro in Cádiz, I'd read quite a few rave reviews of the tapas at Bar Enrique Becerra, which is run by the fifth generation of the celebrated Becerra family restaurateurs.

The menu was in Spanish only, so I used the eeny-meeny-miney-mo method of choosing our dishes. We had *pez espada al amontillado*, which I later discovered was swordfish cooked in dark sherry, smoked salmon, cod wrapped in pastry, prawn salad and *espinacas con garbanzos*. I ordered this last dish simply because I loved the sound of it—it turned out to be spinach with chickpeas. Even though it was all absolutely superb, Dad only liked the cod wrapped in pastry.

As we walked out, the great connoisseur uttered another of his immortal bon mots: 'The only problem with tapas is that straight afterwards you need a crapas.'

We went to an Irish pub in the heart of old Seville to watch the England-Croatia game. The place was bursting at the seams with Brits and three very nervous-looking Croatian supporters. It felt good to scream and chant along with all the England fans again. Thankfully, England won, so the fans didn't beat the hell out of each other. They just did a lot of hugging instead. Dad and I have never hugged each other as much as when England scored the winning goal.

Back in our room, Dad couldn't help himself and turned on the TV again. Boy can he watch some crap. After flicking through every channel he settled on a show that was devoted to tarot reading. This program, which was live and ran twenty-four hours a day, showed a phone number at the bottom of the screen that people dialled to get their cards read live on air. Even more bizarrely, there was a competing tarot card show on another channel. One had a female reader, the other a fellow.

'What happens if no one calls?' Dad asked.

'I don't know. They probably do their nails or rearrange their desks.'

When I dozed off to sleep twenty minutes later, Dad was flicking between the two tarot channels eagerly anticipating the confusion, tension and sheer human drama that would unfold if the phone failed to ring.

15

McGazpacho and McTapas

'What do you think of Spain so far?' I asked Dad as our train sped through the Spanish countryside. He considered the question for a moment before giving his thoughtful reply.

'They've got strange eating habits, too many stairs and sausages for pillows.'

'What about the beautiful architecture and the stunning scenery?' I said, motioning out the window of the train. We had been passing through the scorched Andalucían countryside of neat olive groves and snug stone farmhouses ringed by shimmering mountains, but now we were in the Land of Oz. The rolling hills all around us were covered with sunflowers as far as the eye could see. All we needed was the Wizard of Oz's castle and a bloke in a bad lion suit and we wouldn't be in Kansas (or Spain) anymore.

We'd opted for the AVE, or very fast train, from Seville to Madrid. It was a tad expensive but it was the difference between six hours spent trundling along stopping at every Wizard's castle and Munchkin village or flying through in two-and-a-half hours. The train was like a plane, with hostesses, in-flight magazines and even in-flight movies with headphones. I sat and watched the countryside zip by while Dad watched *The Pink Panther* in Spanish.

The *Wizard of Oz* soon gave way to *The Good, the Bad and the Ugly*. We were passing through the parched desert and prairies of central Spain, home to countless Spaghetti Westerns. I waved to a lone *vaqueros* (Spanish cowboy) on a horse herding his cattle and I was sure he waved a colt .45 back at me.

Ahead, the city of Madrid loomed out of the desolate, arid landscape. Although it is six hundred and fifty kilometres from the sea, and separated from the rest of Europe by a formidable mountain range, Madrid became the capital of Spain in 1561 because it just happened to be located near King Philip II's palace.

•

As we clambered up the steep flight of stairs at Hostal Riesco, Dad turned to the old fellow who was showing us to our room and panted, 'Bloody hell, you Spanish are going to kill me!' The old fellow, who didn't speak English, smiled at Dad and said, 'Thunk you.' Our room was on the fifth floor overlooking the Puerta del Sol—the heart of the city and the 'official' centre of the country: all Spanish road distances are measured from the 'kilometre 0' plaque outside the old Post Office on one side of the square.

Dad was disappointed with our room. It didn't have a TV. I took a firm line: 'You'll just have to miss the next episode of *The Flintstones*, then.'

We hit the streets and headed first for the Palacio Real, the colossal Italianate baroque royal palace with over two thousand eight hundred rooms.

'We don't have to see them all, do we?' Dad asked worriedly as I read out a brief history from the guidebook. As it turned out we couldn't even see one of them. In fact, we couldn't get anywhere near the palace at all as the main street, Calle Mayor, leading up to it was closed off to traffic.

Just as we wondered why they'd closed the empty street, a procession of cavaliers in blindingly bright steel armour and towering feathered hats and sitting stiffly erect on handsome horses decked out in matching feathered hats turned the corner in front of us.

'King Juan Carlos is on his way to the palace!' an American tourist gushed before she jumped into the path of an oncoming horse to take a photo. A gilded carriage swept past with a regally dressed gentleman inside.

'There's Juan Carlos,' Dad said. 'He's been on holidays and got burnt to a cinder.' The regally dressed gentleman was an African dignitary of some sort.

After we'd watched a succession of lavishly costumed men and horses pass by without a crown in sight, we decided to spend the rest of our budget for the whole trip on a glass of wine. Madrid's handsome and historic Plaza Mayor, with its café terraces, was reminiscent of Piazza San Marco in Venice—well, in the sense that it was a square and that it cost a King's ransom to drink there. We got our money's worth, though. We sat on our one glass of wine each for over an hour, much to the waiter's obvious chagrin, and watched the cavalcade of locals and tourists strutting around the square. I may have been ripped off blind for a rather average glass of wine, but I loved this vast, cobbled, traffic-free chunk of seventeeth-century Spain with square, uniform sides as if a grand palace had been turned inside out. If only Australian major cities had been designed by a bunch of Spanish (or Italian) architects instead of the English, we too could have had magical spaces like Plaza Mayor. Instead, we have wide, soulless streets and nowhere decent to burn heretics at the stake.

Some of Spanish history's most dramatic events have been played out on the stage of Plaza Mayor, including commemorative bullfights and joustings, fires, royal and religious pageants, political executions and the Spanish Inquisition. During the Inquisition, the guilty would be paraded around the plaza—bleachers were built for big audiences but the wealthy rented balconies—carrying sandwich boards listing their many sins. They were then slowly burned to death, which was for the good of their own immortal souls, remember.

In the evening, after our now compulsory siesta, we caught the Metro to Restaurante La Paella Real. This was according to my guidebook, 'the place for paella if you can't get to Valencia, the home of paella'. Dad was very sceptical about eating paella, even when I told him that it had mushy peas in it, which it sort of does.

As usual we were first in when the doors opened at 8.30 and, as usual, Dad immediately complained about the bread. I was very happy that the waiter couldn't speak much English as I was saved the embarrassment when Dad held up his bread to the waiter and asked, 'Have you got a chainsaw for this?'

It was actually quite a salubrious establishment with eminently dapper waiters, crisp linen napkins and cutlery that wouldn't be out of place on King Juan Carlos' table. Within half an hour of our arrival the restaurant was half-full. Mind you, none of the diners were locals. Going to a restaurant before 10.00 is frowned upon by the Madrilenos. The 'early sitting' was made up of two tables of giggling Japanese, some Germans and Italians and a smattering of Brits.

The old English fellow sitting two tables from us was even more pissed off with his bread than Dad. He kept shaking his head in disgust every time he took a bite. In fact he was ropable about everything: he took a sip of his wine and shook his head; while reading the menu he kept shaking his head; and he even got steamed up about the state of his cutlery, shaking his head even more vigorously in apparent disgust. I thought the paella was decidedly tasty but the English fellow kept shaking his head with every bite.

What was wrong with this guy? As he and his wife left, Dad put it to the test by asking if he'd liked the paella.

'It was lovely,' he said, shaking his head again. It was then that we figured out what his problem was. The poor fellow had a rather unfortunate tic.

•

We spent most of our second day in Madrid shuffling around the hot city trying to find places to cool off. I was struggling to talk Dad into going to a gallery until I told him how refreshingly cool it would be inside. We just had to choose which one of the three major galleries to visit. The area known as the 'golden triangle', centred around the Paseo del Prado, contained the world-famous Museo del Prado (with its treasure-house of works by Velazquez and Goya, the Prado is often regarded as Europe's second-best art museum after the Louvre); the Queen Sofia Art Centre, home of Picasso's famous 'Guernica'; and the Museo Thyssen-Bornemisza, considered to be the world's finest private collection of paintings and sculptures from the thirteenth century to the present.

Dad wasn't fussed about which one we visited as long as it had good air-conditioning. I opted for Museo Thyssen-Bornemisza because it had an impressive collection of works by some of my favourite artists, including Cézanne, Pisarro, Monet, Manet, Degas, Van Gogh, Matisse, Dali, Magritte, Renoir and Warhol. And besides, the Prado was just too big and too full of boring religious art and Picasso is, in my humble opinion, crap. Mind you, according to Dad, just about every painting in the entire Thyssen-Bornemisza museum was crap.

'He's crap!' Dad grunted as he stood in front of a Matisse painting. 'I wouldn't give a tuppence for one of those,' Dad remarked about a Dali. 'Oh, look, Jasmine [my three-year-old daughter] did that one,' Dad gushed excitedly in front of a Jackson Pollock painting.

'That's a bit harsh,' I said to Dad. 'Jasmine can do better than that.'

Our next respite from the hot sun was in the shady Parque del Buen Retiro. I do love my parks and make a point of visiting the main park in each city I visit. Not only are they often glorious spaces, it's fascinating to watch how locals 'retreat' from their bustling city. Buen Retiro means just that: 'good retreat'. The original palace was so named because in the sixteenth century the Royals used to spend their Christmas and Easter holidays there.

Madrid's most famous park is a vast expanse of green, encompassing formal gardens, fountains, lakes, outdoor cafés and, apparently—and this is something the city should be very proud of—some of the most talented and nimble pickpockets on the planet. We strolled down a long path, past families relaxing in the shade, to the *Estanque* (lake), which is presided over by the grandiose equestrian statue and mausoleum of King Alfonso XII. Couples in rowboats drifted lazily on the lake in front of us while the steps to Alfonso's mausoleum were lined with people basking in the sun. We didn't see any pickpockets picking pockets, but we did see a potential pickpocket pissing on a pot plant. Try saying that fast!

After our siesta we went for a *tapeo,* or tapas crawl. Our plan—well, to be more accurate, *my* plan—was to saunter from bar to bar, nibbling on a selection of tapas and washing it all down with a *cañas* (small beer) or two. Our first port of call was one of Madrid's oldest and most famous bars, Casa Labra. As our *croquettes* arrived, Dad suddenly gasped and said, 'I've forgotten my teeth!' He hadn't realised that he'd gone out without putting in his dentures.

After a quick trip back to the hotel, and with fangs now firmly in place, we stopped for some delectable *patatas bravas* (spicy fried potato) at Las Bravas and then moved on to the exquisitely tiled Viva Madrid for some fried cod fritters. Not surprisingly, that was Dad's choice. It was 9.30 by the time we got to Viva Madrid and—

surprise, surprise—we were their first customers for the evening even though, according to my guidebook, 'Viva Madrid is one of the most popular and busiest bars in Madrid'. Hemingway was right when he said, 'In no other town is there so little going to bed for sleeping purposes'. Even on weekdays, Madrilenos don't go out till after midnight. The first flamenco performances in nightclubs don't start till 12.30!

Dad was ready for bed by 11.00 but I wanted to find the Fiesta de San Juan. Before we left Australia I did an Internet search on all the places we were visiting to see if there were any festivals taking place. After the wonderful time I had researching my last book, *The Naked Man Festival*, I have become an even bigger fan of festivals than I was already. That was how I discovered the Fiesta de San Juan, a Catholic celebration of Saint John that also marks the longest day of the year. 'People come together for a night of mystery', the story I found on the net claimed. The only mystery was where in the hell everyone was. According to my research, 'all the action happens around Plaza San Juan'. We stepped into the tiny Plaza San Juan a little after 11.00 and the only signs of action were a rather dodgy-looking fellow sitting on his moped smoking and a dero rifling through the bins.

Rather despondent, we turned back towards the hotel—only to round a corner and walk smack into the middle of a raucous street procession. A troop of rowdy musicians, jugglers, stilt-walkers, fire-eaters and jesters was slowly making its way towards Plaza San Juan down the narrow Calle de Santa Maria, followed by a swarm of merry locals. Everyone was rolling drunk, because the procession had a roving bar. Every fifty metres or so, a fellow would set up a ten-litre drum of sangria on a concrete bench and dispense free drinks in plastic cups. Before I knew it, I had a cup of sangria in my hand and a very inebriated Spanish fellow had his arms around me.

We followed behind the band who were playing song after song while the growing crowd of revellers danced and sang along. The crowd was multiplying along the way as a fellow on stilts dressed as a faun would stop at every bar, bend down to poke his head through the door, and invite the patrons out onto the street. Just in case they didn't hear him, another chap dressed as a clown would throw a firecracker through the door.

At 12.30 the riotously rowdy procession still hadn't reached Plaza San Juan yet the drummers and trumpet players were already plastered after stopping every few minutes to skol sangria. We couldn't hang around until the finale, however. It would be three o'clock by the time the fiesta hit the plaza and Dad and I were not only knackered but also quite tipsy after half-a-dozen sangrias. As we laid in bed trying to get to sleep, it seemed the entire city was still up eating dinner, partying and drinking. They must sell a hell of a lot of Beroccas in Spain.

•

'Shit, I feel old,' Dad groaned as he stumbled out of bed.

'Happy birthday!' I chirped. It was Dad's seventy-third birthday. It's quite weird that I never really consider Dad being old. Possibly it's because he acts about twenty-five, but it's also because he seems exactly the same (only greyer and plumper) as when I was a kid.

We had a few hours left in Spain before we were due to fly to Malta so I took Dad shopping to buy him a birthday present. This turned out to be more difficult than I imagined. I wanted to buy Dad a shirt but the directory board in the department store looked more like a tapas menu. The choice of departments (or bar snacks) included *Bricolage*, *Cocinas*, *Muebles*, *Vajillas*, *Juguetes*, *Listas de boda*, *Guantes*, *Gafas* and *Piesdelpato*. After traipsing up and around every level we discovered that the 'clothes section' was actually in another building across the road. Later, I did a *babelfish* check on those 'departments'. They were Do-it-yourself work, Kitchens, Furniture, Sets of dishes, Toys, Lists of wedding, Gloves, Glasses and—I may have spelt the original name wrong here—Duck's feet.

We eventually found Dad a nice stripey number almost identical to the one he'd swapped with the English fellow at Butlins. On our way back to our hostal, we talked about birthdays and Dad told me that he missed his 21st birthday entirely.

'I was at sea. Someone told me that it was July the 4th and I said, "Oh, I've missed my birthday". My birthday was ten days earlier. We never had any idea what the day or date was when we were at sea.'

Dad was feeling tired (he was seventy-three, after all), so while he had a rest I went out to get us some lunch.

'I've got you some traditional Spanish food,' I said when I returned hiding the bag of food behind my back. 'It's hamburguesa con patatas fritas,' I said in an exaggerated Spanish accent. Dad's face dropped then immediately lit up when I revealed a McDonald's Meal Deal with cheeseburger, fries and Coke.

'I was almost tempted to eat McDonald's, too,' I said—this is quite a statement from me as I'd rather eat my own toe-jam than McDonald's. 'They had McGazpacho on the menu!' Dad screwed up his face. 'They didn't have any McTapas, though.'

'That's the best meal I've had since I've been in Spain,' Dad announced after polishing off his last French fry.

•

On the packed Metro train to the airport Dad got all romantic and held hands with a petite and pretty Spanish lady. She was rubbing herself up against Dad when he felt something in his pocket. For an old bugger he was quick. In a flash he had her hand in a firm grip while it was still in his pocket clutching his wallet. 'I've got a BLOODY PICKPOCKET!' Dad announced to the carriage, revealing her arm poking out of his pocket. The she gave out an almighty squeal. She squealed because Dad was doing his old steel-cap-in-the-finger-on-the-wrist trick. Dad often used this instant pacifier on us kids when we were misbehaving—and sometimes just for the hell of it—and boy oh boy did it hurt. Under the skin at the tip of one of Dad's chopped off fingers there's a steel cap which he would pummel into the centre of our wrists. Dad was giving the pickpocket a good screwing (so to speak) and her face was bright crimson as she tried not to scream out again and attract any more attention.

When Dad finally let go of her hand she pretended it was an accident and that her hand had just accidentally fallen into his pocket. As the train pulled into a station, and before Dad had a chance to do his old cracking-the-steel-cap-on-the-top-of-the-skull trick, she bolted through the open door.

'Happy bloody birthday!' Dad said.

Malta

16

Maltese cave pizza

Dad first went to Malta by accident. It just happened that when he was arrested for going AWOL from the navy the nearest appropriate jail was in the then English colony of Malta. It was 1949 and Dad was aboard a ship taking part in manoeuvres off the south coast of England when they docked in Cherbourg, France. There were no leave passes given out because the ship was only in dock for a few hours, but that didn't stop a curious and cocky eighteen-year-old from going ashore.

'I'd never been out of England before and I wanted to see what another country looked like,' Dad explained. He also managed to talk five other equally naïve sailors into joining him on his clandestine expedition. A quick walk through town was followed by a 'quick' drink in a local bar. By the time they got back to port, their ship was gone.

Luckily, or unluckily as it turned out, another Royal Navy ship pulled into the dock not long after their ship left. The new arrival was the titanic aircraft carrier *HMS Illustrious*, which was on its way to Malta. Dad and his gallivanting cohorts were arrested and thrown into detention aboard the ship until it reached Malta. They were then locked up in the Corradena Naval Detention Centre just outside the capital Valletta. Funnily enough, Dad wasn't the only Thacker to do time in the Corradena Naval Detention Centre. Dad's brother Gerry spent a couple of weeks banged up after pushing a lieutenant overboard into Valletta's Grand Harbour.

After three weeks in detention, Dad was commissioned to stay in Malta as there were no ships heading back to England at the time. He worked as a cook at Valletta Barracks for nine months.

Our journey to Malta, like Dad's voyage in detention, was full of stress, apprehension and worry. England were playing Portugal in the quarter finals of Euro 2004 and the match kicked off just as we flew out of Madrid. At half-time I asked the English co-captain (of the plane, not the team) if he could find out the score. Fifteen minutes later he announced over the PA that England were 1–0 up. Only a handful of people cheered because most of the passengers were Spanish—or were English and determined not to get too excited until England were at least 5–0 up. True to form, England then tried to protect their slim lead and conceded a late goal to finish up with a draw at the end of extra time. The ensuing penalty shoot-out took place just as we taxied into the terminal (cum garden shed) at Malta International Airport. As we stepped off the plane, the co-captain was waiting for us at the top of the stairs.

'England lost on penalties,' he said, shaking his head solemnly. 'Beckham missed his penalty shot.' England were out of the Euro championships.

'Bloody England!' I grumbled as we collected our bags.

'Bloody Beckham!' Dad added.

Our disappointment with bloody England and bloody Beckham was forgotten, however, as soon as our taxi pulled away from the terminal. The driver was obviously a budding rally car driver and he was honing his high-speed turns around tight corners and death-defying dashes across oncoming traffic. As we desperately held onto our seats so we wouldn't get thrown into the driver's lap, Dad turned to me and said, 'I've just taken up religion again. I've already said three Hail Marys!'

There was one good thing about our life-threatening journey—the half-hour drive into the city of Valletta took only ten minutes. The streets were dark and empty (it was almost midnight, after all) when we were dropped off at the top of the sloping and cobbled Triq Sant' Orsla (St Ursuline Street). We were dropped at the top because the street is so steep that the taxi couldn't get down it, although I was quite surprised our taxi driver didn't do a *Streets of San Francisco* and simply jump the entire street. It was only a short schlep down the steep, wide steps—Dad only mumbled 'Bloody hell' three times—to our accommodation, a three hundred and fifty-year-old former convent that is now Asti Guest House.

I banged on the massive oak door and we were greeted by a diminutive silver-haired lady of Dad's vintage, who was wearing a nightie and fluffy slippers. Her name was Annie and she owned and ran the guest house. She didn't seem to mind having to get out of bed, though, and chatted to us cheerfully as she escorted us up to our room.

The Asti was neat, spacious, and decorated in that particular style your grandmother loves, with pots of flowers, lace doilies and faded black-and-white photos of ancient relatives with bad haircuts. Our room was on the fifth floor and Annie bounded up the high marble steps ahead of us while Dad huffed and puffed and muttered 'Bloody hell' whenever he could catch his breath. Annie doted on us, making sure our sheets were folded back just so, we knew how to close the curtains, we were happy with our towels (and the way they were folded) and we knew when breakfast was. She was just about to help Dad put on his pyjamas when we ushered her out the door.

•

I don't think I'd ever seen my Dad look so happy. For breakfast he had a bacon butty, with *soft* bread, and a nice cup of sickly sweet milky tea. Annie had already been up for a couple of hours as she prepared the food and served it to the dozen or so guests in the cavernous dining room. As we walked out the front door after breakfast, Annie followed us. Like an over-protective grandma she grilled us to make sure we had sunblock and hats, then lined us up and brushed our hair.

We strolled down the pedestrianised Triq ir-Repubblika (Republic Street), which was swarming with camera-wielding tourists. We passed Malta's most impressive AFC (St John's Cathedral) and the rather grand Grand Master's Palace. The palace is the official residence of the Maltese president but in a former life it was the residence of the Grand Masters of the Knights of St John, who are not to be confused with Monty Python's Knights Who Say 'Ni!—We want a shrubbery or else you will never pass through the wood alive!'

The Knights of St John built the city of Valletta in the sixteenth century—the entire city is now a World Heritage site—and were a crack squad of European blue-blooded troubleshooters and 'Soldiers of Christ' who devoted their lives to the Christian faith, either as monks or as warriors, during the crusades. Mind you, you wouldn't have wanted to get on the bad side of these devout Christians. During the Great Siege of 1565 in which thirty thousand Turks attacked the city against only seven hundred knights and around eight thousand Maltese troops, the good knights used the severed heads of captured Turkish prisoners as cannonballs and fired them back at the Turks.

After fighting off the Ottoman hordes, the Knights were hailed as the saviours of Europe and grateful monarchs bestowed honours and, more importantly, heaps of money upon them. They used that loot to build the magnificent city of Valletta. The Knights are still around today and the current Grand Master is Fra' Andrew Bertie (a Scot), who sadly doesn't use heads as cannonballs anymore. The Knights of St John are now known variously as the Knights of Rhodes, the Knights of Malta, the Knights Hospitallers and the Knights Who Say Ecky-ecky-ecky-ecky-pikang-zoom-boing-mumble-mumble.

After tramping across the entire old city we reached Fort St Elmo, which was closed. This now rather dishevelled fort was used as the forbidding Turkish prison in the 1978 movie *Midnight Express*. It's just one of many movies filmed around Malta. In the last five years alone, a total of twelve major films had been shot on the islands—including *Troy*, *The Count Of Monte Cristo*, *Alexander* and *Gladiator*, in which Valletta played the role of Rome. In fact, more films per head are shot on Malta than in Los Angeles.

We virtually abseiled down one of the almost vertical cobbled side streets that lead off Triq ir-Repubblika towards the Grand Harbour, passing buildings that were packed together in a dense and picturesque jumble. Most of the buildings were made of golden sandstone, giving the city an overall a beige complexion.

We stopped first at the Siege Bell Memorial, which commemorates those who lost their lives in the Siege of Malta during the Second World War. Malta's strategic location in the middle of the Mediterranean and its magnificent Grand Harbour allowed whoever controlled it to control the sea lanes traversing the length of the Med. That's why Malta was seen as so important, and why it was so fiercely defended by Britain. It provided the base from which Rommel's supply lines were interrupted, giving rise to his final defeat at El Alamein and the conquest of North Africa. Malta's giant Allied naval base also played a major role in the invasion of Sicily. Although the friendly, gentle Maltese people were bombed mercilessly by the

Germans—Valletta itself was more severely bombed than London was at the height of the Blitz—suffering severe casualties and famine (at one point there were only three weeks of supplies left), they stubbornly refused to surrender. Their gallantry earned the entire country the British George Cross.

As Dad and I stood in front of the touching monument a German tourist turned to Dad and said, 'Ah, hello . . . can you tell me vot ze vord "siege" means?'

'Um . . .' Dad started. Oh no, I thought, what is he going to say?

'The Germans . . .' Dad continued, 'they . . .' Then Dad started imitating a machine gun. I was waiting for him to say something like, 'but we got you bloody Nazis back in the end,' but luckily he called it quits after a superb imitation of a dropping bomb.

After failing to not mention the war to the German, we scampered up the steep steps to the breezy Upper Barakka, a public garden perched on top of the fortifications with a fine view of the Grand Harbour and the mediaeval townscape. Mind you, we couldn't actually get near the view. The gardens were packed with British tour bus passengers from the nearby seaside resorts. (Four hundred thousand Brits come to Malta every year because it's such an easy country to visit: it has plenty of sun and sea, English is the second official language, driving is on the left, you can find British dailies with page 3 girls on the newsstands and the supermarkets stock cans of mushy peas.

Each group of tour bus lemmings was following a tour leader holding up a board with a number on it. We couldn't get near the lookout because group number 10—the passengers were also wearing stickers with their group number on it—had taken over the entire area. Suddenly, there was a mild panic. Groups 7, 9, 12 and 13 had got themselves into a gridlock and the passengers were accidentally mingling with the other groups and becoming disoriented. If groups

14 and 15 turned up, there was a good chance hysteria would break out and some of the lemmings might jump off the lookout into the sea. I probably didn't help either. Particularly when I shouted, in my best tour-leading voice, 'Okay, can group numbers 10 and 7 come over here!' As the panicked passengers got themselves in a right tangle, Dad and I squeezed onto the viewing platform.

'There used to be up to forty navy ships at a time in the harbour when I was here,' Dad said. The massively impressive (and impressively massive) harbour was now home to two cruise ships and a bunch of rowboats.

'That was the barracks,' Dad said pointing across the harbour, 'and they were the officer's quarters . . .' A fellow from Birmingham, who was standing next to us (group 12), interrupted and said, 'Actually, the officer's quarters were over there and the barracks were on that side.'

'Oh, that's right,' Dad said. It had been over fifty years, so Dad was a little confused. Plus he probably thought we were in Gibraltar. When we told the Brummy that we'd just come from England he said, 'England is the pits.' As we went to leave he said, 'The English football team are the pits, too.'

By the time we were leaving, groups 14 and 15 *had* turned up and it took us fifteen minutes to squeeze our way out through the crowd. We headed to the other side of the narrow peninsula and jumped on a fifteen-minute ferry ride across Marsamxett Harbour to the town of Sliema or, as I dubbed it: the Costa del Malt. The seaside resort was full of ugly concrete hotels and sunburnt Brits. We were meeting a couple from Dad's bowls club in Australia. Joe Attard (which is the Maltese equivalent of John Smith) and his wife Sandra were waiting for us as at the ferry terminal and we walked through town to a private club overlooking the Med. Joe had managed to wrangle temporary membership of the club because he is Maltese. Well, he was born in Malta and this was his first return 'home' since he left for Australia as a seventeen-year-old in 1965. Joe and Sandra had already been in Malta for six weeks and had spent their time visiting his countless relatives and walking around the entire coastline.

'When I left,' Joe said, 'Sliema was where the upper class lived in huge mansions.'

We grabbed a table on the club's outdoor terrace, overlooking the ocean-size ocean pool and ordered some lunch.

'So, did you like Spain?' Joe asked Dad.

'No, the bread was like bloody concrete,' Dad huffed. I shook my head. After all our wonderful experiences visiting the grand cities, stunning white villages and pristine beaches and tasting all that amazing food, Dad's lasting impression of Spain was determined solely by the texture of the country's bread.

For most of the lunch, Dad, Joe and Sandra talked about people from the bowls club. 'You know George Dick with one arm . . . well, he's dead.' 'What about Cecil?' 'Oh, he's dead, too.' 'Doris is still playing, though.' 'No, she died two weeks ago.' It sounded like the last three surviving members of the bowls club were all in Malta.

•

Annie was waiting for us back at the guesthouse. After checking to see if our fingernails were clean, she made us a cup of tea. Annie hadn't had a day off in five years.

'My husband ran the guest house for twenty-eight years,' she said, 'and when he passed away in 1999 I took over and I haven't had a day off since.' Annie looked very sad for a second. 'I'm like a bird in a cage.'

After our 'Spanish siesta', we ate a delicious pizza dinner in a cave that forms the basement of a hotel, then hit the streets to find The Gut. The Gut is the nickname of Valletta's bustling and boisterous nightlife district. There wasn't much bustling going on when we headed into the centre of the city, though. It was only nine o'clock and the streets were virtually empty. Almost eerily so. We saw nothing except for a stray cat here and there. The silence was broken only by the odd conversation or television clatter overheard through shuttered windows. When we did find The Gut, Dad wasn't sure we were in it.

'This was a bar that always used to be full of drunken sailors,' Dad said, scratching his head. We were standing in front of Rextel Office Supplies. The strip club on the corner had become an HSBC bank. So where had The Gut gone?

Most of the bars and nightclubs were now over in Sliema and neighbouring St Julian's with all the package tourists. All the partying sailors had left when the British Navy was thrown out of Malta in 1979. (Malta achieved independence only in 1964 after one hundred and fifty years of British rule, ending over three thousand years of foreign rule altogether). Although sailors swarmed to The Gut, it was officially out of bounds and Naval Patrol would drive around in jeeps searching for wayward lads in uniform.

'The jeeps would come along and hundreds of sailors would hide in doorways or duck into people's houses,' Dad said.

It was in The Gut on one of those drunken nights that Dad bumped into his brother John, who came waltzing down the street towards him dressed in navy uniform. Dad not only didn't know that his brother was in Malta, he didn't even know that he'd joined the Royal Navy. Dad had last seen John when his little brother was a thirteen-year-old schoolkid. Dad and John hugged like . . . well, long-lost brothers, then went for quite a few ales at a place called The Pub. Dad and I trudged up and down the steep streets and endless stairs in search of that famed watering hole.

Not only was The Pub the venue for Dad and John's reunion, it was also where the renowned hell-raiser, actor and bon vivant Oliver Reed not only drank himself under the table but under a tombstone as well on 22 May 1999—maybe he was Annie's husband! Ollie started that fateful evening with a casual eight bottles of Löwenbrau beer. Then, when a bunch of British sailors turned up, Ollie shouted the bar and a rum-drinking, arm-wrestling contest ensued. By the time he'd downed his twelfth double rum, the sailors couldn't keep up and moved on. After they left he drank half a bottle of scotch, lay down on his favourite seat in the corner and slowly turned a nasty shade of blue. The owner of the bar called an ambulance and he died on the way to hospital.

'My only regret,' Oliver once said, 'is that I didn't drink every pub dry and sleep with every woman on the planet.'

Oliver Reed would have had a bit of a problem drinking every pub in Valletta dry (quite apart from the fact that he is dead) the night we went looking—they all seemed to be gone or closed. The Pub was still there—but closed.

We eventually did find *one* pub and, even though it was a Friday night in the capital of Malta, the only patrons were a canoodling couple in the corner. We stayed for a beer and watched the first half of the Greece–France quarter final of Euro 2004. At half-time, when I suggested to Dad that we try to find a place that was a bit more lively, he nominated the city morgue.

Just a few doors along from the bar we came across the entrance to the offices of the Valletta Football Club. We could hear the TV commentary and people talking and laughing upstairs, so we crept up the marble staircase for a look. I poked my head around the door of the football social club bar and every patron in the room stared at me. All ten of them.

'Come in!' chorused half the room.

The room was straight out of the sixties, with formica tables and chairs and bright fluorescent lights. The patrons, fittingly enough, were mostly in their sixties too. Charlie, the youngest of the group, invited us to his table and shouted us a beer.

'I was born in Malta,' he said, 'but in 1958 I emigrated with my parents to Canada. In 1991, I slipped on some ice and ended up in a coma for six weeks. When I woke up, I thought "fuck this, I'm going somewhere warm" and moved back to Malta.'

Charlie told us The Pub was closed because the owner Kathleen Cremona won the Lotto and she only opened it now when she felt like it.

'Where are all the Valletta football players tonight?' I asked Charlie.

'Well, Joe here's the goalkeeper,' Charlie said, pointing behind him. Joe was about seventy-five and blind in one eye. Joe smiled and pretended to parry a ball away.

We watched the match on the large screen. When the whistle blew and Greece had won, knocking out the defending champions France, Charlie jumped out of his seat with joy and yelled, 'Fuck the French! Fuck the lot of them!'

17

Freshly cooked cute fluffy rabbit

I almost lost Dad under a Maltese bus. He was a bit slow hopping on and, as he attempted to scramble aboard, the bus pulled out of the terminus. Dad had to run alongside the now moving bus and hurl, then haul, himself onto the step. He was only centimetres away from being dragged under and mashed while the bus driver just smiled and waved him to a vacant seat.

The bus, like most buses in Malta, was an old 1950s British workhorse painted yellow. Each bus was individually owned and adorned with whatever slogans, symbols and pictures (mostly religious) the driver fancied. They had no air-conditioning—apart from the open windows and doors—the gears crunched, the suspension rocked and the engines often had a bad case of smoker's cough, but I loved them. They were simultaneously Maltese icons and relics of a bygone Britain.

We were catching the bus to the port of Cirkewwa on the northern tip of the island, where we were going to catch a ferry to Comino. Comino, Gozo and Malta make up the three islands of Malta. In the nine months Dad lived in Malta he didn't once venture out of Valletta, let alone off the main island. So this was a new adventure for both of us.

We didn't have to travel far on our first journey, as the furthest you can travel in a straight line on Malta without toppling into the sea is twenty-seven kilometres. I was quite thankful we only had an hour on the bus—the driver had gone to the same Swerve-all-Over-the-Road Driving School as our taxi driver from the airport. We drove through the seemingly endless suburbs of Valletta, stopping every five hundred metres to pick up and drop off passengers. Almost all of them crossed themselves as they jumped aboard the bus.

'They must either be very religious here,' I said to Dad, 'or they know the driver too well.' We passed fourteen churches on our bus ride. I knew it was fourteen because the nun sitting opposite us crossed herself every time we passed one.

The main island of Malta is sometimes referred to as a 'city–state' because its jumble of towns create an almost unbroken urban sprawl. When the bus finally left these suburbs it continued through barren countryside and tiny bays overgrown with holiday apartments where package-holiday suntanners slowly cooked themselves out on the stony lidos.

Suddenly, we rounded a bend (as in swerved recklessly around a bend) and there was Comino. It looked as if someone had thrown a large rock into the middle of the clear turquoise waters between Gozo and Malta.

Comino is only two-and-a-half square kilometres in size, with one four-star hotel and a permanent population of five—four humans and a donkey. When the Comino Hotel was built in 1995 the island had a population of fifty. The hotel was expected to attract more people to Comino but it worked in reverse. The locals thought the hotel would bring swarms of noisy tourists so most of them left.

I wanted to stay on Comino because I wanted to go frolicking in the Blue Lagoon. The Blue Lagoon is a sheltered cove with a white-sand seabed and impossibly clear blue water that has been described as 'the most scintillating and transparent in the Mediterranean'. During the day the bay is inundated with day-trippers but in the early morning and evening the hotel guests have the bay—which is a fifteen-minute walk from the hotel—to themselves

We were staying one night in the hotel so we had our very own private launch—a little chug-chug boat that was only one step from a tinny—to Comino. We checked into our room, which had a wide balcony overlooking a large pool and yachts bobbing in the shimmering aquamarine bay. While I admired the view, Dad spent fifteen minutes trying to get the television to work.

'Have you tried this?' I asked as I stepped back into the room and nonchalantly plugged in the power cord.

After dragging Dad away from the TV I took him for a swim at one of the hotel's private beaches. It was only about twenty metres wide but we had the tiny bay to ourselves. The water was delightfully clear and warm and Dad was soon splashing around like a twenty-year-old. It would have been over twenty-five years since Dad and I had last gone for a swim together and, just as he had when I was fourteen, Dad splashed water all over me before I had a chance to get into the water.

The hotel had mountain bikes for loan. We had never been on a bike ride together so we decided to break the habit of a lifetime and go for a ride. It would also help to fulfil my other agenda on Comino: I wanted to track down the island's entire population (including the donkey).

Comino doesn't have any roads as such, just rough dirt tracks—although the main 'track' is rather grandly named Triq Congreve. Dad was a bit shaky even on fat tyres to begin with, but he was soon trundling happily up Triq Congreve.

As we came over a rise the Blue Lagoon came into view. It looked so picture-book perfect it could have passed for a spectacularly designed spa pool. However, it was hard to imagine this stretch of water as 'the most scintillating and transparent in the Mediterranean' when it looked as if half the population of Malta was floating in it. As well as day-trippers from all the seaside resorts, it was also full of locals from the mainland in their yachts and powerboats. Instead of cruising in a car, the Maltese teenagers went hooning in their powerboats. They were lounging on their boats, smoking and listening to thumping doof-doof music—no wonder most of the locals left. I was so glad we were staying the night so I could visit the bay in the morning without the day-trippers and doofheads.

Away from the sea, the barren island was sweltering hot in the blazing sun. There wasn't a drop of wind and the air was rich with the smell of thyme and wild flowers that came in bright shades of red, white, purple and orange. The only sign of life when we first started out was the odd skylark playing amongst the spiky aloes.

Just when we were feeling like the only people on the island, a tractor with a boat in tow suddenly appeared on the track. The driver, an old fellow who I guessed was one of the hotel staff, waved to us as he chugged by. Not long after that we came across a large stone farmhouse. Attached to the farmhouse was a double garage where a tanned young man was sitting on an empty crate cutting up a large mackerel. Our first local, I thought. Except he wasn't a local. His name was Joe and he lived in Gozo. He came to Comino six days a week to work for 'the local population' as Joe put it.

'What do you do?' I inquired.

'Anything,' he shrugged. 'Whatever jobs need doing. I always find something to do.'

The something he was doing today was cutting up slices of mackerel for bait.

'Where are the locals?' I asked.

'You would have passed one on the way here. He was taking his boat down to go fishing. Another one is having a sleep inside and the two old ladies live up the road next to the old hospital.'

The average age of the population was sixty-four—the eldest was one of the ladies, who was seventy-six, and one of the men the youngest at a mere sixty-one. I'm hazarding a guess that none of the local folk will be adding to the population in the near future, so in only a few short years there will probably be no one left on the island except visiting hotel staff and teenagers playing doof-doof music.

A little further down the track was the crumbling Edwardian hospital that once housed wounded soldiers during the Second World War. The two ladies lived in a low building attached to the main one, which at one time had probably housed hospital staff. Most of the building looked all but deserted, with dusty windows and broken doors, but there were three spotlessly clean windows hung with pretty lace curtains. Naturally I got off my bike and had a peek through one of the windows. A large wooden kitchen table, equipped with two chairs more than the entire population would need if they came to a dinner party, sat in the middle of a neat country-style kitchen.

At the front of the hospital was a rather grandiose courtyard, or formerly grandiose, at least. It was now overgrown with a jungle of weeds covering the rusted remains of old machinery. I got quite excited, though. Standing in the middle, munching on his lunch was *the* donkey. I wandered into the courtyard to take a photo and spotted movement from the second-floor balcony. An old lady with silver hair was hanging out her washing. When she saw me, I waved and she gave me a cursory wave in return before ducking inside. I spotted the other lady sitting in a doorway on the bottom floor, but when she saw me she quickly shut the door. Gee, you'd think they'd be hanging out for someone to talk to. They must be sick of talking to each other about the weather for the past sixty years—especially when you consider the climate: 'Oh, I think it's going to be hot today!'

I later read an interview with one of the ladies who said that her kind consent to give the interview should not in any way be interpreted as indicating a willingness on her part to meet visitors on the island. She urged people to respect her right of privacy and not to trespass or linger around her residence. Her name is Marija Said and she was born on Comino to Maltese parents in the late-twenties. Back then, the island had a population of over a hundred and there were 162 hectares under cultivation, growing onions, potatoes and watermelons. All her relatives have moved on, some to Gozo and Malta but most to Britain and Australia, leaving her to put out all the washing.

As we continued on the dirt track around the island we met some of its other population. Lizards and snakes scuttled off the track in front of us as we rode high above the water's edge along dramatic rock walls that dropped spectacularly into the magically clear waters.

'I hope I can still do stuff like this when I'm seventy-three,' I said to Dad as we trundled up a steep track that was littered with rock landmines. To be honest, I was very impressed with my father. Yes, he wouldn't eat any foreign muck and whinged and moaned a bit too much, but he had been willing to go along with just about everything I had wanted to do on this trip so far. It was hard work for him to ride over dirt tracks in stifling heat, but he gave it his all and only twice did he complain about me trying to kill him.

On the way back to the hotel we passed the farmhouse again and met the fifth and final local. He was sitting with Joe, watching him cut up the mackerel. All we really got out of him was that his name was Salvu Vella and that he liked fishing. Like Marija, he wasn't keen for visitors to 'linger around his residence'. We'd done well, though. In the space of an hour we'd managed to see the entire population of Comino and even managed to get five words out of one of them that weren't about the weather.

I dubbed the dinner at the hotel, 'The Battle of the Buffet'. We had to fight off a horde of German tourists to get to the food. The tussle over the dessert trolley was particularly nasty. After dinner, we had a drink at the outside disco—where the only person who danced the entire night was the DJ—with Julie and Terry from Manchester. It was the couple's twelfth visit to Malta and their first stay on Comino. They were staying for ten days and were more than happy to laze by the pool each day and knock back a few beers on the terrace at night. Julie told us that for the past six years they'd been staying in a villa on Malta. On their last visit, the family who owned the villa took them out for dinner.

'We'll take you to a *real* Maltese restaurant with no tourists and *real* Maltese food,' the villa owner told them. When they sat down at the table in the restaurant, Julie felt something at her feet. She squealed at what she initially thought was a rat. Closer inspection revealed that it was only a cute fluffy rabbit with long soft ears and a twitching pink nose. Under the next table was another adorable bunny. When she looked around the room she noticed bunnies hopping all around the restaurant. It was at this point that the waiter waltzed over and asked whether they were ready to order.

'Which one would you like?' the waiter asked, casually pointing to the little bunnies hopping around his feet. The restaurant's house speciality was very fresh rabbit.

•

I awoke at seven in the morning and headed straight to the Blue Lagoon—Dad wasn't interested—he just grunted a few times, rolled over and went back to sleep. I wanted to fit in a swim before breakfast and our 10 o'clock ferry to Gozo. The low sun was already warm as I strolled past purple, white and fuchsia oleanders to the blissfully empty and deserted bay.

The Maltese refer to the Blue Lagoon as *Bejn il-Kmiemen*, literally 'betwixt the Cominos', as the bay is actually an inlet between Comino and its uninhabited smaller sister Cominotto. I waded into the clear, crisp water and swam across to Cominotto—I wanted to be able to brag that I went to all *four* Maltese islands. The water was deep, but so incredibly clear that I could see my shadow on the sea floor far below, just as if it was within arm's reach. I stepped ashore on Cominotto, stood there for a minute, then jumped back in.

Not long after, I suddenly thought I was going to die. I felt an intense pain in my forearm and within seconds my hand went numb. A jellyfish had stung me. I clutched my forearm in pain and squealed like a schoolgirl while treading water. Then I began to panic. I was halfway across the inlet and the numbness started creeping up my arm. Oh, this is going to be good, I thought—the paralysis is going to spread up my entire body and I'll sink to the bottom. The joy of having the bay to myself had suddenly turned into, 'Where the HELL is everyone?' I lay on my back, still clutching my aching and now useless arm, and slowly propelled myself back to shore.

When I finally got back to the hotel with a massive red welt up my arm, Dad said, 'Don't die on me yet, I don't know which ferry I have to catch back to Malta.'

18

Lemon f___king chicken

Our taxi from the port of Mgarr on Gozo travelled only a bit faster than brisk walking pace.

'I've had this car for over forty years and I never go over thirty kilometres an hour,' Joe the taxi driver told us while softly patting the dashboard of his immaculately kept 1960 Mercedes. It took us twenty minutes to drive (or potter) the seven kilometres to the tiny inland village of Xaghra (pronounced Shaa-ra).

Two Piaggio mopeds were sitting on the back of a trailer waiting for us out the front of Xaghra Lodge. I'd organised the bikes—via the Internet from Australia—to be delivered to the lodge at eleven o'clock that morning from a place in the seaside resort of Marsalforn. There was only one small hurdle still to be overcome if my well-organised side-trip was going to be a success—I still had to persuade Dad to actually get onto a moped!

When I'd told him back in Australia that I was planning to hire mopeds in Malta, he'd told Mum, 'There's no bloody way he's getting me on one of those.' That's why I decided to use the last resort of a desperate (and unscrupulous) son: a guilt trip.

'You have to come for a ride with me,' I pleaded as we pulled up in front of the lodge. 'I've already paid for the bikes and they weren't cheap!'

'If you're trying to kill me, I've got bad news', Dad said. 'There's no money left for you.'

After meeting Dave, the proprietor of the lodge, I didn't think I was going to get the chance to ride the moped (or to kill Dad) anyway. Dave wouldn't let us out of the lodge. He cornered us for forty minutes while he told us his life story.

'I got ou' ov Englund in 1995 cos the country is fucked, know wha' a mean?' Actually, he didn't get out of England because it was fucked: he had to leave because he was an east London gangster on the run. Or so I figured. After forty minutes with him I ascertained that he was, 'well dodgy, know wha' a mean?'

Dave had slicked-back dyed hair and was dripping with gold, including a necklace as thick as a dog chain and Elvis Presleyesque diamond-encrusted rings on every finger.

'This one 'ere,' he told us, 'cost me free fousand quid!' Photos of his 'beloved one' adorned the walls in the entrance hall. His beloved was his bull terrier. Dave had the same build as his dog.

'I'm 58 years old and I work ou' evree fuckin' day, know wha' a mean?' he said, flexing his biceps. He was wearing a 'Xaghra Lodge' body-builder's singlet, which were for sale in reception.

After Dave had told us how much the lodge cost him, and that he'd recently split up with his wife and that he knew the Kray twins who were 'fuckin' nice lads who only beat up people they didden like', we finally headed for the mopeds.

'I haven't ridden a motorbike in over fifty years!' Dad said nervously as he got on his moped. He wobbled tentatively around the square for ten minutes then said, 'I'll only come for a bit and only if we go really slow.' Five minutes later we were out on the open road and I sped up a little, hoping I wasn't going too fast for Dad. A minute after that, Dad shot past me at high speed with both his legs in the air whooping loudly with delight.

It was a Sunday and the streets were empty, so we just about had the island to ourselves. We rode through terraced fields that formed steps up to tabletop hills and down into deep valleys. The first town we passed through was Nadur. Like all Gozitan towns, it was dominated by a massive parish church, around which was clustered concentric rings of amber-hued townhouses.

Gozo was about a third of the size of Malta (with a tenth of the population), so it didn't take us long to hit the coast. During his stay on Gozo in 1866, the English poet Edward Lear described the island's coastal scenery as 'pomskizillious and gromphiberrous—there being no other words to describe its magnificence'. San Blas Bay was truly pomskizillious. A steep track from the small car park led down to a sandy cove with impossibly blue water. I'd planned a rather packed itinerary for the afternoon, so we simply admired the view for a minute then chooffed off.

The next stop on our whirlwind tour of Gozo was Xlendi Bay (other tongue-twisting Gozitan town names included Xewkija, Xwieni, Ghajnsielem and the romantic beach resort of Hondoq ir-Rummien). It took us only half an hour to scoot across the entire island up steep narrow roads lined with pink and white oleanders, past the outskirts of the capital Victoria and through endless dusty fields.

Xlendi Bay was almost gromphiberrous. The delightful sea inlet lay at the end of a deep, lush ravine that until the mid-twentieth century was a small fishing port. Colourful fishing boats still bobbed around in the glorious blue-green waters of the land-locked bay, but they were now overshadowed by towering apartment blocks. We sat in the Winston Churchill restaurant with our backs to the apartments, taking in the magical view while we stuffed our faces with seafood.

The Inland Sea at Dwejra on the south coast of the island was both pomskizillious and gromphiberrous. Set in a deep recess in the rocky coastline, the Inland Sea is a large expanse of shallow water linked to the sea by a narrow hundred-metre cave in the cliff. The only buildings near this refreshingly undeveloped natural wonder were a few fishermen's boatsheds and a small restaurant. A large gaggle of children was splashing noisily in the perfectly clear waters.

As we wandered around the shore of the Inland Sea, we were politely importuned by fishermen to go for a ride with them—fishermen supplement their income by taking tourists on boat trips through the cave out to the open sea. We took up fisherman Joe's offer because he had a cousin in Melbourne. Hawkers the world over must do the same 'How to Win Over Tourists' course since no matter where you are someone will use the old, 'I've got a cousin in [insert your city of residence] trick—although in Malta's defence, the entire population really does have a cousin in Melbourne (Australia's Maltese population is 180 000, half that of Malta itself).

The boat trip was 'fabquackilliant'—as soon as we entered the narrow fissure the air turned delightfully cool and only seconds later we were in total darkness. It was eerie yet magical and as we came out of the tunnel into the open sea, the cave became a kaleidoscope of vibrant colour—the light transformed the water into a deep cobalt blue, while bright pink and orange coral clung to the cave walls below the water.

As we motored past the magnificent Azure Window—a massive natural stone arch—Dad said, 'I'm so glad we did this.' I was, too. I was having the most marvellous day, and it wasn't just thanks to the amazing sights of Gozo. I was really enjoying Dad's company and it didn't feel like I was travelling with my septuagenarian father—it felt like I was having a ball with my best friend.

On the way back to Xaghra we stopped at the imposing baroque parish church in the village of Gharb to send a letter to God. Well, not exactly, but they did have a postbox next to the altar. 'I wonder if they have guaranteed next-day delivery,' I whispered to Dad as we shuffled past the altar.

•

I wanted to go to the Oleander restaurant for dinner but Dave threatened to smash our fuckin' heads in if we didn't eat in his restaurant at the lodge. Actually, he didn't threaten us with physical violence. He didn't need to. He just told us that we were eating in his restaurant and I was too scared to say no. The interior of the lodge was furnished in quite an eclectic mix of styles: most of the rooms were filled with magnificent antiques—more than likely off the back of a truck, know wha' a mean?—but there was also a mini mock-English pub and a Chinese restaurant with full oriental regalia. Dave had somehow got two young Chinese guys and their girlfriends sent over from China and then thrown them straight into his kitchen to prepare sweet and sour pork for English tourists. Dad asked Dave if he could have something that wasn't 'too Chinesey'. Dave suggested we have the full banquet. I said that was an excellent idea, since the rings on Dave's fingers looked as if they could tear a lot of flesh from my face.

We were the only diners in the restaurant and, I later discovered, the only guests staying in the lodge. As we ate our standard prawn crackers starter, Dad told me about his visit to the famous Floating Restaurant in Hong Kong. He was stuck at the end of a long queue with a large group from a cruise ship he was on—as a passenger, not the cook—when he called over one of the staff.

'Can you tell the manager,' he said curtly, 'that the Prime Minister of Australia Bob Hawke and his party are here for dinner.'

'The manager gave us the best table,' Dad smiled cheekily, 'and he personally waited on our table for the entire meal.' No doubt 'the PM' did all Australians proud by asking if his Number 24 could be served with chips.

The manager of Xhagra Lodge personally waited on our table too, but I bet the manager of the Floating Restaurant didn't tell stories about beatin' the fuckin' shit ou' of people until they was almost dead. As we dug into our lemon chicken, Dave told us about his spell as a bouncer in a club in Stepney.

'On me life this is true,' he said, kissing one of the massive gold rings on his finger. 'This huge fella asked this tiny little girl, an' I mean faaaaarkin' *tiny* little girl, furra dance and when she said no he punched 'er and tore 'alf 'er fuckin' nose off. We beat the fuckin' shit ou' of 'im, we did.' Dave then screwed up his face and clenched his teeth, 'He was a fuckin' big heap of shit.'

There were more pleasant dinnertime stories over our dessert of banana fritters.

'I knee-capped this dirty fucka' cos he tried t' get in the club wiv the wrong shoes on!' It was something like that, anyway. I was pretending to listen while I tried to enjoy my meal without being put off by visions of bodies being beaten to a pulp. He did tell us something useful, though, and it didn't involve rearranging people's faces. He told us that there was a *festa* taking place in the next village.

'You can ride there on ya scooters,' he said. Dad wasn't keen on riding at night, though.

'It's fuckin' easy,' Dave growled. 'Turn left, bosh, bosh and ya' there!'

'I think it might be too dangerous riding at night,' Dad said.

'This is Malta, not FUCKIN' AFRICA!' Dave cried.

'We better go,' I whispered to Dad, 'or he might string us up by our balls.'

Actually, I was quite excited but not that surprised to discover that there was a *festa* on. Every weekend in summer there is a *festa* in Malta. They are usually noisy three-day affairs involving fireworks, brass bands, and inebriation—all in commemoration of parish saints—each village celebrates the feast day of its patron saint. Faith is very strong in Malta, and Christianity has been the dominant religion since St Paul shipwrecked there in 60 AD. Practically everyone, young and old, attends mass, many even attend daily. Statues of the Madonna are everywhere and houses have names like Visitation, Assumption, Blessed Virgin, Bethlehem and Santa Maria. With a population of only twenty-two thousand people living in fourteen villages, Gozo has sixty-one churches and just about every single one of them had been built on a grand scale.

The village of Xewkija, where the *festa* was being held, was dominated by the Parish Church of St John the Baptist, which has a higher dome than St Paul's Cathedral in London. With enough pews to hold four thousand people, it also has the largest seating capacity in the Maltese islands. The church was built by local parishioners and paid for by the whip-around at Sunday Mass.

What I found most impressive was the church's resemblance to the Griswold house from *National Lampoon's Christmas Vacation*—the entire, vast building was covered with rows and rows of coloured lights. The view of the church rising above the town across the valley as we rode down the steep road out of Xaghra was simply amazing. And best of all, we'd have a hard time getting lost with the Griswold church as our beacon. We also had frequent flashes of daylight as fireworks exploded and sizzled into the air above us so we could see the bumps in the road. Each town lets off fireworks day and night for an entire week, so there must be a lot of nervous cats in Malta. They use so many skyrockets that each village in Malta has its own fireworks factory, and practice really does make perfect: Malta had won the previous four World Fireworks Championships.

After a day of scooting around the island I was feeling quite cocky on my moped, so I rode right into the centre of town, with Dad wobbling behind me, slaloming our way through the swarm of locals and up the narrow streets leading to the town square in front of the church. The entire village was adorned with coloured lights hanging across the street—a massive display that would give the Christmas lights in Regent Street, London, a run for their money. To complete the festive spectacle, huge, intricately designed flags of Saint John were draped from many balconies and windows.

As we got closer to the square, the streets became so crowded that we had to park our bikes and continue on foot. The parading locals were all in their Sunday best: the men in suits and the women in floral dresses. It was easy to spot the few tourists because they were all in shorts. Some of the local teenagers on the other hand, looked as if they were off to the St John the Baptist disco and nightclub: the girls were in tight white pants with brightly coloured G-strings poking out the top, while the boys were in 'disco' slacks and each one smelled like an aftershave factory.

A fifty-piece brass band, who were wearing uniforms that made the Salvation Army band's uniforms look cool, were playing dirges in the town square. The ground was blanketed with streamers from a procession earlier in the evening, while crowds of people stood on the steps of the church drinking and gossiping.

Suddenly the crowd cleared to make way for a parade of priests. The procession combined pomp, sanctity and almost funereal solemnity as the priests dressed in white robes with hot pink shawls made their way up the wide steps to the entrance of the church.

'Look!' Dad said excitedly, 'they've got the Euro 2004 cup.' The leading priest did look as if he had the Euro cup perched precariously on top of a long pole. Behind him, a large and sweaty flock of priests lumbered past carrying a towering gilded statue of St John on their shoulders. The entire crowd started singing a song to what sounded like the tune of 'Bob the Builder'. We stayed for a bit more singing (' . . . Jesus and his Disciples have so much fun, working together to get the job done'), then went for a wander.

On the way back to our bikes we witnessed some locals in an emotional display of religious fervour. Shouting and screams of joy and pain were emanating from inside a small doorway. I snuck my head in the door to see a large bunch of drunken men watching the Czech Republic score the winning goal against Denmark in the Euro quarter final.

•

Before we went down for breakfast in the morning I made my bed. I didn't want the lads sent after me. While Dave served us up his homemade and deliciously fluffy and light scrambled eggs, he told us about when he 'punched some big fuckin' bastard in the mowf and hacked his arm off wiv a butta knife.' When Dad told him that I was writing a book and that his lodge would appear in the book, Dave leant over and—I kid you not—said, 'You'd betta giv me a good write up or I'll tear ya' fuckin' ears orf!'

So I hope you've enjoyed Dave's sparkling repartee, although I'm sure I've failed to do it justice. All I have to add is that the Xaghra Lodge is far and away the best place I've ever stayed. Oh, and Dave, in case you're looking for me, I've moved to South America.

19

KFB (Kentucky Fried Bunny)

By the time we got to Mdina in the centre of the main island of Malta I needed a good chiropractor and a skin graft. The bus took almost three hours, via Valletta and just about every single house on the island. My back was screaming with pain from the bumpy ride and my legs were stuck (by melting) to the seat in the searing heat.

Both Dad and I were a bit grumpy during the bus trip and when a fourteen-year-old boy got on the bus and asked to see our tickets I told him to go play on a busy road. The very confident and well-spoken teen then presented his 'Ticket & Bus Inspector' badge. After checking everyone's tickets, he filled out his little blue book and began grilling the driver. I watched amazed as a fifty-year-old bus driver grovelled to a pre-pubescent bus inspector.

After prying ourselves off the bus seats, we checked into Hotel de Vue and had a spot of lunch on the verandah with a Vue of a large carpark. On the other side of the car park was a section of the handsome fortifications that surround the old city. Situated on a rock ledge in the geographical centre of the island, Mdina has only four hundred inhabitants and is one of the best-preserved baroque towns in the world. Thanks to its meandering alleys, it is also virtually car-free. Inside the baroque gates are historic convents, St Paul's Cathedral built in 1697, and mediaeval townhouses, the oldest of which dates back to 1233.

Traipsing around the ancient capital of Malta wasn't our main reason for visiting Mdina, though. I had timed our visit to coincide with Malta's biggest festival, the Festival of L-Imnarja, which celebrates the feast day of saints Peter and Paul. The festival dates from before the coming of the Knights in 1530 and is essentially the same folk festival and piss-up it was five hundred years ago.

All of the action takes place in Buskett Gardens, a wooded park ten minutes by bus from Mdina. By the time we'd psyched ourselves up sufficiently to get back onto a bumpy hot bus it was 4.30. The bus dropped us off at the entrance to the heavily wooded gardens that had suddenly appeared out of the surrounding parched fields. On the long path down to the festival site, food and drink vendors were selling traditional Maltese food such as 'American Hot Dogs' and 'American Popcorn'.

Stone paths meandered through the groves of Aleppo pine, oak, olive and orange trees to a dusty open space where a stage was set up—along with bars, food stalls and the Agricultural Show with its displays of animals, fruits and vegetables. Then we spotted a crowd of people and I realised we were at the wrong festival. We'd somehow stumbled into the World's Ugliest Person Competition. Must be something in the water round those parts, because those folk looked as if they all claimed direct descent from the offspring of Quasimodo and the Bride of Frankenstein. There were lots of steep foreheads, boxer's noses and ears like mainsails. This lot hadn't been touched with an ugly stick, they'd been hit with an ugly baseball bat. It was all the more disconcerting because a bunch of them kept staring at me. To them I probably looked like Brad Pitt.

We weaved our way past the cast of *Monsters Inc.* to the Agricultural Show. In the middle of an open shed was a long three-tiered display of just about every fruit and vegetable under the sun. I picked up a program at the entrance which listed all the sections and classes for the Agricultural Competition, including prizes for the Best Straw and Best Bastard Saffron.

The first display was French Beans, where the winning beans looked identical to the beans that took second place. They looked quite nice as far as beans go, but they didn't look any different from the beans at my local supermarket. We waltzed past the Best Wrinkled Peas and what looked like the Best Weeds and stopped at the Best Banana section—there had only been one entry, so therefore it had won first place. Sadly, the banana in question wasn't even at *its* best—it looked about a week past its use-by-date.

There was a large crowd, including a TV news crew, milling about a line of cages containing very nervous-looking rabbits. I was always under the impression that there was just one type of pet rabbit: cute white ones with fluffy ears. But there were hundreds of the buggers. There were Flemish Giants, Netherland Dwarfs, Siamese Sables, Vienna Blues, Californian Rexes, Dutch Lops, Dwarf Lops, Mini Lops and Lop Lops. One scary-looking bunny was the size of a German Shepherd.

After filming the rabbits, the TV crew moved on to the leeks and filmed the winner and runner-up for about ten minutes. That was all a bit too much excitement for us so we wandered back over to the food stalls. In between stands selling sheep dip and chicken feed, there were food stalls selling fried rabbit, stewed rabbit, rabbit fricassee and rabbit burgers—no wonder the rabbits looked so nervous. I had some KFB (Kentucky Fried Bunny) and chips. The rabbit seemed to be mostly bone, but it was quite nice. Dad just had the chips.

We sat at a table with a bloke who looked like Jabba the Hutt in a suit and, over a few of the local Cisk Lagers, watched the hordes of people streaming into the park. Jabba told us that marriage contracts in Malta included a clause requiring the husband to take his new bride to L-Imnarja at Buskett Gardens in the first year of their marriage. They must have a Newlyweds Ugly Competition.

As the shades of evening fell slowly on the gardens, folks sought out prime spots under trees draped with fairy lights, where they could spend the night after they'd lavishly indulged in plenty of food, wine and song. Other people had set up chairs in front of the stage waiting for the entertainment. Entertainment is probably the wrong word, though. It was more akin to fingernails on a blackboard. The Addams family, complete with Lurch on guitar strumming the same chord over and over, were playing traditional Maltese 'Ghana' or folk music. Four old blokes, including Uncle Fester, took it in turns to groan into the microphone.

After two painful ballads we'd had enough of the Melody-less Munsters, so we joined the throng of locals doing laps of the park. The pathways were jammed with people going round and round and round, but no one actually looked that happy. I'd read that L-Imnarja was 'Malta's most boisterous fun festival', but the only boisterous fun I saw happening was in a large cage of guinea pigs.

We left at 11 o'clock as streams of people were still pouring into the gardens. We stopped at the entrance to ask a 'handsome' policeman where to get the bus and Dad, who doesn't mind a chat, bailed him up for fifteen minutes. In that time we found out that his name was Joe and he had a relative in Melbourne. Joe lived in Rabat, a sprawling suburb of Mdina, had five children, had been in the police force for twenty-eight years, worked twenty-four hours on then had twenty-four hours off, and had never shot anyone while on duty, but he did once get punched in a fight. We also found out that everyone gets rolling drunk at the festival and most people don't leave until at least four in the morning.

'Only the old people leave early,' he said. The bus was full on the way back—there was me and a busload of seventy year olds.

•

'We have to get to Buskett Gardens early,' I said to Dad as I urged him to finish his breakfast.

'What for?' Dad asked through a mouthful of toast.

'The Goat Milking Competition.'

'You're bloody kidding!' Dad huffed.

'No, apparently it's the highlight of the festival.'

Sadly, by the time we got to Buskett Gardens the Goat Milking Competition had finished. At least the World's Ugliest Person Competition was still in full swing—the morning's event was a subsection of the main competition: The World's Ugliest *Fat* Person Competition. We hung around till noon to watch His Excellency Dr Edward Fenech Adami, the President of Malta, hand out the prizes in the livestock and other animal sections, including Best Maltese Nanny Goat, Best Bob White Chicken and Best Long Face Pigeon, but by 12.30 he hadn't shown. The judges were probably still having trouble deciding which was the Best Maltese Heifer.

We got back on the bus and continued fifteen minutes up the road to the south coast and Dingli Cliffs, one of Malta's most celebrated beauty spots. The bus driver dropped us and eight other tourists in the middle of a deserted town and gestured vaguely off into the distance when I asked where the cliffs were. An old English couple headed off first and the rest of us followed some distance behind them. We straggled down a narrow road out of town and along a path lined with dry-stone walls flanked by barren fields.

'They must grow stones here,' Dad said. It did look like that, the surrounding fields were scattered with white stones as if they'd grown up from the ground.

After fifteen minutes of plodding through fields with no sign of a cliff anywhere, the couple stopped and we caught up with them.

'We've got no idea where we are,' the man said. I laughed. Like lemmings (except we couldn't find a cliff), we'd all been blindly following them. Everyone looked at each other dumbfounded for a minute, then we all split up and headed off in different directions. We followed a Belgian couple. They had no idea where they were going either, but if we were going to spend the entire day hopelessly lost they seemed like a nice couple to spend it with.

The four of us followed a rocky track, then suddenly the land fell away in a spectacular two-hundred-metre drop to the sea. We'd found the Dingli Cliffs. We spent fifteen minutes seeing who was game to go closest to the edge, then I said, 'I wonder where the other couples are?' The other couples hadn't turned up and [insert *Twilight Zone* music here] we never saw them again.

The Belgian couple joined us as we hiked down the road along the top of the cliff until we reached a lone building precariously perched near the edge. The Bobbyland Restaurant should have been called Bunnyland Restaurant, since once again there wasn't much on the menu except rabbit. The restaurant was almost full—I later read it was a Gozitan favourite—but we managed to score a table on the terrace with majestic views of the car park. I had a delicious spaghetti alla fluffy (spaghetti with rabbit sauce) and Dad had what he hoped was a hamburger and chips—I suspect the burger had more to do with Bugs Bunny than Porky Pig, though.

After lunch, we searched anxiously for half an hour till we eventually found the bus back to Mdina. I was keen to get back because I didn't want to miss the bareback donkey races at Saqqajja

Hill in Rabat. The races have been part of Festival of L-Imnarja since the seventeenth century, when the event comprised races on donkeys, mules, mares and horses, and races for boys, men and 'negro slaves'.

I was pretty sure we wouldn't be seeing any negro slaves racing, but before we arrived in Mdina I wasn't sure if we'd even be able to get to the racetrack. When we'd first arrived at our hotel, I'd asked the manager where the race took place. I had assumed it would be way out of town somewhere, but he led me out on to the balcony of our room and pointed, 'Down there'. Below us, running through a field of cacti and olive trees, was a busy, steep asphalt road.

'That's the finish line,' he said, indicating a T-intersection directly below us. 'They close the road for the race, though,' he added. That's a pity, I thought. Watching bareback donkey jockeys trying to dodge large yellow Maltese buses would have been fun.

When we finally got to Mdina, the race route was already lined with throngs of people defying the scorching rays of the sun to get a good view of the track. We'd missed a few races but had arrived just in time for the start of the Clash of the Lilliputians. The horses were the size of jockeys and the jockeys, who were sitting on buggies behind, looked about ten years old. They turned out to be twelve years old, so I was close.

The track was a kilometre long and each race would start before the one before it had even finished. It all seemed quite chaotic. Some races had eight horses, while others had only two. Spectators were even wandering onto the track in the middle of a race. You'd think after three hundred years, they might have got the organisation of the race right. We waltzed down to the finish line—when I say the finish line, I don't just mean near the finish line, people were standing *right on* the finish line—to get a closer look. I almost got bowled over by one winning horse, and of course it had to be a normal larger, scarier one. Sadly, we'd missed the bareback donkey race (and the negro slaves), so we trudged up to our room for a siesta.

•

Dad awoke with a fright.

'Oh my God, I've woken up at my own funeral!' A brass band had just struck up a funeral march in our bathroom—that's what it sounded like, at least. A large band was blaring away in the town square, which we could see if we craned our heads out the window. While we'd been napping, the square, which had been full of buses, had been cleared and decked out with a stage and rows of folded chairs that were now full of people. We popped down to have a look and were quite surprised to see that it was the same band from the *festa* in Gozo. It seemed the Dirge Brothers Big Band were quite popular in Malta.

After dinner at our hotel—I had a tasty local dish called *bragioli*, which is thin slices of beef wrapped around a stuffing of breadcrumbs, chopped bacon, egg and parsley, then braised in red wine sauce; Dad had cod and chips—we went to check out Mdina. The entrance to the old city is through the imaginatively named Main Gate, which was built in 1724. As we walked over the stone bridge and across the moat towards the gate, it felt as if we were stepping back in time . . . until I glanced down into the former moat. It now holds half a dozen brand new tennis courts.

The massive original wooden door was open but I gave it a further experimental push. It was surprisingly easy to move. Being a Thacker I couldn't help myself, I began to close the heavy oak door and announced to the people strolling in behind us, 'I'm sorry everyone, we're closing up for the night.'

'A few hundred years ago, that's what they used to do,' a man in a suit said as I closed the door on him. His name was Charlie and he was a retired school principal from the nearby town of Mosta.

Charlie and his wife Mary often came into Mdina for an evening stroll and asked us if we'd like to join them.

'Mdina is called the Silent City,' Charlie told us. Silent all right. The place was like a morgue. The twisting narrow streets and alleys were ominously quiet as we shuffled past closed wooden shutters painted blue, green and brown, empty wrought-iron balconies, and brightly coloured doors with elaborate door knockers. The day-trippers had gone, so all of the shops and cafés were closed.

Charlie certainly knew his Maltese history and seemed to know when every single building in Mdina was built.

'That's the Chapel of St Agatha,' Charlie said, 'which was built in 1417, and next door is St Benedict's Church, which was built in 1418.' Then again, he could have been using my old trick when I was a tour leader, just making up the dates. After a while, Dad started testing him.

'When was that built?' Dad asked, pointing to a green metal rubbish bin.

Charlie pointed out the balcony on Notary Bezzina's house—the balcony on which the French governor was lobbed to his death in 1798. Malta was under Napoleanic rule at the time and the scuffle began a bloody uprising against the French. He also showed us the Nunnery of St Benedict, whose sisters are never allowed to leave—even after death—they are buried in the grounds. No man is permitted to enter the convent and some of the older nuns have not seen a man in over fifty years. Dad suggested to Charlie that we should drop in for a cup of tea.

'I know an easier place to get a cup of tea,' Charlie said.

The Fontanella Tea Garden was on top of the city walls. The Black Forest cake was magnificent, and the view from the terrace wasn't bad, either—you could almost see the entire island. Charlie's hometown of Mosta was easily identified by the massive cupola of the Mosta Dome. Three German bombs landed on the church in 1942 when there were three hundred parishioners inside. Two bombs bounced off and landed in the square without exploding, while the third pierced the dome and rolled across the floor. Amazingly, not a single person was hurt.

Charlie and Mary were just lovely and they even escorted us back to our hotel—although I think that was because they were worried we might have gone back and broken into the convent.

•

We arrived back in Valletta just as the stern of one of the world's largest aircraft carriers slipped out of the Grand Harbour. Dad was gutted. We'd heard that the *USS John F. Kennedy* was in town and Dad was looking forward to hanging out with some sailors and talking about yardarms and scurvy and stuff. There certainly would have been enough sailors to talk to: the ship has a crew of five thousand six hundred, outnumbering the Maltese armed forces and police force combined.

We would have had such a wonderful view of the ship, too. On our last night in Malta we were staying at the formerly quite flash—and formerly too expensive for the likes of us—British Hotel overlooking the harbour. While Dad was disappointed about missing the US Navy, we did get to wander through long, dark and dank tunnels dug into the limestone underneath the city. We were looking for the NAAFI (Navy Army Air Force Institute), the armed forces canteen where personnel could buy discounted cigarettes, grog and bacon butties. At one time there was a huge NAAFI in Valletta, with long rows of bars and mess halls. All that was left now was a tiny fibro shed set aside for the tourists.

It looked as if none of the other tourists could find it since we were the only customers. An ancient tape deck was playing old war tunes and the walls were covered with war posters and armed forces memorabilia, including used gun shells on the tables as vases. It was all very authentic—even the bacon butties tasted like they were from 1948.

After a last diverting stroll through the town, we repaired to the convivial terrace bar on the roof of the British Hotel for an aperitif. For dinner I had one last go at rabbit—when in Rome, etc.—then we retired to the bar to watch the sunset. There was only one other person in the bar soaking up the magical view. His name was Joe Abela and he was born the same year as Dad and had emigrated from Malta to San Diego in the USA in 1967, the same year we emigrated to Australia. He was in Malta on holidays staying with his nephew David Montabello who owned and ran the hotel—David's family had run the hotel since 1932.

When Dad told him I was a travel writer Jo said that *I* should read one of *his* books. He was the author of nine books, including one on the theories behind psycho-cybernetics—which I'm guessing is 'crazy robots'.

'It's a book about the history of Malta,' Joe told us about the one he really wanted me to read. 'It's called *Malta Explained to Extraterrestrials & Other Aliens*.'

'That should come in handy for Brian, then,' Dad said. 'He has to come from another planet—you should see some of the funny stuff he eats.'

Sri Lanka

20

Fish head curry and brain masala

'Are you Australian?' the fellow at the foreign exchange counter at Colombo airport asked me.

'Um, yes,' I admitted, cautiously.

'Australia are 8 for 162,' he beamed.

'That's, er . . . good,' I said. I thought it was good. I really don't have much idea about cricket, or—as I call it—Standing About. There is also an indoor version called Indoor Standing About.

'Sri Lanka only made 98, though,' he said, shaking his head gravely. He lowered his voice, leaned towards me as if to share a confidence, and said, 'It's a bowlers' wicket.'

'That's nice.' I didn't have a clue what he meant.

The cricket match in question was on the radio in the taxi.

'You are Australian!' the taxi driver gushed excitedly when he heard my accent. He then turned up the not-quite-tuned-in radio and gave us a huge smile and a thumbs-up. My dislike of cricket is hereditary and, even at this early stage, Dad just couldn't take it any more.

'I HATE cricket! It's the most boring bloody game in the world.' The taxi driver looked at him in utter shock. Actually, he looked more confused than anything. How could an Australian not love cricket?

'You can't say that,' I whispered to Dad. 'The Sri Lankans are obsessed with cricket. If you admit you don't like it, they'll think you're bloody mad!' and, of course, the opposite was also true. We'd make instant best friends through our mutual love of the great game of Standing About. I would happily pretend to love the world's most boring spectacle while I was in Sri Lanka and even wax lyrically about very silly cover drives and the state of Shane Warne's off stump.

'That Ricky Ponting sure has a good square leg, doesn't he?' I said, winking at the driver.

•

The streets of Colombo were just how I imagined they would be: chaotic. It took me ten minutes to figure out which side of the road the Sri Lankans were supposed to be driving on. That was partly because I could hardly see the road. Three-wheelers (called tuk-tuks in other parts of Asia) were belching out so much black smoke I could barely make out the bus in front of us belching out its own black smoke screen. The buses were all falling apart, the roads were all falling apart, the houses were all falling apart and our bags were all falling apart in the boot of the taxi as they got thrown around throughout the bumpy ride.

All of a sudden we were in the 'business district' and we shot past modern glass buildings and scurrying people in suits carrying briefcases. Three minutes later, we were back in the black haze of downtown Colombo. Thankfully, the air cleared considerably when we reached the beachfront and the sound of clapped-out vehicles was soon replaced by the crashing of waves and screeching of seagulls.

It was easy to spot our hotel. The Galle Face Hotel would have looked more at home on Park Lane than Galle Road. The grand whitewashed colonial hotel, which opened in 1864, was for years the centre of British colonial life and later the playground of the rich and famous who passed through the island. Lest you forget its illustrious clientele, the hotel had a bronze plaque listing its celebrity guests. The names ranged from famous to infamous: John D. Rockefeller, Emperor Hirohito, Roger Moore, Richard Nixon, Mahatma Gandhi, Bo Derek, Kurt Waldheim and someone named Tigger-Stack Ramsay Brown.

Mahatma Gandhi met us at the entrance. He was wearing a crisp white admiral's uniform and greeted us as though we were long lost friends. He was the doorman and four other hotel staff rushed past him to grab our bags and escort us to reception. Inside the palatial four-storey building, the sweeping staircase and threadbare red carpet bore witness to a glittering past. Here was languid luxury on a grand scale. It had to be conceded that those imperialists had exquisite taste and an attentive eye for detail. The perfectly groomed staff were certainly attentive. By the time we stepped into our room, twenty-seven different staff members had been directly involved in getting us there.

We had a quick lie-down as we were both tired after the long flight from Malta via Tripoli in Libya and Dubai. When we emigrated to Australia in 1967 on a super-ridiculously long flight, we stopped in Colombo for five hours.

'It was bloody hot,' Dad told me, 'and they gave us cups of tea with flowers floating in them! The whole airport smelled of curry.' Dad said the same thing about Amaravathi Restaurant, which was just up the road from our hotel.

'It smells like bloody curry,' Dad winced as we walked in.

'That's maybe because it's a *curry* restaurant,' I observed drily.

Dad spent six months in Sri Lanka with the Royal Navy and didn't once eat anything that even resembled Sri Lankan food. Every single meal he ate was in the mess where he worked as a cook. He had arrived in Trincomalee on the north-eastern coast of the tear-shaped island aboard *HM Submarine Artemis* in 1953. Back then,

Sri Lanka was called Ceylon—it didn't become Sri Lanka until 1972, although the local Singhalese call their country simply Lanka. Even though Sri Lanka gained its independence from Britain in 1948, the Royal Navy kept its base at Trincomalee until 1957. Less than twenty years after Dad left the sleepy town of Trincomalee, that infamous football club, the Tamil Tigers, turned the area into a war zone. Up until a ceasefire in 2002, the town had been under the control of the LTTE (Liberation Tigers of Tamil Eelam).

Our first meal in Sri Lanka was at a Tamil restaurant. Amaravathi Restaurant served southern Indian cuisine—Sri Lankan curries are very hot, so I thought I'd go for a slightly milder Indian curry.

'So, Dad,' I said as we sat down, 'are you going to have chicken curry or beef curry?'

'I'd rather starve!' he grunted. 'I must be able to get a jam butty back at the hotel,' he added hopefully.

'The menu looks good,' I observed cheerfully, 'they've got fish head curry and brain masala.' Dad didn't look up. He was too busy staring at the menu in total disbelief and dismay. I ordered the chicken biryani with roti as sadly, they didn't do fish head curries on Thursdays.

'I'll have a beer for lunch,' Dad said to the waiter.

'Sorry, sir, no beer today,' the waiter said, shaking his head like one of those plastic dogs on car dashboards. There was no beer because it was *poya*, the full-moon public holiday, and it is forbidden to serve alcohol on this day. (Incidentally, Sri Lanka has 26 public holidays a year—including one for every full moon.) Dad looked sorely disappointed. The waiter glanced around apprehensively, then whispered, 'It's okay, I'll get you a beer.' The waiter returned with two metal sugar bowls filled with beer.

'No one will know that you are drinking beer,' he murmured. It sort of worked. The other patrons didn't know we were drinking beer, they just kept staring in wonderment at the weird foreigners sipping from bowls of sugar.

Dad watched me in equal amazement as I took my first bite of what amounted to a simple chicken curry.

'You'd eat dog's balls, you would,' he said with a shudder.

After my delicious 'dog's balls' and Dad's liquid lunch, we went for a stroll. Not far from the restaurant was the Seema Malakaya Temple, perched on an island pavilion in the middle of the murky Beira Lake. The temple is accessible only from a narrow wooden jetty and as soon as we stepped onto it and over the water, the muggy oppressive Colombo air turned delightfully cool.

We'd been in the open-sided Buddhist temple only for a minute when a barefooted and withered old man dressed in his bedding asked us politely to take our shoes off. And no, he was wasn't a beggar angling for some new footwear, he was the resident Buddhist priest and he was just pointing out that we should have removed our shoes before entering.

While he gave us a brief tour of the temple and its many statues of Buddha—most posed as if the Great Man was adding a pinch of salt to his plate at dinner—he told us that he woke at six every morning and tended the temple all day until ten at night. He then pointed out his 'home'. It was a straw shack on stilts, attached to the temple by a rickety wooden landing. His entire residence wasn't much bigger than the thin mattress on the crude wooden floor inside. Not that we had to cross the landing to look inside the room; the walls had gaping holes in them.

After I'd retrieved our shoes Dad said, 'He just told me that tomorrow he is having his first day off in twenty years.'

'Wow, really?'

'Yeah, he's going to the dentist!' Dad chortled.

The priest had only four teeth.

At the next Buddhist temple Dad refused to go in.

'Someone will steal my shoes,' he protested. The Gangaramaya is one of Colombo's most celebrated temples but there was no way Dad was leaving his shoes out on the street.

'I'll stay and guard your shoes,' he said. My shoes were a five-dollar pair of rubber thongs—that's flip-flops for you Poms and jandals for you Kiwis.

I had to walk past the old and very large resident elephant to get into the temple grounds. Not only did the poor creature have his trunk painted purple, he was constantly tugging at the chain wrapped around his foot. The temple was abuzz with white-clad worshippers—a *poya* holiday is a big day for prayer—burning candles, laying flower petals at the feet of Buddha, throwing metal cups of water onto the 'sacred bo tree' and eyeing off my rubber thongs at the entrance.

The most impressive sight of the many in the temple grounds was a collection of at least a hundred identical metre-high statues of Buddha set in neat rows, all adding pinches of salt to their dinners.

Dad went back to our room for a nap while I went parading with the locals. In front of the Galle Face Hotel and stretching for almost a kilometre along the seafront is Galle Face Green. It was absolutely chock-a-block with well-dressed folk out for a stroll. It was blowing a gale and, although the skies were clear, people were dotted all over the lawn snuggled under umbrellas. I later discovered that the young lovers canoodling under the umbrellas were hiding from the police—apparently kisses stolen in public are a crime.

Every thirty metres or so along the boardwalk trundle carts were selling hot snacks and dispensing soft drinks that were artificially tinted a dyspeptic green. Every single one of the countless stalls was selling exactly the same snacks: bright orange squishy patties with three (and always three) shrimps on top. Some astute entrepreneur could make an absolute killing if they sold something different like, say, bright orange squishy patties with four shrimps on top.

Back at the hotel, I grabbed Dad and headed for the wide marble-tiled verandah with whirring ceiling fans for a pre-dinner aperitif. Well, we would have except the bar had a sign on it that read: 'Today is Poya day—alcoholic beverages will not be served'. I asked the bored-looking barman, who was lazily polishing beer glasses with a cloth, for an orange juice and he leant over and whispered, 'I can accidentally slip some vodka in if you like.'

'Can you accidentally slip some beer into a glass as well?' Dad asked. He couldn't, but he did accidentally slip some gin into a glass of tonic.

We had dinner at the hotel's Seaspray restaurant, where we soon discovered that the name couldn't have been more apt. I had planned to dine alfresco but even from the verandah the crashing waves of the Indian Ocean were so close, and the wind was so fierce, that we could taste it. Sitting outside would have been like dining in a shower.

The inside of the restaurant was virtually empty but the staff were super-friendly and the food was superb. I had the 'BBQ Banquet', which involved choosing from an incredible array of meats and seafood. You took your selection to the chef, who cooked it in front of you in a large wok-like barbecue. There were also salads, vegetables and a dozen hot dishes, including coq au vin and, much to Dad's delight, roast beef.

After finishing my whopping plate of food, I dozed off. Dad was in the middle of talking to me when I dropped off to sleep at the table. It must have been five minutes before Dad realised.

'Who's the old man, then?' Dad said mockingly as he shook me awake. I was instantly wide awake again when the waiter brought out the dessert. I stopped at all the stations and tried a morsel of eight desserts on offer.

'Which one was the best?' Dad asked. They were all good so I wasn't sure. I went back and tried all eight again in reverse order. Returning from my third visit to the sweet spread, I made an announcement.

'And the winner is . . .' I began, and revealed a plate piled high with the passionfruit mousse.

We went for an after-dinner toddle to walk off my dessert frenzy. Not that weight control was my principal motive, I'd read that there was a karaoke bar at the nearby Hilton Hotel and I wanted to add Sri Lanka to my world tour of karaoke bars. I think I've now sung karaoke, and no snide chuckles please, in twenty-seven lucky countries. We were halfway there when I turned to Dad and said, 'I need a toilet.' Two minutes later, now clutching my stomach, I said, 'Quick, I need a toilet bad.' One minute later it was 'I need a toilet NOW!' I rushed down a handy side-street, ducked behind an even more handy parked truck and, well, exploded.

I gingerly waddled back to Dad on the main street and said, 'Well, I've finally found a good use for *Lonely Planet*!' I had torn out quite a few pages, too. Luckily we weren't travelling to the south, north *or* west of Sri Lanka. While I hunched over in obvious pain, Dad began gloating about his sensible beer diet versus my reckless experimentation with chicken curry.

My alfresco toilet stop could have been avoided because the karaoke bar was closed. Because there was no alcohol, and therefore no drunk people, no one obviously had any desire to sing—except me, of course. We caught a taxi back to the hotel just in case Krakatoa decided to erupt again.

•

'You can't spend the rest of your life in bed!' I said to Dad, who was propped up in bed watching television. That was one of Dad's favourite sayings when I was a kid, along with, 'You've got two brains: one's lost and the other one's looking for it' and, when we were particularly annoying, 'Go play on the train tracks' (or alternatively, the freeway). As it turned out, we both could have stayed in bed. By the time we got downstairs, the city was awash with a monsoonal downpour—the first rain we'd seen in over a month.

After we'd waited out the deluge, we hopped into a three-wheeler and headed to Fort Train Station to pre-book our tickets to Kandy for the next day.

'Ah, Shane Warne, very good!' our driver squealed with delight when I told him that we were Australian. When he dropped us off, his original quoted fare of one hundred rupees had magically doubled.

'You Australians are *very* rich!' he said, holding out his hand.

'No, only Shane Warne is rich!' I said, handing him a hundred-rupee note.

After getting our '1st-Class Observation Saloon tickets' to Kandy we went for a wander around the small market near the station. We didn't last long, though. We were the only potential customers, so every stall holder was pleading for our patronage: 'You want . . . garish jewellery? badly made shirts? ill-fitting shoes? limp lettuces? fly-infested slabs of meat? rusted engine parts?'

Near the front of the market there were stalls selling tasty looking 'lunch packets'. These parcels of rice and curry (chicken, beef, fish or vegetable) are sold on street corners all over Sri Lanka.

'They're only fifty cents!' I said to Dad.

'If they were one cent, I wouldn't bloody buy one,' Dad huffed.

I couldn't let Dad have a liquid lunch again, so we walked to the nearby World Trade Centre, which was home to the very western and very sterile Deli Market Coffee Shop. Dad ordered a sausage roll and a pastie for lunch.

'I don't like them,' he said, pushing his plate away. The sausage roll was only slightly spicy and the pastie had a hint of curry in it. He raided the basket of bread rolls instead and put a few in his pocket.

'So I don't bloody starve later,' he grumbled.

Dad wanted to buy a ring for Mum so we flagged down a three-wheeler and raced to the 'jewellery district'. And I mean raced. Dad looked absolutely petrified on our cross-town journey as the driver, who I'm guessing was an escaped lunatic, swerved madly all over the road dodging traffic. I didn't even flinch. Even when he lurched in front of an oncoming bus on the opposite side of the road. It was like being on a scary amusement park ride—without the queues.

We tumbled out of the three-wheeler into the crowded, narrow streets of Pettah and were immediately hit by the suffocatingly clammy air, thick with flies and dust. On either side of the street was an endless row of tiny jewellery stores. The first one we wandered into had enough room for four customers only.

'Shane Warne bought a ring here!' the proprietor told us. Just after he mentioned to us that he was a Tamil, what sounded like loud machine-gun fire rattled out from directly in front of the shop. I instinctively ducked down and Dad dived headfirst under the counter. It wasn't the Tigers on a rampage, however, just firecrackers being set off to announce the imminent arrival of one of the candidates in the upcoming local election, who was out and about pressing a bit of flesh. A very smarmy fellow in a suit, accompanied by a large entourage, squeezed into the shop, shook our hands and, with a big cheesy smile, said, 'Please vote for me.'

After checking out half-a-dozen shops, Dad finally found a ring that he liked and was big enough—most of the rings were made for slender Sri Lankan fingers, not chubby western ones. Dad paid in Australian dollars and the salesman studied the one-hundred-dollar note before asking, 'Who is this person on your money?'

'That's Merv Hughes,' I said. It was General John Monash, but he did have the same big bushy moustache.

'Ah, yes, the fast bowler,' the salesman gushed excitedly.

It was my turn to do a bit of shopping, so we made our way to Odels department store. Many major fashion labels have their clothes made in Sri Lanka so the goods are for sale here without the ludicrous mark-ups that get added by the time they reach our stores. We ambled around for over an hour, but I didn't buy a single thing. I'm hopeless at clothes shopping. I need my wife to tell me what to buy and it was no use asking Dad. His knowledge of fashion is strictly limited to drip-dry slacks and body shirts.

When we returned to the hotel to indulge in a spot of quaffing on the verandah, dining tables were being set up on the lawn for what looked like an extravagantly swanky wedding reception. A seven-piece band of hip young Sri Lankan lads were also setting up—saying 'check, one, two' over and over again must be in some international muso's handbook. While I ordered our drinks, Dad went over to chat to the band.

'You're singing at the wedding party tonight,' Dad said when he returned. 'You're going to be the special guest singer from Australia.' Dad had told Sanjeewa, the lead singer of 'Spark', that I was a famous singer from Australia. (I do sing in a band in Australia, but only playig four times a year at small parties doesn't quite make me famous.)

'You're on at eight o'clock,' Dad added. The band, who were bashing out 'To All the Girls I've Loved Before', gave me a big cheery wave as we left.

We had dinner at the German restaurant across the road from the hotel, where the interior looked as if it had been transported from a bier cellar in Munich. There wasn't much oomp-ahing going on, though. There was only one other German couple sitting in the corner. I suggested to Dad that we have *wurst mit gestampfte kartoffel und halbes Mass* and he screwed up his face in disgust right on cue. Then I explained that it was actually bangers and mash with a mug of beer.

After our *Abendessen* (dinner), we sat at the bar to finish our beer and the barman told us that in peak season (December to March) the restaurant would be full of homesick Germans eating sauerkraut. The bar staff knew only some very basic German pleasantries, so before we left I taught them how to say 'you have beautiful breasts' in German.

I was a little bit nervous about my Sri Lankan singing debut, particularly when we wandered back to the wedding party to find two hundred and fifty of the city's elite dressed to the nines—the men resplendent in suits and the women in elegant saris—sitting on long, lavishly decorated tables on the lawn. What made me feel even more uncomfortable was that the band, who were dressed in jeans and t-shirts when we saw them earlier, were now wearing suits. I was in shorts, a t-shirt and thongs. When the band finished their set, Sanjeewa came over to see me at the verandah bar, which overlooked the entire wedding, and asked if I would sing a song for the wedding waltz. Bloody hell, what had Dad told him? Sanjeewa probably thought I was John Farnham. Five minutes later, after Sanjeewa had introduced the very special guest singer from Australia, I was up on stage singing 'I Can't Help Falling in Love with You' while the bride and groom waltzed around the dance floor. I looked over at Sanjeewa at one point and he gave me a beaming smile and the thumbs-up, but no one else danced and when I finished only one person clapped. Dad.

'That was great!' Sanjeewa said, as I walked off-stage. 'I've got a surprise for you,' he added. 'There's someone I think you'd like to meet.' Sanjeewa dragged me down into the thick of the party and introduced me to a man in a smart black suit with a tongue-twisting name.

'Nice to meet you,' I said shaking his hand. Then it clicked who it was. It was The Chucker—it wasn't until I got home that I found out his name is Muthiah Muralitharan. I might not follow cricket but I knew he held the world record for most Test wickets—settle down cricket fans, I know Warney has since passed the record—and that he was famous, or infamous, for chucking. I was almost about to say, 'Ah, you're The Chucker!' but luckily I stopped myself and said instead, 'Why aren't you playing against Australia?'

'I've got an injury,' he said clutching his elbow. I later learnt that his withdrawal from the tour was as much a matter of insult as injury. It was partly a protest against the attitude of the Australian media—and even the prime minister, who had just added his own condemnation of Murali's action.

'You were good,' he said, 'you should sing again.' I sang 'Suspicious Minds', but once again not a single person danced. At least two people clapped this time, though: Dad and Murali.

After I sang, an old fellow from the wedding party got up on stage and groaned and howled his was through a syrupy Sri Lankan love song. Before he was more than two bars into the song, the dance floor was jumping. When everyone applauded at the end of his painful ballad, I took it as a sign that I should go to bed.

21

Dead spiders covered in pubic hair

'There's our train!' I shouted to Dad over the pandemonium that was Colombo Fort Station.

'That's not our train!' Dad cried as we rushed up the platform. 'That's been abandoned!'

At least we didn't have to run up the entire platform, the '1st-Class Observation Saloon' was the first carriage—or rather the last, since it was at the rear of the train. The carriage was only small and its twenty-four seats all faced the large back window, which had a mighty crack right down the middle of it. The seats were faded and in need of a good clean.

'I thought we'd be in a big glass carriage with table service and a movie!' Dad whined. To be honest, so did I. Well, not quite the in-flight movie, but I was expecting at least a bit of luxury and perhaps seats that weren't covered in dust and smelled of stale chicken curry.

'Look Dad, it's got air-conditioning!' I said excitedly. Attached to the ceiling were two very old fans that made it sound as if a light plane was about to land in the luggage rack.

The train coughed and lurched forward just as we got into our reserved seats. We did have a wonderful view, though. We sliced through the suburbs so closely we saw a series of snapshots of daily life: women bathing, dogs fighting in the dirt, children fighting in the dirt, and lots of men sitting on wooden crates. The further we moved away from central Colombo, the smaller and more run-down the houses became.

'My garden shed is bigger than most of these houses,' Dad remarked.

I went for a wander up the train after twenty minutes of having the back of my head buffeted by the wind rushing through the open windows. The second-class carriages had clean seats (albeit wooden ones) and, even more surprising, everyone was smiling and chatting and having a grand old time. In most trains around the world, passengers look as if they are off to a funeral.

'I found the restaurant car,' I said to Dad when I returned to my buffeting. 'It's actually quite nice considering. I had a fresh baguette with smoked salmon and cream cheese.' Dad looked at me suspiciously.

Once we'd left the sprawling ramshackle suburbs of Colombo, the track ran through a stretch of jungle, then past rice paddies and the odd cow, and eventually started to climb through the dense native and lush hardwood forest of the first range of hills around Kandy. As the train puffed asthmatically up into the hills, immense rock formations and thundering waterfalls were visible in the distance. Best of all, though, the oppressive humidity of Colombo began to lift. By the time we reached Peradeniya, the rail junction for Kandy's short spur line, the air was noticeably cooler.

The air may have been cooler but every time the train went through a tunnel—and there were lots of them—our carriage would fill up with toxic diesel fumes. I went for another trek up the train to find some fresh air but the only person who seemed to be getting any was the driver. I returned to our carriage just before we pulled into Kandy.

'You should have gone to the restaurant car,' I said to Dad while trying to suppress a grin. 'They were serving fresh scones with jam and cream.'

We were going to catch a three-wheeler to our hotel from the train station but a fellow with a sparkling new van offered to take us there for the same price. He introduced himself as Blacky.

'I'd get arrested if I called you that in Australia,' Dad said to him.

The Queens Hotel is even older than the Galle Face Hotel and it was showing its age. The faded establishment was still clinging to a hint of former grandness, though. Its many lingering vestiges of the colonial era included dodgy plumbing and the original bed linen from 1849.

Before we went to find some breakfast we took a quick exploratory stroll around town. Within a few minutes I'd decided I loved the old Singhalese capital. The charming town was tucked in a ring of wooded hills, overlooking the captivatingly lovely Kandy Lake, which was across the road from our hotel.

We had breakfast at the hotel, although we didn't even realise that the café we were in was part of that rambling establishment until we got the bill with the Queens Hotel logo on it. The café had incredibly high ornate ceilings, a long teak bar and a glass cabinet stuffed with pastries. I had vegetable curry puffs for breakfast.

'Bloody hell,' Dad muttered. 'Curry puffs for breakfast and the shits for dinner.' My health-conscious father had a large slice of chocolate cake.

I was keen to visit the Pinnawela Elephant Orphanage, which is about an hour's drive from Kandy, so we booked a driver (and his car of course) from the hotel to take us there. Our driver's name was Jaya and he looked like Lionel Ritchie, circa 1977, with long permed hair, a porno moustache and a pale-blue silk shirt.

Jaya wanted to get us to the elephants in time for the 1.15 feeding, so he was playing a bloodcurdling game of chicken. In order to overtake, he would pull out into oncoming traffic, then wait until the very last second to see who would lose their nerve and swerve over to the side of the road first.

'I've been driving for twenty-two years and I've never had an accident,' Jaya beamed as he forced a three-wheeler and an oxen and cart off the road. Jaya *was* very good at chicken and he ended up winning 27 to 3—the three showdowns he, quite sensibly, chickened out of were *very* large trucks.

At one point we forced a learner driver in a 'Scientifical B-grade Driving School' car off the road. I imagined a driving lesson in Sri Lanka would be interesting (particularly a B-grade one): 'Okay, we'll do some reverse parking first, then we'll do a bit of death-defying driving into oncoming traffic, and finish up with practice in overtaking on blind corners while waving to friends on the side of the road'.

When we were game to open our eyes there was plenty to see: tractors that looked as if they were put together from defunct lawnmowers, statues of the Buddha rising from masses of vegetation, whipsnakes fluttering on the road like pieces of green celluloid, the odd monkey and endless stalls selling a plethora of strange fruits.

We made it in time for the feeding of the baby elephants, who were downing super-sized bottles of milk. Occasionally they'd also have a swig of beer, although it was me who needed a swig of beer after our hair-raising car trip.

The elephant orphanage was set up to save abandoned or orphaned wild elephants and there are now over seventy privileged pachyderms plodding about in the reserve—it's estimated that there are only three thousand wild elephants left in the whole country.

I'd never seen so many elephants in one spot before and they were all different shapes and sizes, including one poor sod who had only three legs. The other leg had been blown off after the elephant stood on a land mine. One of the *mahouts* (elephant trainers) told us the elephant's Sri Lankan name, and when I asked what it meant in English he said, 'Three Legs.'

While we were standing next to one mammoth fellow, he unloaded a crap that was as big as me. Now that I've got us onto the subject of elephant poo . . . I recently took my three-year-old daughter Jasmine to the zoo to see the elephants (amongst other critters). We were in the middle of the whole messy toilet training thing and my wife and I were encouraging Jasmine to use the toilet by telling her that she wouldn't be starting ballet school if she kept pooing on the rug. When the elephant at the zoo dropped a steaming big load on the ground in front of us, Jasmine yelled out to the elephant: 'No ballet school for you!'

After the feeding, we wandered back through the main gate and down to the river. To get to the river we had to pass through a tiny village full of souvenir stores selling elephant statues, wooden elephant mobiles, elephant hats, elephant handbags, elephant drums, elephant chairs, elephant jigsaws and even elephant pyjamas. One shop was selling, according to their sign: 'Elefant souvenirs'. Maybe they got the shop next door to help them with their sign. That shop had an even larger sign that read, 'We Spoken good English'.

Each afternoon, the mahouts tramp their charges right through the middle of the village and down to the river to bathe and play. The best place from which to watch jumbo bathtime was the Elephant Restaurant, but the best tables on the verandah overlooking the water had already been reserved.

'Good afternoon sir, my name is Brian,' I said ever so cheerfully to the waiter. 'I rang this morning and reserved a table.'

'Ah yes, of course, sir,' the waiter chirped as he led us to a prime table on the verandah.

'You didn't ring, did you?' Dad whispered as we sat down.

'Nope,' I smiled.

As we sat with beer in hand, we could hear the elephants stampeding through the village. Well, it was more like a gentle stomp but they still sounded like an approaching army. Within a minute the entire street was jammed with lumbering elephants as they splashed into the wide river directly in front of us and immediately turned it into a huge, sloshing bath.

We clambered down to the river bank to get a closer look and as I stood next to a one-month-old baby elephant it wrapped its trunk affectionately around my leg.

'I'd stay away from that one,' Dad said, pointing to a rather exuberant male with a willy about the size of my leg.

One of the mahouts told us to stay well clear of another very large bull that was chained to a rock.

'He killed a tourist last year,' the young mahout told us. 'Oh, but it was *only* a Sri Lankan tourist,' he added quickly. The mahout's name was Chandana and he was very excited because he was only two months away from finishing his two-year traineeship. He would then become a fully-fledged mahout with his very own lovable giant to handle. Chandana knew the name of every single one of the seventy elephants.

'Is that one over there,' Dad said, pointing to the excitable elephant, 'called Biggus Dickus?'

After a more leisurely drive back to Kandy—Jaya only played chicken a dozen or so times—Dad headed back to our room for a nap while I went for a quiet stroll around the lake. It was actually quite nice having a little break from Dad. We had, after all, been living out of each other's pockets for seven weeks. Mind you, we hadn't had a single argument in that time and I hadn't wanted to strangle him more than twice a week. All-in-all things weren't going too badly.

My nice quiet walk around the lake wasn't that quiet, though. On my forty-five-minute trek I was asked by different touts if I'd like to attend a Kandyan dance, go to a nice restaurant, buy an ice-cream, visit some elephants, see a cultural show or buy some buttocks.

'Buttocks?' I asked incredulously.

'Oh yes,' the tout gushed. 'Men's or women's! We have both!'

'No thanks,' I said. 'I'm fine for buttocks at the moment.'

'But I have the best buttocks in Kandy,' he pleaded.

I later discovered that he was actually talking about batiks, which are traditional dyed pieces of fabric.

•

'Because of those bloody drums I couldn't get any sleep,' Dad groaned when I returned to our room. Loud drumming and chanting was emanating from the Temple of the Tooth across the road from the hotel. The Temple of the Tooth is a place of pilgrimage for millions of devout Buddhists from all over Sri Lanka, who regard it as the country's greatest treasure. The tooth itself is claimed to have been brought to Sri Lanka some sixteen hundred years ago by a princess from southern India. Legend has it that the tooth was taken out of the Buddha's mouth when he was about to be cremated and brought to Kandy in 344 AD. The storybook city has enjoyed lavish patronage ever since, and while the actual miraculous molar is displayed only once every four years, the gold coffer that holds it is on display daily. Each evening it is locked away for the night with a lot of pomp and ceremony. I wonder if that includes brushing the tooth before it goes to bed . . .

We sauntered over to see what the fuss was all about, and had to pass through three security checks before we even got into the grounds—the temple sustained damage from a terrorist bomb in

1998. Inside the grounds a Buddhist ceremony was taking place. Swarms of worshippers were sitting on the gravel surrounding the smaller temple. A guide tried to latch himself onto me so I threw off my thongs and stepped inside the temple. It worked. I lost the guide but I also lost Dad. I found him fifteen minutes later, after the guide had dragged him around the entire complex.

'He took me into one of the temples and told me that if I didn't donate my life savings to Buddha, terrible things would happen to me.'

'So, what did you do?' Dad shrugged his shoulders.

'I gave Buddha twenty cents.'

Dad didn't want any more guides hassling him so he waited at the entrance of the main temple while I went in to see the tooth box. The main temple, which was built in 1687, was painted a pale shade of rose pink and adorned with elephant carvings. There was an entrance fee so I did one of my usual tricks and snuck in with a tour group—I'm sorry, I can't help myself! I joined the never-ending line of worshippers and tourists shuffling through the decorated halls and eventually moved into the darkened, gilt-roofed relic chamber, which is the temple's holy of holies. Inside, two monks stood before a gold reliquary while three very skinny fellows played drums. There seemed to be a lot of ear-shattering drumming going on and not much else happening. After ten minutes I skipped the locking away of the venerable fang—and really, how exciting could that be?—and went outside to see if any terrible things had happened to Dad yet.

•

Finding a restaurant for dinner where Dad could (or would!) actually eat anything proved quite difficult. The guidebook suggested one place that did a 'good curry' and another that did a 'nice curry', as opposed to the one that did a 'very nice curry'. I opted for the Old Empire Hotel restaurant, which apparently did a 'delicious curry'. It seemed, however, that most people preferred just a 'very nice curry', as we were the only customers.

The Old Empire Hotel was certainly old.

'This place needs a good maintenance man,' Dad said as we sat down. I had to stop him from getting up to fix the power points that were held together with sticky tape.

Dad ordered a bowl of chips—there was fish *and* chips on the menu, but the fish was off (so to speak).

'There's a dead spider in my beer!' Dad yelped as he stared with dismay at his mug of beer. As he pushed his beer aside with disgust, the waiter placed his bowl of chips on the table.

'Bloody hell!' he squealed after eating a handful of chips. Sitting in the middle of his chips were two long dark curly hairs. 'It's good we've only got one night in the hotel,' Dad grumbled as he pushed his bowl away.

'Why is it good?' I asked. Dad stared at the chips with disgust.

'I'll probably shit my bed.'

My two-dollar chicken curry came out with six other plates of food, including curried vegetables, pickles, shredded coconut, dahl, fried sardines and rice. It all looked wonderful but by the expression on Dad's face you'd think the waiter had just plopped down a plate of dead spiders covered in pubic hair.

22

You can stick your devilled chicken right up your Kyber Pass

My original plan for the next leg of our journey after Kandy was verging on the preposterous. I had it in my mind that we would reach Trincomalee via leisurely stopovers in Nuwara Eliya and Sigiriya. After studying the bus and train timetables more closely I realised we would have to zigzag all over the country to basically end up back where we'd started. And we would be trying to squeeze at least four days' worth of travelling into three. So instead of heading for the station on the morning of our departure we hung around the hotel reception waiting for Blacky to pick us up in his sparkling new van.

Blacky had given me his card and told me he would drive us anywhere we wanted—Dad suggested Melbourne. For only US$100, he was going to drive us all the way to Trincomalee with overnight stops in the mountains of Nuwara Eliya and the ancient fortress of Sigiriya. Dad was happy. He wouldn't have to sit in hot, dusty trains and he'd get to call a dark-skinned person Blacky for three whole days.

Blacky had been leading tours for almost twenty years and he'd just about won me over on that first ten-minute trip to our hotel from Kandy Station without even opening his mouth. In the pocket behind the driver's seat was a thick, bound book full of glowing reports from satisfied customers from all over the globe. He's a smart man that Blacky. He offered cheap transfers from the station and when potential punters picked up his book, they inevitably asked about his tours.

Blacky was also very busy on the home front. He had eight children ranging in age from eighteen down to just nine days.

'You'll be bloody happy to get away, then,' Dad remarked. Blacky had lived in Kandy all his life, had met Shane Warne and, funnily enough, was a huge fan of Lionel Ritchie. Thankfully, he didn't look like the singer or drive like the lookalike driver.

Not far out of Kandy, the landscape changed dramatically. We rounded a bend and suddenly the vast tracts of native forest were gone. In their place stood forests of tall pines cut by rivers stained brown with the rich soil and Sri Lanka's best-known export: tea. From that point on, we rarely lost sight of the dark green mottled patchwork of tea estates spread across the hillsides like slightly worn felt. Think of the name Ceylon and you think of tea. Although it is just over one hundred and fifty years since the British introduced tea to the island, it is the largest exporter of tea in the world.

As we twisted our way up the narrow roads we'd catch the occasional glimpse of Tamil women picking the tea, which made a colourful contrast to the all-pervasive green. Blacky told us that picking tea is one of the most highly prized jobs in Sri Lanka. So good, in fact, that new vacancies rarely come up because when a picker retires she passes her position on to one of her daughters—only the women pick; the husbands work in the tea factories and their jobs are handed down to their sons. Not only is the pay quite high—well, US$4 a day is quite high for the average Sri Lankan—but they also get a house, free schooling, free medical treatment and bottomless cups of tea.

We drove through the heartland of former British plantations and 'high-grown' teas—those that grow above 1200 metres—where the estates had such very British names as James Finlay Brookside Estate, Royal Park Estate, Glen Loch Estate and the Rothschild Estate, the logo of which was a spiffy-looking fellow in a safari suit and walk socks smoking a pipe.

'Would you like a cup of tea?' Blacky asked us.

I couldn't believe that we'd been in Sri Lanka for four days and hadn't had a single cup of tea—particularly Dad, who is normally a four-cups-a-day man; fifteen-a-day man when he's with our relatives in England. He also likes a bit of sugar in his milky tea. 'I have four sugars,' he says, 'but I don't stir it, because I don't like it sweet.'

The Mackwoods Labookellie Estate sat on a bluff overlooking tiered tea plantations that crept up over the surrounding steep hills and cascaded down the slopes in a carpet of green. On our guided tour of the factory we learnt that Mackwoods Fine Tea has been around since 1841 and is one of the world's most highly regarded blends; and that it takes a lot of plucking, withering, fermenting, rolling and crocheted tea cosies to make the perfect cup of tea. Best of all, we discovered you could drink as many brews as your bladder could handle because the tea served in the delightful café was free. The scrumptious chocolate cake wasn't free, but that was probably a good thing—I would have tried to eat my body weight in cake.

As we inched our way up the steep climb towards Nuwara Eliya we entered Little England. And it really was just like England. It was drizzling and the hills were shrouded in a damp fog. I couldn't hear a lot of whinging going on at that moment, but if the locals let me down I'd be able to rely on Dad as dinner time approached. Even most of the cars we were now passing on the road into Nuwara Eliya were English.

'Look!' Dad said in wonder, 'there's an Austen A35.'

'No, I think it's an A31,' Blacky chipped in.

'It's only got two doors, though.'

'It must be an A30 then,' Blacky said musingly.

This went on all the way into Nuwara Eliya and in the end they both concluded that it was definitely an English car of some sort.

Arriving in the high-altitude town of Nuwara Eliya (pronounced 'Noo-rely-er') was like entering into a time warp: a 1930s Devon village transplanted to the Sri Lankan hills, complete with racetrack, golf course and a country-club ethic long since forgotten in the mother country. The main reason I wanted to visit Nuwara Eliya was to stay at the Hill Club Hotel. For joyful anachronism and sheer jolly Britishness at its most charmingly absurd, I couldn't pass up the opportunity to stay at a place where the spirit of the Empire lived on with exaggerated respect for all things British.

The long sweeping driveway took us past manicured lawns, rose gardens and perfectly clipped hedges to what looked like an old English country estate. Stepping inside was like stepping into a natural history museum—the Hill Club was formerly a hunting club and stuffed animal heads, including bears, deer, buffalo and leopards, were peering down from every wall.

One of the many liveried staff escorted us to our room past the hushed library, the men-only bar, the billiard room, the darts room and the women's entrance—up until a few years ago, women were allowed to enter through the side door only. Our large room had French windows that opened onto a mature garden scented with frangipani and jasmine trees. Dad was agog at all the furniture: 'That wardrobe is walnut . . . and the beds are teak!'

I tipped the bellboy, who took my money without a moment's hesitation. As he left, I noticed a sign on the back of the door that read, 'Please do not break our hundred-year-old tradition of *not* tipping staff'.

After snooping around the hotel and peeking into the kitchen, the office and the staff quarters, we wandered into town. It was still drizzling, so after checking out a few shops we adjourned to the Lion Pub for a Lion Lager.

'They also have Lion Lager in South Africa *and* New Zealand,' I said to Dad while I stared at my bottle. 'And Germany has a Lion Brew, too,' I added. After seven weeks of travelling together, we'd just about run out of conversation—yes, there was a limit to how many times we could dissect the Manchester United and England teams. We'd talked about Dad's family, our family and the parts of Dad's life he could remember, but we never talked about anything really personal or emotional. Neither of us are like that—just ask my wife about the trouble she has talking to me about emotions—and we weren't suddenly about to change. Instead, we spent the first half-hour in the pub trying to think of beers from around the world that have an animal in their name. We came up with quite a list, including Elephant Beer from Denmark, Tiger Beer from Singapore, Emu Beer and Mountain Goat Beer from Australia, Moosehead from Canada, Eagle Beer and Kingfisher from India and Camel Beer from Mongolia. See, that's a lot more fun than talking about emotions. And no one gets hurt.

Just as I came up with the brilliant addition of Reindeer Beer from Greenland, an old Ceylonese gentleman sat next to us.

'I am not Sri Lankan,' Charlie told us in a clipped English accent, 'I am Ceylonese.' Charlie was wearing a tweed suit with a cravat. 'Sri Lanka was *so* much better when it was British.' Charlie went on to tell us how much he loved the Queen, that he had even met her once, and that Britain was full of gentlemen. He obviously hadn't been to Blackpool or Butlins. When Dad told Charlie that he had been in the Royal Navy, the Ceylonese gent just about jumped out of his seat to hug him.

When we left the pub, Charlie told us, 'It was jolly nice to meet you both.' We took a different route back to the hotel and strolled down an English country lane past mock-Tudor mansions and Victorian cottages flanked by hedges and stone walls. I wouldn't have been at all surprised if a fox hunt led by a pack of yelping hounds had run across our path.

The men-only bar at the Hill Club was very much like England, too. Especially the prices of drinks. The same Lion Beer we had in the pub was six times as expensive. A glass of scotch was US$30, although one did have the choice of ninety types of whisky and seventeen different cognacs. We were the only patrons in the tiny wood-panelled bar and the only sounds were the ticking of a grandfather clock and the two barmen wiping the bar every time we lifted our glasses. Rajah, the older of the two, had been tending the bar at the Hill Club for nineteen years. We were suitably impressed until he told us that the other barman was actually born at the hotel because his father had been a chef at the Hill Club for thirty-six years.

Rajah kept glancing up at the clock because it was getting close to seven. That was when the dress code came into force and every gentleman within the confines of the hotel was required to don a jacket and tie. At seven on the dot, a butler came into the bar to escort us to the 'jacket' room. Inside the large room was a single walnut wardrobe full of dusty jackets, some of which dated back at least sixty years. Dad grabbed a fetching grey velvet number with a purple silk tie that made him look like Hugh Hefner. I went for the checked jacket and orange paisley tie. I looked like a pimp.

'I'm sorry, sir, jeans are not allowed,' the butler said ever so politely as he eyed off my scruffy and faded jeans.

I had no choice. I had to borrow a pair of Dad's beige drip-dry slacks. The waist was a little generous, so I had to bunch up the top with a belt. If it wasn't for the addition of my dusty hiking boots, I would have looked very dapper indeed.

Before we headed back to the bar, we toddled over to the library to relax in the saggy leather armchairs and discuss Wordsworth and Byron. Actually, we just pretended we were tea barons and said 'Jolly what, dear boy?' and 'Frightfully nice, old chap!' a lot while propping against the fireplace. We could have read a bit of Wordsworth or Byron, though as the library's collection of dusty books was like a who's who of British literature. The distinguished authors included Wordsworth, Byron, Dickens, Shelley, D.H. Lawrence, Jane Austen, Emily Bronte, T.S. Elliot and Ben Elton.

The men's bar was still empty when we returned for a drink, but there were now a few people in the 'mixed bar' having pre-dinner cocktails, including a table of nodding Japanese men and two gorgeous tall Dutch girls wearing nice dresses and hiking boots. At exactly eight o'clock, the butler walked into the bar and announced, 'Ladies and gentlemen, dinner is served'. In the baronial dining room, liveried waiters glided past the stags' heads, yellowed engravings and starched linen tablecloths escorting guests to their tables.

'I've got cutlery coming out of my ears!' Dad said when we sat down. The table was set for five courses. Although everything did look quite grand, there was a hint of faded splendour. The waiters' clean white gloves had small holes in them and the crisp linen tablecloth had a few stains. The food was nice, if a bit boarding school. We started with a seafood pancake, then asparagus soup and rump steak for main—'I'll have mine well, well, *well* done,' Dad told the waiter. As soon as we finished our main course, the dessert was plopped down in front of us—it was really just like England. Dad almost wet his pants when he saw the dessert. It was his all-time favourite: trifle.

After dinner we adjourned to the lounge area for cheese and biscuits and a spot of tea. Only the day before we had been sweltering, and now we were sitting in front of a roaring fire. We attempted to have a game of darts, but when Dad speared the cheek of the stuffed boar that was mounted on the opposite wall I thought we had better move on.

'I can't throw the bloody darts because of my fingers,' he moaned. He didn't fare much better at snooker, either. In front of a large audience of stuffed animal heads and fish, Dad was only fifteen points down with the game not even half over when he threw in the towel.

'That's it!' Dad cried when I potted another ball. 'You've won. Let's start again.' Ah, so that's where me being a sore loser comes from.

By ten o'clock, the hotel was eerily quiet, with only the odd staff member scurrying about—most of the people at dinner had just been visiting the hotel. We went back into the bar, but Rajah was closing up.

'Is there anywhere else open?' I asked.

'I think the Lion Pub might still be open,' he said, 'but just be careful on your way into town.'

'Why's that?'

'Oh, sometimes leopards come into town at night to take a dog back to the hills,' he remarked casually.

'I think I might just go to bed,' Dad said.

When I jumped into bed I felt something furry and warm under the sheets. I was just about to scream out that there was a leopard in my bed when I realised that it was the crocheted cover of my complimentary hot water bottle.

•

As we waited for Blacky to pick us up in the morning—he had been staying with a friend in town—I added my two bobs' worth to the visitor's book:

'Frightfully nice, jolly what? Tally ho!

Retired Colonel Cecil Smiggenbottom Smyth-Jones'.

•

As we drove down the busy road out of Nuwara Eliya I finally figured out the complicated car-horn etiquette. Two short beeps meant move over; one short beep indicated a thank you and a long beep meant: 'If I was you, I'd move over rather quickly or we'll both die!'

I was quite amazed that there was never any sort of aggression at all on the road. Blacky told us that it was part of the Buddhist doctrine to be calm, relaxed and happy. It was hard to tell with Blacky, though, because he was so relaxed and happy the whole time anyway. He just about had a permanent smile plastered on his face and he was so jolly that he even laughed at Dad's jokes.

Dad, on the other hand, wasn't happy with his toast. I'd refused to pay US$10 each for breakfast at the Hill Club so we'd stopped at a roadside café. The toast, which was actually toasted roti, was fresh and delicious, but as soon as Blacky told Dad that they were a 'traditional Sri Lankan breakfast' he pushed them aside.

'I don't want to eat any foreign muck for breakfast,' he grumbled. Now I wasn't happy.

'Just because it's a "traditional Sri Lankan breakfast" doesn't mean that it's foreign!' I screamed at him, not entirely logically. 'It's just toast!' I knew that I was never going to change my grumpy Dad, but that didn't stop me from getting frustrated with him. Still, with less than a week of our trip to go, this was our first real argument and it lasted all of one minute.

As we hairpinned down the mountain, we passed more tea estates and more women dressed in shimmering saris picking tea. When the tea plantations came to an end, we entered a jungle-covered plain strewn with exotic plants and granite boulders. In what seemed like only a few minutes the cool misty mountain air was replaced by blue skies and a stifling muggy heat. For quite a spell after that we drove through corn fields and then rice fields that were dotted with palm trees. When we entered yet another totally different landscape—this one looked like the plains of Africa—it felt as if we'd driven across the entire country on fast-forward.

The 'African plains' were home to a string of national parks. I had contemplated doing a safari in one of them, but I'd read that the guides were expensive and that you could spend a few days in the park and only spot the odd elephant or monkey.

'You don't need to go to a national park to see some animals,' Blacky told us. 'I'll take you somewhere where there is many animals.'

Half an hour later we drove around a bend into the middle of a narrow, marshy clearing that was teeming with wildlife. It was absolutely incredible. There was a large herd of elephants, numerous troops of noisy monkeys (toque macaques), water buffalo, chital deer, painted storks, egrets, ibis and large, menacing fish eagles.

'You see!' beamed Blacky. 'This is the place for animals.' It *was* amazing, however I'm not sure that it would ever become a big tourist attraction. The problem was that we were in the middle of the rubbish dump for the town of Kenelulu. The herd of elephants was foraging among polythene bags and battered oil drums while the monkeys were fighting over the remains of the previous week's vegetable curry. When I went to hop out of the van to take a photo, Blacky cried, 'No! If the elephant charges you, he might damage my car.'

•

We stopped for lunch at the Resthouse Hotel overlooking the Sea of Parakrama, a rather grand-sounding name for what is essentially a man-made lake. Across the road from the hotel stood the ruins of the ancient city of Polonnaruwa.

'I'm having the devilled chicken,' I said to Dad as I perused the menu. 'Shall I order that for you as well?'

'You can stick the devilled chicken right up your Khyber Pass,' Dad muttered. He had the roast chicken and chips. When my devilled chicken came out, Dad stared at it for a minute and said, 'You'll need the rest of the *Lonely Planet* after you eat that!'

The remains of the once great city of Polonnaruwa were spread out over a wide area so Blacky drove us from ruin to ruin. Polonnaruwa first came to prominence when the city became the residence of Ceylon's kings in the fourth century. Then the city replaced Anuradhapura as the capital of Sri Lanka in the tenth century and became the most important city in Sri Lanka for the following three centuries. The city's golden age came during the reign of King Parakrama Bahu the Great, who embellished the capital with impressive temples, stupas and huge stone images of Buddha.

Today, however, all that remained of Polonnaruwa were grey stones and partial monuments to a city that once was great. Time and wear had levelled them and neat little ivy roots had eaten their way into the structures for so many years that I had trouble distinguishing what might have once been a palace wall from what might have always been just a pile of bricks.

By the time we got to the second pile of bricks I was ready to kill someone. We couldn't walk ten metres without a tout trying to sell us a coconut shell carved into the shape of a monkey's head. These buggers, who were mostly kids, were a particularly persistent bunch, too. I've spent years fine-tuning my techniques for getting rid of touts, but none of my tactics seemed to work. I tried being polite but that was a waste of time. I'm very good at completely and utterly ignoring touts, but Dad couldn't get the hang of it at all and would strike up a conversation with them. I also tried my pretending-to-speak-an-obscure-foreign-language and my old favourite, which I'd first used to resounding success in the Moroccan souks: putting my arm around their shoulders and singing love songs to them.

In the end, I was so hot and bothered that when one fellow just wouldn't go away I resorted to the tried and tested, 'FUCK OFF and leave us alone, or I'll shove that monkey's head up your arse!'

'Are you Australian?' he asked sheepishly.

'Yes,' Dad said.

'You Australians *always* tell me to fuck off,' he sighed.

The final stop on our tour was the twelfth-century Buddha statues at Gal Vihara, which were carved out of a granite cliff face and included two seated Buddhas, a standing Buddha and a reclining, dead Buddha. We shared the statues with a group of improbably well-behaved schoolchildren escorted by a Buddhist monk in an almost luminous orange robe. The girls wore gingham dresses that belonged in the fifties while the boys were dressed in grey flannels and white shirts. All of them had bare feet. Best of all, though, not a single one of them asked us if we wanted to buy a coconut monkey's head.

After our extensive tour of the world's most annoying touts, we drove an hour up the road to what Blacky described as 'a *very* nice hotel'. It seemed that not many people agreed with him, though, as we were the only guests staying at the Eden Garden. After a quick dip in the pool, which was *very* nice, we adjourned to the terrace for dinner. We both had our standard fare: I had chicken curry and Dad had roast chicken and chips. Our meal was also accompanied by Dad's standard gripes: 'That looks like diarrhoea', 'You'd eat bloody dog's balls' and, 'You'll be shitting through the eye of a needle after that'. There were two good things about us having the hotel to ourselves: we had four waiting staff each and no one else had to listen to Dad.

After dinner, Blacky very kindly offered me a massage. Well, he offered to drive me to the 'herbal massage' centre we had passed on the way to the Eden Garden. Dad declined the massage as he didn't want 'a bunch of strange foreigners touching him'. If he had gone, at least he wouldn't have had the surprise that a friend of mine's father got when he agreed to a massage from 'a bunch of strange foreigners'. My friend Chris was visiting his brother Matt in Ho Chi Minh City with his father when Matt took them both for a massage. Halfway through his massage, Chris's rub suddenly turned into a rub 'n' tug. When he'd finished (so to speak), he was too embarrassed to share his exploits with his Dad, who in turn was even more embarrassed, but didn't say a word. Neither of them has mentioned the episode since.

I sincerely hoped I wasn't getting a rub 'n' tug. A parade of elegantly-dressed and gorgeous masseuses kept shuffling past me in the reception area of the massage centre, but I got the tall lanky fellow with the bony Andre-the-Giant hands. Five minutes later I found myself lying naked in a small room getting smothered with sandalwood oil. This was followed by my head getting pummelled with some—and I'm guessing here, but I think it was—curry powder. The massage concluded with my face getting rubbed with boiled pomegranate leaves. By the time I finished I smelt (and felt) like a chicken curry.

•

I got up early so I could climb a large rock. I wanted to beat the crowds and the heat and climb to the top of the spectacular rock fortress of Sigiriya. Dad stayed in bed because he didn't want to 'climb another bloody rock and see any more bloody ruins'.

It was a fifteen-minute drive to the rock, but even from kilometres away the two-hundred-metre-high rock fortress loomed large over an expanse of flat scrub and jungle. As we got closer, the massive red-stone edifice seemed to rise from the centre of the earth.

I've been to many a fortress and castle in my travels but none of the others would have been half as hard to storm as the fortress in the sky at Sigiriya. The whole dynastic drama that led to the building of the fortress began when the fifth-century king Dhatu Sena was killed by his son Prince Kasyapa. Fearing the revenge of his brother, the Prince built the impregnable palace and remained a self-imposed prisoner there for eighteen years.

To get to the Prince, his brother would have had to first get past the wall around the rock, which was guarded by an entire army. If he got past them, he'd have had to weave his way through the maze of gardens and somehow get over the wide moat, teeming with man-eating crocodiles. That was the easy bit. Even after he'd clambered up the twelve hundred steep steps on the far side of the moat he would have come to a dead end. The final leg was a sheer cliff. The only way up was if someone above threw a rope down. Then again, the Prince's brother may have been deterred from going any further before he even got to the first wall. The annoyingly persistent touts wanting to be your guide or to sell you wooden elephants would have scared off even the most determined attacker.

Being one of the first people there, I was lucky enough to have the place to myself. Unfortunately that also meant that I had every single wannabe guide to myself. A long line of them were waiting just inside the entrance. This looked like a job for Getting-rid-of-touts Technique No. 14. As soon as I walked through the entrance I grabbed the first guide in line. Then, and this is the clever part, we tottered past all the other guides and not a single one of them hassled me. When we'd hiked a suitable distance away from the gaggle of guides, I threw the second part of Technique No. 14 into action.

'Where are you from?' my guide asked.

'Estonia,' I said.

'Ah, Estonia is very beautiful country,' he said nodding his head. 'Is this your first time to Sigiriya?'

'No, this is my fifth!' I said brightly.

'Fifth?' he squawked.

'Yes, I live in Colombo.'

'Oh, what do you do there?'

I glanced around as if to make sure no one else was listening. 'I work undercover for the Sri Lankan police,' I whispered.

'Oh . . . well, bye, bye then,' he said before scampering back.

Halfway up the rock, I took a detour to the Cave of the Heavenly Maidens via a shaky spiral staircase with open wrought-iron steps and a vertical drop of a hundred or so metres directly below.

'Very safe!' said one of the cave's custodians. 'It was a gift from London Underground.'

The Cave of the Heavenly Maidens is basically ancient porn with frescoes of shapely contenders for the Miss Sigiriya 500 AD crown.

'Nice boobs,' I said to the cave custodian. Most of the women portrayed had massive and perfectly formed breasts.

'Yes,' the guard replied proudly. 'All Sri Lankan women have nice boobs. This one here,' he said pointing to a buxom young lass, 'is just like my wife.'

I struggled up the final cat's-cradle of iron ladders and walkways that clung to the face of the granite massif, then finally stumbled onto the plateau at the top. The entire summit of Sigiriya, nearly three acres in extent, was once occupied by buildings, but all that remains is a few old bricks and an empty in-ground swimming pool. The view was outstanding, though. The jungle that stretched to the mist-shrouded mountains on the horizon was dotted with bunches of enormous flowers that lit up the countryside with droplets of pink, yellow and blue.

I did well on the way down. I managed to successfully tackle the twelve hundred steps with relative ease and to successfully ignore the thirty-two touts who tried to sell me wooden elephants.

•

The final leg of our journey with Blacky was a three-hour drive northeast through Tamil Tiger territory to Trincomalee. As we left Sigiriya behind, the houses became noticeably poorer. Many of them were made from wattle and daub with thatched or corrugated-iron roofs, if they had a roof that is—many didn't, having been abandoned during the years of fighting. And just to remind us how recent that all was, small pillboxes popped up along the roadside with alarming frequency, and the bored-looking soldiers inside pointed machine guns at our heads.

Even the town names sounded like a clattering machine gun. As we bumped our way over the potholed and cratered narrow 'highway', we passed a sign for the town of Galenbindunuwewa. Other machine-gun rattling local town names include: Parakramabahu, Radawaduwa, Pallavarayankaddu and Srijayawardenepurakotte.

We did see a lot of machine guns, but at least we didn't see any severed heads.

'Ten years ago,' Blacky told us, 'I took a tour with two old couples from Belgium and one morning we saw stuck on fence posts almost thirty heads from men who had been executed. I told my clients that the villagers had a pageant the night before and had made these rubber masks. They said to me "Oh, they are not real heads, then?" and I said, "Oh no, they are just made for the locals to have fun".'

Even while Blacky told us this story, he kept smiling. He also smiled at all the checkpoint guards and, when he had dropped us off at the Medway Hotel in Trincomalee, he was still smiling as he drove off down the road.

23

Hoppers and rotty botty

The first place we visited in Trincomalee (Trinco to its friends) was the old Royal Navy barracks just up the road from our hotel. Well, we think they were the old barracks: Dad wasn't quite sure whether they were or not and the army officer at the building's entrance wasn't quite sure what planet he was on. Dad *was* sure about the location of the main harbour, though. Mind you, the dockyard and ships directly in front of our hotel were a bit of a giveaway.

What Lord Nelson once described as 'the finest natural harbour in the world', was once the British naval headquarters for the Pacific campaign during the Second World War. There were no navy ships in the docks now, just a few fishing vessels and a rusted tugboat.

'The Sri Lankan Navy used to be here as well,' Dad said as we stood on the windswept dock. 'They only had two patrol boats. There were six people aboard each boat, so their entire navy was made up of twelve sailors!'

It was only a short stroll from the dock to Trinco's 'main street', which ran parallel to the harbour.

'This looks exactly the same as it did fifty years ago,' Dad exclaimed. The main street was lined with rambling, run-down shops whose goods—chillies, rolls of silk, plastic chairs, pots and pans and fish heads—spilt out onto the footpath. This was the only place we'd visited on our entire trip that hadn't changed since Dad's first visit. There was one modern addition to Trinco, however, they had an Internet café—although the computers inside were at least twenty years old. It was all a bit ramshackle and smelly, but I liked it.

Trinco was well outside the range of the tourist radar—we were staying in the only hotel in town and we were the only guests—so not one single person tried to sell us a coconut monkey's bottom. There was only one problem with the lack of tourists and that was trying to find a restaurant that served what Dad described as 'normal food'. My guidebook suggested Anna's Restaurant; its most outstanding quality being that it was 'spotless'. It wasn't quite McDonald's: spotless, but it did have very similar garishly coloured plastic chairs. No Big Macs either, but Dad was happy to discover they had fried chicken on the menu. I ordered the chicken fried rice, being a little bit curried out. Anna's Restaurant was on the second floor, so we had a fine view of the main street.

There seemed to be a distinct lack of cars in Trinco; the street was abuzz with bicycles, three-wheelers and a few mules. At one point, a flock of goats paraded straight down the middle of the street.

'It's got bloody chilli in it!' Dad spat when he took a mouthful of his fried chicken. 'Why can't they just make plain fried chicken?' The chicken fried rice was actually quite plain, so I offered Dad my meal. He only took a few mouthfuls, though, because 'I'll probably get the plague or something'.

After lunch, we went for our customary aimless wander. Trinco sat on a narrow peninsula with the main harbour on one side and two protected bays on the other. Behind the harbour was Dutch Bay, which had stunning white sand and turquoise waters—and a herd of deer roaming through piles of rubbish on the edge of the sand.

You could barely make out the beach at Back Bay. That was because the sand was covered by myriad colourful fishing boats, fish drying on racks and slapped-together shacks. We wandered through the maze of fish and boats and soon discovered that the shacks were actually people's homes. We ducked up a lane full of sarong-wearing men hunkered down playing cards, women in gossiping gaggles and small children dressed in grubby underwear peering out of corrugated huts with sand floors. We had to watch our step because the middle of the lane was one big open sewer.

'Let's get out of here!' Dad moaned. 'This place is disgusting!' I tried to explain to Dad that, although it wasn't quite the leafy outer suburbs of Melbourne, this was their home. Dad was too busy looking at the dirt to notice that most of the folk we passed had big beaming smiles on their faces.

We had dinner at our hotel even though it didn't have a restaurant. The menu was at reception and the meals were served on the verandah out the front of your room. Dad ordered a bowl of chips and a beer while I went for the curry prawns—daring the deluge. Our meals were due at 7.30, but by 8.00 there was no sign of them.

'Your meals are on their way', the fellow in reception told me when I enquired. I don't know where the meals were actually 'on their way' from, but by nine o'clock there was still no show.

'I don't want my dinner any more!' Dad huffed. 'I'm going to bed!' Dad flicked on the TV just as the Sri Lankan 'English' news started. After a two-year truce, the Tamil Tigers were back at it again and a suicide bomber had blown up a police station in Colombo. It was only about fifty metres up the road from the Galle Face Hotel.

'Looks like we're going to get abducted,' Dad observed drily.

'You'll have to eat curry for breakfast, lunch *and* dinner then,' I said.

I was sitting outside when our dinner finally arrived at 9.30. I brought the chips in to Dad, but he'd already nodded off to sleep. The prawns were delicious but I couldn't eat the rice: it smelt like Dad's socks.

•

'Happy birthday, Brian!' Dad said. Well, it was actually more like: 'Arrrggghhhh erggghhhh!' Dad staggered out of bed at 3 a.m. and threw up all over the bathroom. Dad was still feeling sick in the morning, so he stayed in bed while I had breakfast.

'I'm not eating *anything* till we get to Singapore!' he snorted. Singapore was four days away. Dad would have liked the breakfast, too. I had fried eggs and sausages on toast.

'It was that bloody fried rice,' Dad groaned as we waited for a three-wheeler. Dad did look pale and he probably didn't need a bumpy three-wheeler ride, but there were no taxis in Trinco so we had no choice. It was only fifteen kilometres to the Nilaveli Beach Hotel, but the road mostly consisted of potholes within potholes. For half-an-hour, our three-wheeler bumped its way around stray cows, girls in saris laughing under umbrellas, soldiers brandishing large guns and stalls selling coconuts.

As I signed us in at the front desk of the hotel, the receptionist said: 'Oh, it's your birthday today! Happy birthday!'

'That's right,' Dad croaked. 'Happy birthday.' He had totally forgotten.

Dad hopped straight into bed as soon as we got to our room. The room was clean and modern with a magical view out to sea through hammock-slung palm trees, but Dad asked me to close the curtains.

'It was that *bloody* fried rice!' Dad groaned again. I'd eaten nearly all of the fried rice in question and I was fine. When I suggested that it could have been a number of things that made him sick—like the fact that he doesn't wash his hands after he's been to the toilet—he barked at me: 'Those bloody Sri Lankans are trying to kill me!'

A large basket of fresh fruit, including pineapple, mangoes, papaya, coconuts, oranges, apples and bananas, was delivered to our room as a birthday present from the management, but Dad refused to eat any of it.

'I'll just have a sleep,' he said. There wasn't much I could do. I left Dad a large bottle of water with strict instructions to 'keep his fluids up' and headed for the beach.

The beach was simply stunning: kilometres of fine white sand, fringed by palm trees that stretched as far as the eye could see in either direction. I'd decided what I was going to do for my birthday before I left Australia—I was going to hire a boat and go snorkelling off Pigeon Island. It was such a pity that Dad wasn't with me because I had been looking forward to doing this with him.

I felt a little guilty leaving Dad in the room but I have to admit I had a marvellous time. I had my own chartered boat and its skipper took me out to a bay with clear blue water on the tiny island five hundred metres off shore. I snorkelled among a rainbow of fishes—that's my own collective noun. I did almost shit my pants, though, and it wasn't the dodgy fried rice. A ten-metre moray eel popped its head out from behind a rock and snapped its teeth at me. Okay, it was more like two metres long, but it still scared the hell out of me.

Back in our room, Dad was still in bed. He still wouldn't eat anything, either. He'd been sick again but he refused outright to let me find a doctor for him. Even at home he shunned doctors. I remember one time he almost lost one of his remaining fingers while he was sawing a piece of wood. Even as the blood squirted to the ceiling he reached for a Band-aid.

'You're a stubborn man,' I said when he refused to eat any of the fruit, then realised that sounded very familiar—that's what my wife says to me all the time.

I stayed for a while, but when Dad dozed off to sleep again I went for a walk along the beach. Not far up from the Nilaveli Beach Hotel was the burnt-out shell of a larger tourist resort that had been bombed in the 1980s. A bit further up again was a military base of some sort. The barbed-wire fence ran right down the middle of the beach and two armed guards sat at either end in tin shacks looking out to sea. Little did we know then that all these traces of the destruction caused by the Tamil Tigers over more than twenty years were themselves about to be swept away by the tsunami that hit this coast just five months later. As I write, it is still very difficult to get precise details of what happened, but in the area around Trincomalee alone over nine hundred people were killed and almost fifteen thousand were left homeless. The Nilaveli Beach Hotel was completely destroyed. Three waves hit the hotel and the seawater receded up to a kilometre into the ocean before returning with a vengeance and a towering ten-metre wave that literally crushed the hotel. Of the one hundred and eighty guests staying at the hotel, only sixty survived.

I trudged for almost an hour past endless palms with their lacy crowns turned upwards toward the sky and their long necks stretched towards the ocean. When I was just about ready to turn back, I spotted a lily-white couple sitting on the sand. They were English medical students who had just finished a two-month placement in the countryside. They had arrived in Trinco by train and had told a three-wheeler driver to take them to a 'cheap' place to stay. He'd taken them to his sister's guesthouse in the middle of nowhere.

'Is there anywhere to eat around here?' Anthony asked me.

'There's a resort about an hour that way,' I said, pointing down the beach.

Their guesthouse did have meals, but they'd had curried vegetables for both breakfast and lunch. They were quite content with their seclusion but were also more than happy to tramp up the beach for an hour to down a few cold beers by a swimming pool.

Dad was still asleep when I returned to the room to check on him, so I found him some soft bread rolls in the restaurant, then joined Anthony and Emma at the Beach Bar, where we met two other English medical students. I ordered a pina colada.

'It's my birthday today!' I said, justifying my exotically decorated drink when it arrived.

Dad would have run screaming back to the room if he'd come to dinner with us. The 'theme' for the night's buffet was Mongolian BBQ. The food was delicious and nothing like the Mongolian BBQ I had in Mongolia (fried mutton fat and bones).

I told the four medical students about Dad's condition and they recommended that he drink a lot of water and try to eat some plain food.

'He should go back to England, then,' I said. They also examined the red welt left on my forearm after my Maltese jellyfish sting. Emma's professional diagnosis was: 'That's weird!'

'It should be fine,' Anthony said reassuringly. ' . . . Or your arm might fall off.'

•

After I had threatened to send in four medical students to dissect him, Dad finally crawled out of bed to go to breakfast. He nibbled on some toast and took a few sips of tea while I had the most luscious pineapple, papaya, passionfruit and lemony bananas with buffalo milk yogurt and palm treacle. After breakfast, Dad hobbled back to the room and I went for another long walk, this time in the opposite direction.

For over an hour I ambled along an endless line of perfectly art-directed swaying palms until I came across a whole village of palm-leaf thatched huts with their backs to the beach. Brightly coloured fishing boats were anchored just off shore while a line of fishermen looked as if they were playing a game of tug-of-war with the ocean. Straddling a thick rope, they were hauling a heavy fishing net in from the water.

I pretended to join in, but they gratefully received my lame joke as an offer of assistance, so I ended up spending half-an-hour helping the twenty-odd fishermen pull in their wide, horseshoe-shaped net. It was a long, hard haul and the resultant catch, just a few kilos, seemed scant reward for the amount of backbreaking work involved.

On my walk back to the resort, I thought about our trip so far and whether I'd achieved my aim of getting to know and understand my father better. I thought I had. I'm no psychologist, but I kinda now understood why Dad turns just about every situation into a joke. He has used humour as a crutch to get through difficult times, which started with not having any parents to speak of from the age of seven. Being separated from his brothers and sisters, living in a home during the war, going out on his own to face the world at only fourteen, and even losing his fingers would have all contributed to Dad's never-ending comedy routine. It also helped explain why he still keeps his emotions in check. I don't know if it's hereditary or whether it has to do with my Mum dying when I was young, but I too have trouble expressing my emotions and often use humour to deflect conversations away from sensitive subjects. My friends would probably also suggest that, again like Dad, my sense of humour maintains a high rate of production with very little quality control.

Using humour is one trait I've obviously picked up from Dad, but he has one or two others that I was now absolutely determined not to pick up, like being narrow-minded—yes, I know I am a little bit opinionated, but not *that* much. On the other hand, I also discovered attributes that I hope to possess if I get to seventy-three. One of them, which I really admired him for, was his willingness to try new things—or things he hadn't done in fifty years—such as going to a Shakespearean play, riding a mountain bike, hooning around on a moped, eating tapas and hanging out in a nightclub. He had been a real sport, too, about being rushed around on such a busy itinerary. It was actually only now that he had started genuinely complaining—and that was mostly because he was sick and just wanted to go home.

After taking two steps forward in my estimation, though, Dad was about to take two steps back. When I returned to our room he was watching Sri Lankan soaps on the television. If his mental health was under question, at least he hadn't actually been physically sick for twenty-four hours. He now just had a mild case of the trots.

•

I had been hoping to go back to the room with some good news, but the Tamil Tigers stuffed up my brilliant plan. I inquired at reception about a flight from Trinco to Colombo but all the flights between the two airports had been cancelled for a month due to the Tamil's recent bombing. My original plan was to catch the train, but Dad was in no state to spend nine hours in a dusty, hot train with dodgy toilets. It might even have been the end of him. I decided to get a driver, but there was no way I was paying inflated hotel prices. I wandered out of the resort and hit the streets. After asking a few people and a couple of goats I found a driver who would take us to Colombo for US$35.

I spent the rest of the day swimming, lying on the beach and checking up on Dad. By late afternoon, he said he was feeling a little better and that he would join me for dinner. I dropped into the restaurant on the way to the Beach Bar to check the culinary theme for the night. It was 'Sri Lankan Night'. They did have a few western dishes at the buffet, but Dad would have to walk past a dozen different curries to get to the roast chicken and chips.

I met Anthony and Emma for a drink before Dad was due to join us in the restaurant at seven o'clock. At eight, he still hadn't shown. Anthony suggested that I was travelling with my 'pretend Dad' and that he didn't really exist.

'He does exist,' I insisted, 'and I should take him some food.'

I took him a plate of boiled potatoes, some (soft) bread and butter and a large slice of pineapple cake.

'I almost got to the restaurant,' Dad sighed, 'but I had one whiff of a curry and bolted back to the room.'

When I returned to the dining area, Anthony and Emma were still sceptical about the existence of my father.

'You didn't give that food to your Dad,' Anthony said, 'you just went outside and gave it to the crabs.'

I thought I might surprise Dad with a rotty botty after dinner. I ordered the Sri Lankan staple called a hopper, which was a wafer-thin, bowl-shaped pancake made of rice flour, yeast and coconut milk with a crisp surround and soft spongy centre. It was then filled with a blistering chicken curry that was called, rather worryingly, rotty. I had nothing to worry about, though: not only was there no rotty botty, it was incredibly tasty and by far the best meal I'd eaten in Sri Lanka.

•

'This is my first job as a driver,' Sumeda beamed. He was certainly keen—he'd arrived to pick us up an hour before our scheduled departure time.

'Did you like the beach?' he asked Dad as he packed our bags into the back of the van.

'Yeah, it was nice,' Dad lied.

Sumeda told us that the main sealed road to Colombo was closed, so we went on the secondary papier-mâché and straw road instead. There must have been quite a newspaper and clag shortage when they built it, because after a while the road shrank to only a couple of metres wide. Even as we were being thrown around like rag dolls, Dad was flaked out in the back. I was quite worried about him now. He was extremely weak after missing so many meals.

After two hours we stopped for a drink and Sumeda disappeared for five minutes.

'I rang my boss,' he explained when he returned. 'I gave you the wrong price. It should be seventy-five dollars, not thirty-five dollars.'

I scoffed. 'Ah, that old chestnut!'

'I make mistake,' he pleaded. 'I in big trouble.'

For the next twenty minutes I argued that he should 'honour' his original price while he argued that I must give him the extra money so he could fix his 'big' mistake. We only stopped quibbling when he pulled up in front of his brother's house and ran inside with a pile of gifts. The battle continued when he returned and I grilled him about the 'closure' of the main road to Colombo. 'I think it was closed,' he stammered uncertainly. I suspected that the convoluted detour was just an excuse to drop into his brother's place.

Sumeda pulled over a taxi driver in the next town.

'How much to Colombo?' he asked. The price was forty dollars. 'See!' Sumeda squeaked. 'We have already driven three hours, so you must pay me seventy-five dollars or go with the taxi driver.'

'I only *have* fifty dollars,' I lied. 'If we go in the taxi, I can only give you the ten dollars that's left.'

This squabbling, and Sumeda stopping at every town to get a price from a taxi driver, continued all the way to Colombo. It was incredibly draining but I tried not to remonstrate too much in case he decided to throw us out. If I was travelling by myself I wouldn't have cared less, but in Dad's weakened state I couldn't make him stand on a dusty, hot road waiting for another lift. It was a fine line as to whether we were going to make it all the way to Colombo or not, but I outright refused to pay the full price. I thought I was already compromising enough by offering him my 'last' fifty dollars. My guess was that this was a well-rehearsed scam and not Sumeda's first driving job at all.

Sumeda was still pushing for the inflated price and I was still worried he'd ditch us when we hit the suburbs of Colombo. The traffic was as madcap and harrowing as ever. When we caught sight of the Galle Face Hotel, I finally relaxed. Our 'four-hour' trip had taken us over eight hours. What should have been a pleasant journey had turned into a very stressful marathon argument. I handed Sumeda fifty dollars while the bellboys removed our luggage—and Dad—from the van.

'You must get me the rest of the money now!' Sumeda persisted. 'I wait here and you use your credit card inside the hotel.'

'Okay,' I answered warily. 'I'll be back in a minute.'

An hour later, Sumeda was still waiting out the front of the hotel while I was downing a desperately needed beer in the verandah bar. And boy, had I been looking forward to that beer. Dad was so tired and weak that he went straight to bed. I did, however, manage to talk him into eating something. I ordered a toasted cheese sandwich and a pot of tea from room service. I didn't want to put Dad off his food, so I went downstairs to the restaurant for my last chicken curry in Sri Lanka.

When I returned to our room, Dad was already asleep. At least he'd eaten half a sandwich and about three chips. It was only eight o'clock, and my last night in Sri Lanka, so I went for a wander in search of a bar. The streets were empty—there was no sign of Sumeda and his van—and the first two bars I tried were closed. Eventually, halfway along a run-down street I found a little slice of Dublin. There were only two couples inside Clancy's Irish Pub with the eight barmen.

'Everyone is at home watching the local election results on the TV,' one barman told me. Well, I suppose live Sri Lankan politics would be a lot more action-packed and exciting than live cricket.

On the way back to The Galle Face Hotel, a man smiled at me and said, 'Hello, would you like to fuck a Sri Lankan girl?'

I smiled back. 'No, I'm okay thanks.'

'Sri Lankan girls are the best fuck in the world. I can get you one if you like.'

'I think I'll just go to bed, thanks,' I said. 'But it was very kind of you to offer.'

Singapore

24

Volcano burgers and exploding arses

It's amazing how just being upgraded to Business Class can suddenly make you feel better. Dad was still incredibly weak but he chirped up considerably once he'd sunk back into his commodious seat. Best of all, he finally ate something. Mind you, it wasn't just the salubrious surrounds of Emirates Business Class that encouraged Dad to eat. The doctor sitting next to him scolded him like a naughty little boy and almost force-fed him his lunch.

This was my seventh visit to Singapore, but it would be the first time that I had actually left the confines of the airport. Although the transit lounge at Changi Airport is quite lovely, I was looking forward to seeing a bit more of Singapore than perfectly neat and orderly shopping malls surrounded by perfectly neat and orderly steel, glass and concrete buildings.

Our taxi from the airport to our hotel drove us past perfectly neat and orderly shopping malls that were surrounded by perfectly neat and orderly steel, glass and concrete buildings . . .

I'd heard somewhere that 'It's fun to stay at the YMCA', so I'd booked us into the Singapore branch. It wasn't too much fun to begin with, though. Dad didn't want to leave the room. He was still very tired and it was mid-afternoon, so the city was like an oven.

After a lie down Dad was feeling well enough to go for a walk, so we jumped on a perfectly spotless bus and drove down a perfectly spotless road lined with perfectly spotless footpaths.

'Most of the population must be cleaners,' I said as the bus pulled into the perfectly spotless bus stop on the perfectly spotless Orchard Road.

The city looked as if it had only been built the week before. And they hadn't finished, either—there were perfectly spotless construction sites all along Orchard Road. Singapore *is* actually new. In 1819, when Sir Stamford Raffles arrived at the small island (forty-five kilometres across at its broadest point), no one lived in its swamps except a few pirates and fishermen. Britain saw the need for a strategic 'halfway house' to refit, feed and protect the fleet of their growing empire and by 1824, just five years after the founding of modern Singapore, the population had grown from a hundred and fifty to ten thousand.

The population today is four million and most of them were shopping on Orchard Road. We even had to queue just to cross the road. While we patiently waited to cross—as a Pom, one thing Dad never complains about is queuing—a tourist waltzed past us and, in the space of a few seconds, racked up S$1640 worth of fines for jaywalking, smoking on a public street and littering. Singapore is known as 'the fine city', and that's not because of its spotless streets. Over the past thirty years, the city has introduced draconian penalties for the most minor of offences. There are fines for pretty much anything, including selling or importing chewing gum (AU$800), jaywalking (AU$40), dropping litter (AU$800), dancing in public (AU$4000), skateboarding (AU$400), smoking on the street (AU$800), public speaking without a permit (AU$1600) and not flushing a public toilet. Not putting down the toilet seat is, as in the rest of the world, punishable by constant nagging. Even partial nudity in one's own house is illegal—a law enforced by the special Peeping Tom Division of the police force. I imagine the Peeping Tom Division would also be responsible for detecting anyone partaking in a bit of 'unnatural sex'—no swinging from the chandeliers, then—which is also punishable under the *Public Environment Health Act*.

I restrained myself from throwing in a quick two-step as we entered Raffles City, one of the massive and immaculate air-conditioned multi-storey shopping complexes that are jammed side-by-side all the way down Orchard Road. Most of the shops in the complex sold stuff that was either way too expensive or way too cute. There were shops full of oh-so-sickly-cute 'Hello Kitty' accessories for everything and anything. Hello Kitty is so popular, in fact, that a few years ago a Hello Kitty doll caused mayhem in the city. The main McDonald's in Singapore—there are, and this is frightening, 113 of them!—decided to offer a Hello Kitty doll for S$5 to any customer who bought a Big Mac Meal. On the first day of the promotion so many Singaporeans showed up that McDonald's ran out of dolls and traffic was blocked around the entire island. The police had to step in and tell them they couldn't run the promotion any longer because it had too much impact on the flow of traffic. At least the people who were buying the dolls with their meal were sensible about something: they were throwing the Big Macs into the perfectly spotless rubbish bins, as they left.

Dad was quite happy to find a McDonald's in the Raffles City Hawkers' Market, which was really just one big food hall. As we sat in the packed dining area, Dad gagged on his drink and proceeded to have an uncontrollable coughing fit. As he spluttered and spat, a mass of people from the surrounding tables got up and moved.

'They all think you've got SARS,' I said, trying not to laugh.

Back at the YMCA, just as I was about to doze off to sleep, Dad piped up in the dark: 'I think these pillows are bags of cement with pillowcases on them.' He was feeling better, then.

•

Dad came to Singapore with the Far East Fleet in 1953, only days after Hillary and Tenzing had conquered Everest and Elizabeth had been crowned Queen. For three months, Dad was stationed at *HMS Terror*. The chappies at the Admiralty back then were obviously not au fait with the public relations value of signalling the extreme peacefulness of your intentions and eschewing anything smacking of aggression. *HMS Terror* was part of such a huge British naval presence that Singapore was called the Clapham Junction of the Eastern Seas. During the Second World War, the city was considered an impregnable fortress—until it was overrun by the Japanese in 1942. When Singapore gained its independence from Britain in 1965, the Royal Navy was booted out and the Americans moved in.

After a good lie-in—Dad was still feeling quite weak—we jumped in a taxi and headed to what used to be *HMS Terror* in Sembawang on Johore Strait.

'This was all coconut groves and villages!' Dad exclaimed, as we drove past endless rows of neat apartment blocks on the way to the north of the island.

The main gate into the docks was still there, it was now manned by the American navy.

'Which ship are you visiting?' the crew-cut and chiselled-chinned guard asked as we pulled up.

'Umm . . .' Quick, think of a state! '*USS Montana*?'

'Sorry, there's no *USS Montana* here,' he replied.

'Oh, I mean . . . um . . . *USS Wyoming*!'

'No. Look, can you move on, please?'

He didn't laugh when I said: 'I've still got another 48 states to go yet!'

The taxi driver dropped us off next to the old officers' barracks and the former British officers' club. The latter was now an American officers' club, but they'd kept the old name: Terror Club.

'Shall we see if we can get in?' I asked Dad.

'I couldn't even go in there when I was in the Royal Navy. Only officers could!' he huffed.

'That's all right, I'll just tell them that you were a commodore.'

'No, no! They won't believe that,' he cried. 'Make me a sub lieutenant.'

Our chances didn't look too good, though. The entrance was like Fort Knox. Beyond the small reception area was a heavy steel revolving gate guarded by Arnold Schwarzenegger. I told the guard at reception that I was writing a book about my Dad who used to come to the club when he was a lieutenant (I promoted him) in the Royal Navy and asked whether we could possibly get an escorted tour. He gave our passports a cursory glance, then said, 'Yeah, just go in and wander around for as long as you like.' It was as easy as that. They didn't even check our bags for bombs. Dad was very excited—after fifty years, he was finally getting into an officers' club.

Most of the outdoor space was taken up by a huge swimming pool where a group of ladies was taking an aqua-aerobics class. Dad couldn't help himself and stopped and chatted to the first white-bellied man lounging on one of the sun lounges. His name was Paul and he was a *real* Lieutenant. 'I come here every Tuesday to watch the show,' he said, motioning towards the officers' wives doing their exercise class. He was all set up for the 'show', too. He had a massive bowl of popcorn.

We wandered up to the verandah bar for a drink. A television with the sound turned down was showing *Wheel of Fortune* from America, while a stereo was blasting out The Eagles' greatest hits. Our small cans of Budweiser came with complimentary buckets of popcorn.

Once we'd tired of seeing how the other half played, we caught the MRT (Mass Rapid Transit) back to the city centre. We only bought one ticket and Dad followed right behind me through the turnstiles. It was quite a big risk considering punishment for not having a ticket was probably twenty years in a labour camp—but we saved five dollars.

Dad went back to the hotel for a rest while I went to check out Chinatown. I didn't stay long, though—it was like a spick 'n' span Disney version of Chinatown. My guidebook said that you could eat on the streets, but I think they meant that you could actually eat *off* the streets because the footpaths were so immaculate.

•

The British may have lost Singapore, but they still have a prominent presence. There's a large expat population and, by the look of the British Club, a lot of them were well cashed-up. I'd managed to score us an invitation to visit this private club in a jungle setting at the top of Bukit Tinggi hill in the poshest suburb of Singapore.

'Do you live here?' Dad asked the taxi driver.

'If I did, you'd be walking!' he quipped. 'These are A1 people,' he added as we drove past rows of large houses with three or four cars parked in each driveway.

'What's A1 mean?' I asked.

'A1 people live in a big houses in Singapore. A2 is a small house, B1 is a big apartment, B2 a condo, C1 a small flat, C2 a tiny government flat and C3 is . . . God help them!'

Security at the main gate of the British Club was tighter than at the US navy base—the taxi was checked inside and out and even underneath for bombs using big mirrors on poles. 'The security's even tighter here,' Dad said, as we walked inside the entrance of the sprawling clubhouse. On each side of the main entrance was a knight in shining armour. Well, minus the brave knight.

We were met at reception by the lovely Shakila, the marketing manager for the club, who took us on a guided tour. The club was a home-away-from-home for homesick Brits and had a soccer pitch, cricket pitch, bowling green and billiard room, tennis courts, restaurants serving bangers and mash, mediaeval banquet nights and a transplanted English pub called the Windsor Arms. Mind you, this little slice of England doesn't come cheap. The joining fee alone is S$20 000. Then you have to pay another $3 000 on top of that every year. It costs so much, in fact, that the members can't afford towels. A sign on the noticeboard asked politely if anyone 'might' have accidentally taken one of the club's pool towels home, since 332 of them had gone missing in the previous two months.

After we'd downed a quick half-pint in the Windsor Arms with Shakila, she left us to have dinner on the verandah overlooking the rich expats stealing towels from the pool.

'Look, they've got a Volcano Burger on the menu,' Dad said. 'Do you know why it's called that?'

'No,' I said.

'Cause when you eat one, your arse explodes.'

Dad had the non-explosive cod and chips and I had the potentially volcanic chilli crab.

Even though there are another 9 999 taxis in Singapore, we somehow managed to procure the same taxi driver that had taken us to the British Club. As we went back past the A1 houses with their three or four cars in the drive, our taxi driver told us that it costs more to get a permit to own a car in Singapore than it does to actually buy the car. And even then you can only keep a car for seven years before you have to buy a new one. Taxis only have a five-year life.

'So which one are you?' Dad asked, referring to the A1 system.

'I'm about an F6,' he smiled.

•

I had a surprise for Dad.

'I've booked us in somewhere a bit nicer.' This was our last night in Singapore and the last night of our eight-week trip, so I'd decided to lash out. And I mean really lash out. It's fun to stay at the YMCA, but it's a darn sight more fun to stay at Raffles. I was looking forward to it. The Raffles Hotel is consistently ranked as one of the finest in the world. I felt confident Dad could look forward to very soft bread rolls and even softer pillows.

The original Raffles was established in a sprawling colonial bungalow known as the Beach House in 1887 by the famous (and just about only, I imagine) Armenian hoteliers, the Sarkies brothers. When the hotel opened it boasted Singapore's first electric lights and fans and Singapore's first French chef. For a century it was *the* place to stay in Singapore until time, wear and a downturn in tourists in the early 1980s left the hotel looking a bit shabby. In 1989 the hotel closed for three years of restoration. When it reopened its doors to the public in 1991, it looked much as it had in 1915 during its elegant heyday.

It was a pity that Dad was still feeling sick because he didn't fully appreciate our grand entrance as the taxi swept up the driveway and pulled up in front of the whitewashed colonial grand dame. By the time we'd reached reception, eight staff members had shaken our hands and personally welcomed us to the hotel.

Our 'suite' was in the Palm Court wing overlooking tropical gardens and the most perfectly clipped and perfectly green lawn that I'd ever seen. A petite lady was waiting for us outside the door to our room.

'Hello, my name is Janice,' she said. 'I'm your valet.' Now this was luxury. We had our very own twenty-four-hour-a-day valet.

'You can buzz me anytime for anything you want,' she said with a beaming smile.

Our suite was palatial, with a taste of old-world opulence including a private parlour and a dining area. The entire suite was full of period furnishings with oriental carpets spread over polished teak floors. The two double beds combined were bigger than my whole apartment back in Australia. It was certainly a step up from the saggy bunk beds at the Malham Youth Hostel or the falling-apart room in the Cannon Hotel in Gibraltar.

'Look,' Dad pointed, 'there's a button for the valet above my bed. I might call her in the middle of the night. She did say to buzz her for "anything you want".'

After going through every drawer and cupboard—you never know—a rich person might have accidentally left a large bag of cash—reeling in shock at the price of drinks in the bar fridge, eating all the complimentary fruit for lunch (and a few of the complimentary chocolates for dessert), we went for a wander around the hotel.

The Raffles complex is massive, taking up an entire city block, so it didn't take us long to get lost in the labyrinth of restaurants and shops.

'Bloody hell!' Dad muttered, as we stood in front of a shop window. Bloody hell, alright. The shops were so expensive even Bill Gates would baulk at the prices. A plain old t-shirt—with some fancy-schmancy label was reduced *to* S$795!

'I don't spend that much on clothes in an entire year,' I said.

The Raffles Museum was marvellous—and free! I love looking at old travel memorabilia and the museum was chock-a-block with old brochures, guidebooks, postcards and restaurant menus from the Golden Age of Travel (1870 to 1939). Some of my favourite pieces included a Raffles Hotel brochure from 1910. On the inside cover was a timetable for carriage trips to 'sights around Singapore', including the Botanical Gardens, French Church, Singapore Club, Ladies' Lawn Tennis Ground, the Criminal Prison and the Lunatic Asylum. A Bradshaws Overland guidebook (the *Lonely Planet* of the 19th century) to 'India, Turkey, Persia, China and Australia' from 1873 recommended that one should take a few bottles of good port and champagne when travelling in case of depression. Nowadays, you'd get very depressed when you saw the price of a good bottle of champagne at Raffles. Then again, the best bottle of champagne in the Long Bar was still cheaper than a fancy-schmancy t-shirt. We had to have a Singapore Sling, though, even if I did have to sacrifice my daughter's education to buy one.

One of tourism's great rites of passage is to have a Singapore Sling in the Long Bar at Raffles. The famous tipple was created there by bartender Ngiam Tong Boon in 1915 (the recipe is gin, cherry brandy, Cointreau, Dom Benedictine, pineapple juice, lime juice and grenadine with a dash of Angostura Bitters and garnished with a slice of pineapple and cherry). It was originally meant to be a woman's drink, which explains why it is a rather garish shade of pink. There wouldn't have been too many women drinking it, though—in 1915 the men outnumbered women in Singapore eight to one. Dad wasn't quite ready for a fancy sickly-sweet expensive cocktail, so I got him a plain old expensive orange juice instead.

'The orange juice was nine dollars!' I gasped, when I returned from the bar.

'You could buy an orange plantation in Sri Lanka for that,' Dad grunted.

We both sipped our drinks very slowly.

'The bar is exactly the same as it was in 1953,' Dad remarked, looking around the crowded bar. I later found out that the bar was originally on the other side of the hotel and the bar itself was about twice the length. About the only things that really had remained the same were the cane and rattan chairs.

'Well, Dad,' I said. 'We made it.'

'Not quite,' Dad observed drily.

'What do you think has been the highlight of the trip?' I asked. Dad thought about it for a minute.

'Leaving Sri Lanka.'

Even though we were in one of the best hotels in the world, Dad had had enough and was ready to go home. I knew he was ready because he kept going on about shepherd's pie and 'normal' bread.

Dad went back to our suite while I went to the spectacular rooftop pool for a dip. When I rejoined him, Dad was sitting up in bed with a tray of tea and biscuits.

'I buzzed Janice,' he beamed. 'It took her two minutes and twenty seconds to get here.'

The 'bathroom' was so big that it was actually three rooms. I could have run laps in the shower and the towel was so enormous that I got lost in it and had to call Dad in to get me out. I dabbed on way too much Floris aftershave—all the toiletries were made by Floris with a specially designed 'Raffles bouquet'—and I even polished my hiking boots on the 'valet table'. My thongs came up a treat, too.

'Feed at Raffles' Rudyard Kipling once said. He didn't specify where, though. The modern Raffles has fourteen restaurants. Our choices were a bit more limited because my cargo pants and hiking boots weren't quite 'smart elegant' enough for half the dining establishments and Dad didn't want to eat any 'foreign muck'. We opted for the Long Bar Steakhouse but we only had an entrée. I would have had to send Dad back into the navy to afford the main course.

The mixed-spice yogurt marinated beef tenderloin entrée was divine and we both ate it so slowly it was like a main course anyway.

Dad chooffed off to bed after dinner while I went to check out all the hotel bars (for research purposes only, of course). The Bar & Billiard Room was where Singapore's last tiger was shot in 1902. As one of the bar staff was closing up, he spotted a tiger which had escaped from the circus lying under a billiard table. The tiger probably collapsed under the table when he saw the prices of the drinks. A glass of Fosters was eleven dollars.

'You can't even give Fosters away in Australia,' I told the barman.

The Writer's Bar had a 'smart elegant' dress code, but no one said anything to me when I waltzed up, possibly because my hiking boots were looking so fabulous after their polish. I was the only writer in the bar, but that was because I was the only patron in the bar. A gold plaque above it read: 'The Writer's Bar commemorates Raffles Hotel's association with great writers, including the novelists Joseph Conrad, Rudyard Kipling and Somerset Maugham'. Most of today's literary talent might have trouble affording the Raffles perspective. Particularly the Million Dollar Cocktail. It didn't actually cost a million dollars, but as I drank one I figured that I'd need to sell twenty books to cover the cost.

I was intending to go back to the room when I bumped into a large group of folk wandering around outside the bar.

'Do you know where the Long Bar is?' a Scottish fellow asked. 'We've been walking around this place for half an hour trying to find it.' The directions were too complex for post-cocktail explanation, so I escorted them to the bar. The group was in Singapore for a conference and it was itself a cocktail of different nationalities. I wasn't intending on staying for a drink, but when the Scot offered to buy a round I decided to hang around just so I could tell my grandchildren I'd been shouted a drink by a Scotsman. The round of drinks cost $235.

A covers band of groovy Singaporeans with pony-tails and loud shirts was playing in the upstairs bar. Mind you, I thought it was a CD. The band were playing 'Stairway to Heaven' when we arrived and it was a note-for-note copy of the original. I stayed till closing—what else could I do, the conference lads kept buying me drinks. When the band finished, I switched allegiances and joined the musos for a drink. Lee, the lead guitarist from the Moodique Band, told me that they'd been playing together for nine years and they'd only had one night off in that time. Nine years of 'Dancing Queen' and 'Stairway to Heaven'! No wonder he needed a few drinks after playing. I'd had quite a few drinks too by the time I left. It took me almost forty minutes to find our suite.

•

Dad missed breakfast because his tummy was feeling a bit dodgy again. When I returned to the room, he was propped up in bed with a cup of tea.

'Janice only took one minute and fifteen seconds this time,' Dad beamed.

Just about the entire staff of the hotel bid us farewell as we jumped in a cab to the airport. Rather appropriately, our English adventure ended in a London cab, although there was nothing London about it inside—we could actually understand the driver and the interior had spotless cream-leather seats and oriental carpets. When Dad sat down, he looked at me wearily and said, 'I'm ready to go home.'

•

We arrived back in Melbourne just after midnight. Although we had scored an upgrade again, Dad didn't have a good flight. He was incredibly tired and run-down. By the time I drove him home it was close to 2 a.m. As we stood in the middle of the lounge room, Dad gave me a big hug and simply said, 'Thank you.'

'Thank you, Dad, for such a wonderful trip,' I replied. 'I love you.'

The trip had certainly created a stronger bond. That was the first time—that I could remember at least—that I'd told my Dad I loved him.

Port Melbourne

25

Calamari with weed salad

One week after we got home, I took Dad out to lunch in Port Melbourne. The migrant hostel in Port Melbourne was our first home when we arrived in Australia in March 1967. We were just one of many new families moving in. In fact, more settlers arrived in Australia in 1967 than in any other single year. In twelve months almost two hundred thousand new immigrants arrived. In the 1960s alone over 1.2 million foreigners settled in Australia. Many of them no doubt spent dismal evenings in the Ladies' Lounge of the local pub, chewing slowly on their ham steaks and pineapple while dreaming longingly of the 'foreign muck' they grew up on. The population of Australia back then was ten million—half what it is today.

Before we headed to the pub for lunch we went for a drive past the spot where the hostel used to be. In its place was a car dealership in the middle of a sea of ugly grey factories. Dad said that the factories were nice compared to the hostel. The hostel had been a collection of green corrugated nissen huts plopped in the middle of what were then bleak, rubbish-strewn fields. It was so bad that when we turned up in our bus, three families immediately turned around and went straight back to the airport. It also didn't help that it was 38 degrees—being inside the huts was like being a future meal in a microwave oven. The hottest day on record in England up till then was only 32 degrees. We were still in long trousers and jumpers—it was a decidedly chilly minus five when we left London.

England must have seemed a million miles away as we spent our first night in Australia baking in our corrugated oven. At least Dad had a job and a house to look forward to. He likes to remind people that we weren't 'Ten-pound Poms'—Dad had got a transfer to Australia with Lucas, the automotive company he'd been working for in Birmingham. Even so, we had to wait three months for all our worldly possessions—including a 1964 Vauxhall Cresta—to arrive by ship before we could move into the house. Even now I can remember thinking that I couldn't understand why we were living in a tin shed.

For the first few months in Australia I thought we were royalty. The day after we arrived, we caught a taxi into the city to have a look around and the streets were decked out with banners and streamers and thousands of people were waving balloons and flags. Dad told us that all these people had come out especially to welcome us to Australia. We waved back, thinking how very special we were. Not surprisingly, the crowds weren't actually celebrating our arrival. They were out in the streets celebrating the annual Moomba Festival.

As we drove down towards the pub, I reminded Dad of our regal introduction to Australia.

'You gave the country a pretty good introduction to us as well,' Dad said. 'We'd only been here a week when you caused absolute mayhem. Your Mum and I went to the shops while the lady next door looked after you four kids. While we were walking back to the hostel, three fire trucks flew past. When we got back, the supply hut was up in flames and we found you hiding under your bed clutching a box of matches.' I must admit, I only have vague recollections of my pyromaniacal introduction to Australia. It was probably Mick, anyway.

We had lunch at the London Hotel and Dad was back to his cheerful, non-stop moaning self. He certainly looked trimmer—he'd lost seven kilos from his Sri Lankan bug. We both ordered the calamari salad then Dad flicked through my photos of the trip. When he'd finished, he said, 'We really did have a great trip, didn't we?'

Yes, we did. Not only did we have a great trip but I felt incredibly lucky and privileged to have been able to do it with my father. On top of that, we now shared a special bond. I have heard many people whose fathers have passed away say that they wished they'd got to know their Dad better. I think I not only got to know my Dad better, I got to know myself better, too.

A few months after we got back, and after we'd talked about our trip a dozen times, we were back to talking about Manchester United and discussing whether Rooney should play as a lone striker. I didn't mind, though. That's the way we've always been. We still shared something very special and we'll never lose that.

When our calamari salad arrived, Dad screwed up his face.

'Bloody hell!' he whined at the waiter. 'It's got weeds in it.' He didn't like the calamari, either. It had been lightly grilled in olive oil.

'I thought it was going to be crumbed,' he grumbled. Dad called over the waiter again. 'I don't want it,' he moaned, 'it's bloody horrible!'

'What's wrong with it, sir?' the waiter asked, looking perplexed.

'Nothing,' I said. 'I'm sorry, he's old . . . and he's a Pom.'

Acknowledgements

This book owes a lot to a lot of people, but first and foremost I'd like to thank me Dad. I feel both lucky and privileged to have shared this journey with my father. Despite his obsessive fear of foreign muck and walking, which I swear on my *Lonely Planet* I have not exaggerated one bit, he was a joy to travel with.

Huge love and gratitude to my wife Natalie. Although you weren't on the trip with me, I couldn't have done this without you.

I would also like to express my genuine gratitude to all my lovely English relatives for their hospitality, entertainment and endless roast dinners: June in Royal Leamington Spa; Margaret, Peter, Wayde, Dean, Kellie, Gerry and Brenda in Manchester; Fred, Ann, Colin, Cheryl, Andy and David in Birmingham; and Rosie, David, Lisa and Lindsay in Devon. And just in case I didn't give you fair warning about the ribbing some of you would receive: I'm sorry.

Many thanks also to the following for their hospitality and generous assistance along the way: Annie Choy at Raffles Hotel; Shakila Samuel at the British Club in Singapore; Lesley Penniston at Butlins; Gail Fifett at Chatham Historic Dockyard; George Athroll at Shotley Museum; Dean Cleaver at Emirates and Peter and Sally Moore.

Special thanks go to James Richardson for adding sparkle—and countless tense-corrections—to my manuscript.

Last, but certainly not least, heartfelt thanks to my agent Pippa Masson at Curtis Brown and Jo Paul, Joanne Holliman and April Murdoch at Allen & Unwin.

If you'd like to view photos of Harry in walk socks or the world's largest roast dinner, you can check out the photo album of our trip at *www.brianthacker.tv*. You will also find useful links to help you book a Butlins holiday, translate a menu full of foreign muck and book a night (and arm wrestle) with an ex-East End gangster in Gozo. Or just drop me a line. I'd love to hear from you.

Brian Thacker, East St Kilda 2005